IN THE FACE OF
UNCERTAINTY

25 Top Leaders Speak Out on
Challenge, Change, and the Future
of American Business

IN THE FACE OF
UNCERTAINTY

25 Top Leaders Speak Out on
Challenge, Change, and the Future
of American Business

MARTHA I. FINNEY

AMACOM

American Management Association

New York • Atlanta • Brussels • Buenos Aires • Chicago • London • Mexico City
San Francisco • Shanghai • Tokyo • Toronto • Washington, D.C.

Library of Congress Cataloging-in-Publication Data

Finney, Martha I.
In the face of uncertainty : 25 top leaders speak out on challenge, change, and the future of American business / Martha I. Finney.
p. cm.
Includes index.
ISBN 0-8144-7161-7
1. United States—Economic conditions—2001–2. Economic forecasting—United States. I. Title: 25 top leaders speak out on challenge, change, and the future of American business. II. Title: Twenty-five top leaders speak out on challenge, change, and the future of American business. III. Title.
HC106.83 .F56 2002
338.0973—dc21   *2002001490*

Printing number

10 9 8 7 6 5 4 3 2 1

To the memory of Daniel Pearl

Contents

Foreword
Ed Reilly, President and Chief Executive Officer,
American Management Association   xi

Acknowledgments   xiii

Introduction   xv

1. GRANT ALDONAS
Under Secretary, International Trade,
U.S. Department of Commerce   1

2. JOHN ALEXANDER
President, Center for Creative Leadership   12

3. CHARLES BARCLAY
President, American Association of Airport Executives   19

4. CURTIS R. CARLSON
CEO and President, SRI International   28

5. MICHAEL P. C. CARNS
General (retired), U.S. Air Force   37

6. PEGGY CONLON
CEO and President, the Ad Council   49

7. LEO A. DALY, III
Chairman and President, Leo A Daly   59

8. RONALD E. DALY
President, R.R. Donnelley Print Solutions   69

9. RALPH DICKERSON
President, United Way of New York City   79

10. GERALD FITZGERALD
President, PB Aviation   85

11. JOE GALLI
President and CEO, Newell Rubbermaid   93

12. STEPHEN G. HARRISON
President, Lee Hecht Harrison   101

13. CHESTER D. HASKELL
President, Monterey Institute for International Studies   108

14. SUNIR KAPOOR
Founder, E-Stamp   115

15. CHRISTOPHER KOMISARJEVSKY
CEO Worldwide and President, Burson-Marsteller   125

16. JAMES LAWRENCE
Chief Financial Officer, General Mills   133

17. HOWARD LEARNER
Executive Director, Environmental Law
and Policy Center   140

18. JAMES C. MADDEN, V
Chairman, CEO, and President, Exult   148

Contents

19. MARILYN CARLSON NELSON
Chairman and CEO, Carlson Companies, Inc.   157

20. MARJORIE RANDOLPH
Senior Vice President, Human Resources,
Walt Disney Studios   166

21. LEONARD D. SCHAEFFER
Chairman and CEO, WellPoint Health Networks   174

22. THEODORE G. SHACKLEY
Associate Deputy Director of Operations (retired),
Central Intelligence Agency   184

23. KEN SMITH
CEO, President, and Founder, Jobs for
America's Graduates   195

24. WILLIAM E. STRICKLAND, JR.
CEO and President, Manchester Bidwell Corporation   205

25. TAI-CHIN TUNG
Chief Financial Officer, Charles Schwab
Investment Management   215

EPILOG:
WILLIAM BRIDGES
Principal, William Bridges & Associates   222

Index   230

Foreword

Like a body slowly repairing itself after monstrous trauma, all of us are gradually regaining our equilibrium after the events of 2001. It is our hope, here at the American Management Association, that this book of dialogue contributes in some modest way to our collective healing and offers a forum for the management lessons learned from these events.

Certainly none of us, no individual and no business, will ever be quite the same. We cannot and should not be. In dealing with the effects of September 11, we have all discovered a lot about ourselves, personally and professionally. We look at the future differently.

Foremost, I think, a more profound respect for the value of the person has been seared into us. What we mourn after the terrorist attacks is not the loss of income statements or business plans, but the irreversible loss of people we knew or could have known, people who were or could have been our colleagues.

We are also learning how resilient the human spirit can be. By picking up the pieces of our lives and our businesses—and some of us are literally doing just that—we express hope for the future. We hear from many companies that they're operating with a greater sense of clarity. They report less bureaucracy and quicker decision-making. If a fundamental innocence has shattered, it has been replaced by something more valuable: an enhanced sense of commitment by employees to the values and goals of their organizations.

In the Face of Uncertainty reflects changes in perspectives of leaders who have thought deeply about the fundamental changes we have undergone. John Alexander, president of the Center for Creative Leadership, put it memorably: "Since September 11, everyone has become more of a leader."

As Mr. Alexander observes in his interview in these pages: "There are no easy answers to begin with.... That's the real definition of leadership anyway. It's not doing the stuff that's easy or clear. It's figuring things out when you hit a wall."

We're especially interested in these reactions at the American Management Association because our purpose has always been to help organizations renew themselves. A key theme of our seminars and books has been the challenge of doing business with incomplete information in a fast-changing world.

Through sheer experience, if nothing else, in recent years American businesses have gotten much smarter about operating and strategizing in the face of uncertainty. Thankfully, all of us have these skills to draw upon now. We knew they were important, but we never realized how crucial they would be. These skills are the well-developed muscles, if you will, that have kept us on our feet and are helping us heal. One of the lasting lessons of 2001 is that all of us are capable of doing far more than we imagined.

The leaders interviewed in this book speak from diverse viewpoints. However, in their own voices, they echo the belief that vision is perhaps the most vital component of endurance. Successful managers instinctively understand that people work best when they work toward a goal: that we crave being part of something greater than ourselves. In these volatile times, the need for vision arises with new strength.

As I write this, workers have almost completed the Herculean effort of clearing the rubble at Ground Zero, and citizens are vigorously debating the form of a permanent memorial. Our geographic and mental landscape is forever altered, but our faith in ourselves endures. The nation's economic health ultimately will mirror our determination and our collective resolve. Our confidence in the future remains firm.

Ed Reilly
President and Chief Executive Officer
American Management Association

Acknowledgments

At the risk of sounding really cynical, here's an inside tip for you: It's quite common to see authors thank their agents, editors, and publishers in these pages. Those sentiments are more often than not code for: A) sorry to have been such a pain in the <u>fill in the blank</u>; B) please take a look at the incoming proposal for my next book idea; C) please don't tell your friends what it's really like to work with me; D) please return my phone calls; E) all of the above.

However, in the case of working on *In the Face of Uncertainty*, I feel I must begin by thanking the entire AMACOM team most sincerely. In the face of an excruciatingly tight deadline to make this book as timely as possible, we had to work as a tightly choreographed team from the start. Many was the time during this whole process that I have thought of those organ-transplant surgical teams racing from one table to the other with steel bowls or Playmates (the cooler, not the person) filled with vital parts still thumping and thriving, having plucked them from one body and getting ready to plunk them into the other...before it's too late.

That's the way it has been with us as the clock ran down, transplanting twenty-six chapters from my hard drive in California into AMACOM's 3,000 miles away in New York. No one lost their mind. No one lost their temper. No one lost their composure. No one lost their faith. I just love you guys!

Since it's impossible to prioritize by importance or value, I'm going alpha here: Andy Ambraziejus; Niels Buessem (I know you dislike semicolons, but there you are); Ellen Kadin; Hank Kennedy; Irene Majuk; Ed Reilly; and Kama Timbrell. I've told you before but now I'm going public with it: It has been an honor and a privilege working on this particular book, and I am so grateful to have been on your team. Every writer should be so lucky. Thank you—for everything.

Many thanks also to these people who helped me with introductions and access: Barbara Burke; Alexander Cailett; Bonnie Carpenter; Fran Charles; Doug Cody; Alan Downs; Rebecca Galli; Ellen Horton; Sian Imber; Steve McElfresh; Judith Myers; Alice Resnick; Sandy Street; Rena Lewis; and Ken Ross.

A huge thank you to Bruce ("two words") Ferguson. Bread sticks are on me next time. Many thanks also to Dallas and Joan for keeping watch over me during the holidays and keeping me supplied with jerk chicken and other yummies. To Kevin and Executive Housewares for this great place to live while the world came to a stop around me. To Mary Foley for changing my life; I drew on what I learned in *Bodacious!* almost every day. To Jennifer Coste for keeping the cats alive while I travel the highways and airways, and for all those evenings exploring the great restaurants of the California Central Coast.

Finally, a big hug and thank you to my esteemed brother and fellow journalist Rick Finney, for reasons my professional dignity will not allow me to divulge. No need to mention the war.

Introduction

Change has long been accepted as a necessary, if not always welcome, part of the business life cycle. It is that vital process in which an established organization can be transformed to produce a new, more profitable and productive future. Business change has traditionally been something over which business leaders exercised control. By and large, they have been able to anticipate most of the major trends that have been the catalysts of change. With the exception of a few historic shocks, such as Pearl Harbor and Black Monday in 1987, they have expected to control—and, more to the point, *were able* to control—the nature, logistics, timing, and pace of changes that had the greatest impact on their lives and work.

But on the morning of September 11 our preconceptions of change shattered instantly. When the initial shock subsided, we began to reassess the way we live and work. In response to overwhelming tragedy and loss, we have shown a remarkable capacity for resilience, strength, generosity, inventiveness, and resourcefulness. It is not our nature to shrink from challenging circumstances.

We have a remarkable opportunity to transform what was once "business as usual" into a more dynamic, agile, productive, and profitable way to meet new and continuing challenges. Perhaps the first step in reclaiming control of our destiny is to ask the right questions.

In the Face of Uncertainty is derived from those questions as presented to America's top leadership in government, politics, private enterprise, academia, and the nonprofit world. In these pages you will meet **Theodore Shackley**, one of the nation's foremost experts on international espionage and corporate security, in an extremely rare interview; **Grant Aldonas**, under secretary for international trade, US Department of Commerce;

Marilyn Carlson Nelson, chairman and CEO of one of the largest travel and hospitality companies in the world; **John Alexander**, president of the Center for Creative Leadership; **Joe Galli**, president and CEO of Newell Rubbermaid; **Charles Barclay**, president of the American Association of Airport Executives; **Sunir Kapoor**, founder of E-Stamp; **Ralph Dickerson**, president of the United Way of New York City; and **James Lawrence**, CFO of General Mills, among many others.

In the pages that follow, you will find discussions around questions such as:

- What is the essential ingredient for resilience?

- What is the U.S. corporation's new role as corporate citizen?

- What does "investing in the future" mean now?

- How can a U.S. company operating internationally help neutralize anti-Americanism around the world?

- Will there ever be such a thing as "business as usual" again?

- How can leaders create an innovative workplace of mission-motivated, passionate people when priorities and objectives are subject to change daily?

- How can we find meaning and value in the change process itself?

My hope is that the conversations you read in this book will encourage similar dynamic discussions within your own personal and business circles. It is not my mission to make everyone feel certain. We may never be certain again. But it is by embracing rather than fearing this reality that we best equip ourselves to shape the future of our businesses as well as our lives.

Martha Finney
Salinas, California
March 2002

Grant Aldonas

Under Secretary, International Trade
U.S. Department of Commerce

Unless we're grappling, and are seen *to be grappling, with the economic issues that confront the developing world, we leave a vacuum for others to fill. That vacuum can be filled by some pretty unsavory actors. As a consequence, September 11 should, if anything, encourage us to redouble our efforts to promote economic engagement and international trade.*

The second jet of September 11 made it clear that this was no accident the world was witnessing as its network television cameras swiveled their lenses south toward lower Manhattan and the World Trade Center. It was immediately obvious that the World Trade Center was an intentional target. True, the tallest buildings in the most prominent city in the world would have made a logical choice for terrorists anyway. But the fact that this was the World Trade Center made it instantaneously clear that this was no attack merely on American hubris. This attack was precisely engineered to knock the foundations out from under the spirit of global commerce—a world of both borderless and fearless transaction.

World trade has never been solely about the cross-border flow of value—merchandise, raw goods, cash, etc. It has also been about the free flow of ideas, ideals, religions, values, information, culture, and priorities. Clashes have always been part of the story of trade, but never in such a short time did so many people, representing so many countries, perish in the span of a mere sixty minutes. From the World Trade Organization riots in Seattle and Geneva to the rubble off Wall Street to the relatively well-behaved rally accompanying the World Economic Forum in February 2002, the issue was really the same for everyone no matter what side of the arguments they were on: What does the expansion of world trade mean to me and the principles I cherish most?

For Grant Aldonas, Under Secretary of International Trade for the U.S. Department of Commerce, the continued opening of international markets for the United States represents all the values the United States traditionally holds most dear: increased employment for Americans domestically, unlimited opportunity for the greatest possible number of people here and abroad, and a better way of life around the world. Before joining the Department of Commerce, Aldonas served as Chief International Trade Counsel to the Chairman of the Senate Finance Committee. During his tenure on the Committee, Congress passed a number of significant trade bills, including the Trade and Development Act of 2000, a grant of Permanent Normal Trade Relations for China, legislation replacing the Foreign Sales Corporation provisions of the Internal Revenue Code, and a series of tariff bills.

In this discussion, Aldonas talks about the larger implications of the U.S. role in international trade:

- How the attacks of September 11 affected overall U.S. trade policy and strategy
- The opportunities of American business to help to rebuild Afghanistan
- Trade relations between China and the United States
- Corporate citizenship lessons to be learned as the Enron story unfolds

How has the Bush Administration changed its agenda regarding international trade since September 11?

The events of September 11 have enhanced the arguments for worldwide engagement on an economic level. What happened on September 11 is a strong rebuttal to the arguments of some who believe that trade is damaging and leads to the impoverishment of workers, as opposed to improving their standard of living and providing a variety of other benefits. Unless we're grappling, and are *seen* to be grappling, with the economic issues that confront the developing world, we leave a vacuum for others to fill. That vacuum can be filled by some pretty unsavory actors. As a consequence, September 11 should, if anything, encourage us to redouble our efforts to promote economic engagement and international trade.

We saw this philosophy reflected in the launch of a new round of talks at Doha. There was a sense among the delegates that we could not afford to fail. This isn't simply because of the economic benefits of or the need to reaffirm the value of the World Trade Organization as a forum for negotiations. It's also because the World Trade Organization is a member-driven institution that includes representatives from all over the world—from Latin America to Africa to North America to Europe to Central, South, and Southeast Asia. The WTO provides a place where governments can come together as representatives of a civilized community of nations where the voice of the people is reflected in what goes on in the trade arena.

How soon do you see us opening up Afghanistan as a venue for American business and economic opportunity?

There's going to be a real commitment to reconstruction by the international community. People from all over the world will show up to rebuild Kabul and its other cities—roads, bridges, power plants, and other infrastructure. American companies will be a part of that effort, and we will be there to help promote our companies' interests. I don't know that that's necessarily "opening it up" for U.S. business, but, as Under Secretary for International Trade, I do hope that U.S. construction companies and contractors get their fair share of the contracts that are going to be signed as part of the reconstruction process.

Where will the money come from for this opportunity?

A lot of the money will come from sources that have been available before, such as World Bank funding. I would expect that some will come bilaterally through our foreign assistance programs. The Afghan Recovery Conference has just pledged almost $3 billion from delegates worldwide. I would call that a great start, but the reconstruction effort will likely require a more sustained presence for some time into the future. It will also require a significant degree of discipline in the eventual bidding and contracting process to ensure that the money is well spent and remains focused on what's essential to Afghanistan's future.

Another region that's intensely interesting to U.S. international trade is China. But China presents whole new sets of issues, not the least of which is a culture that has historically set itself apart from the rest of the world. Is it realistic to expect China to fully embrace capitalism

when the entrenched power structure has so much to lose, and when—and unless the timing is perfect— the resulting social upheaval could be devastating?

I wonder if the leadership itself doesn't worry about a new feudalism. The provinces are growing stronger economically, and the national government still relies on the provinces for the repatriation of taxes collected locally, rather than a system of direct taxation, to finance the national government. As a consequence there's a lot of power that resides with the provinces. Historically, in China, as the center weakens, one of the provinces grows stronger and splits off—or tries to take hold of the center. I'm sure that prospect is very much on their minds as they move in the direction of less central control over the economy.

Additionally, you have 100 million people in the cities, which are rising and prospering from the new economic environment. And, then you have another 900 million people who have historically relied on the land and who are now attracted to the economic vitality in the cities. This creates a certain amount of social pressure that didn't exist before. And that's where the current system could come apart.

But I am more optimistic than that. The Chinese really have a shot at the kind of productivity and economic gains that would allow them to sustain the development of their economy over time and meet the rising expectations of a growing middle class in China. If those rising expectations aren't met, they will find their way into the political environment. People do have a voice now that didn't exist before in China.

At the same time there are still those actions in China that hark back to the bad old days, such as people being executed for bringing Bibles into the country.

When I was the Chief Trade Counsel for the Finance Committee, I made the argument that we would be better off dividing our trading interests from our leadership on human rights issues, particularly with China, in large part because our advocacy of our economic interests generally was perceived to undercut our ability to speak with a strong voice on moral issues. As a practical matter, politicians should, and do, vote their constituents' interests and their pocketbook interests. I was concerned that what the Chinese would read from that was that we weren't necessarily serious about human rights. Frankly, I think we would have more impact if we delinked the two. We would not threaten sanctions, but neither would China or any other country be able to escape international attention for the sorts of things they do, particularly in terms of repression.

I can understand that the Chinese leadership might be concerned with social movements fragmenting their society. There is a historical reason for that. But, at the same time China and other countries are going to have to come to grips with a more open society in terms of statements about politics and about faith if they're going to have a more open economic system.

From the point of view of U.S. government policy, we have an opportunity to speak with a much stronger voice on human rights when it's not undercut by an annual vote that suggests we're more interested in trade. We're interested in both.

There's also a question as to whether China can maintain a closed society and a closed political system in the face of a real need to open up the economy and achieve the level of growth that will meet the rising levels of expectations of their population. Human freedom is not divisible. When individuals attain their freedom economically, it's natural to ask, "If I can make my own decisions about what's good for me economically, why shouldn't I be able to do so politically?" In the face of that fact, authoritarian governments are going to have to open their society and the political process if they want their economy to flourish, because an expanding economy depends on individuals pursuing their own economic destinies and obtaining the direct rewards of their efforts.

We have the business relationship with China, but there are also overtones of enmity. With the downing of the military jet over China in 2001 and the alleged bugging of China's presidential jet, we behave like enemies. How do we reconcile these two different ways of relating to each other?

I don't think the United States treats China as an enemy. There are certainly those in U.S. politics who think we should. But I think it's more accurate to say that you shouldn't define the relationship as enemy, friend, or competitor. It's more realistic to say that this is a country with a dynamic future ahead of it, and a growing role on the world stage economically, militarily, and politically. That doesn't mean that we shrink from defending our own interests, but we have to deal with the reality of it. There are points of convergence, and there are points of conflict in any relationship. There may be more points of conflict in our relationship with the Chinese, like the downing of the U.S. aircraft, but that wouldn't mean that they're an enemy.

To do so would overlook the many points of convergence. I don't, for example, see the Chinese suggesting that capitalism and a market-based economy are an inappropriate system to try to generate important economic returns. You don't hear that from government officials the way you used to hear the rhetoric. When the Party Congress gets together, the leadership sounds some of those notes, but that's not what you hear in day-to-day discourse.

I'm very hopeful for China and for the Chinese people, which is probably one of the reasons I don't want to define our relationship as enemies. It very well may be that China will become the engine for economic growth in Asia. Although we're trapped in this political logic of trading market access between one another, everyone understands that the real benefit goes to the country liberalizing its economy. So, while U.S. exporters and the U.S. economy will benefit from the market access we will get from China's accession to the World Trade Organization, China will see real economic gains as well. They'll get the higher efficiency gains because they're opening up out of the state-dominated economy into one where markets are more likely to flourish. With competition, you always see an increase in productivity and, again, a rising standard of living. That's how the Chinese will benefit.

It's in our interest to trade with China. Through trade, we build relationships that will provide some bulwark against conflict—a bulwark not only against potential conflict between the United States and China but a bulwark against instability in Asia generally.

Considering what has happened with Enron and what it has done to domestic communities, especially around Houston, emerging international markets wouldn't be able to handle such a catastrophe. What kind of moral obligation do we have as a nation or as a community of American businesses to make sure that if we do leave we have left the economy whole?

Let's be clear. Companies don't get up and move because they decide one day, on a whim, that they're going to leave their investment behind. Companies get up and move generally because of changes in the market environment, generally changes that governments have set in motion.

Companies don't bear an ethical obligation to operate in an environment where they can't turn a profit. The way we get the most out of resources—and, incidentally, the way we leave the least environmental damage behind—is the constant pressure that the market imposes on companies to become more efficient. We know that competition regularly drives people out of business. How does that happen? The capital markets siphon capital away from loss-making enterprises and feed it to enterprises generating a higher rate of return. The fact that a company is driven by market circumstances, not government support, is the essence of the bargain in a market economy. If there is a moral obligation, it is to operate in a way that provides for the future of the enterprise, its shareholders, and all who work for it—by turning a profit.

Given that fact, I do get very concerned when either governments or companies mislead people as to the fortunes of the enterprise. For example, when a government raises tariffs, it sends the signal to people to go ahead and make the investment of either their working lives or their money. Knowing that their investment was completely dependent on whether the government would keep those tariffs in place, would someone go ahead and invest their resources? I think the answer is no.

When governments distort markets, what they're doing in fact is misleading people about how they should invest their own lives. And that takes on a moral quotient.

If it's a company that's misleading people, the same moral questions are raised. If, on the other hand, companies are completely open and honest about the economic circumstances under which they're operating, and if they communicate that to their employees and shareholders (which is essential to the market economy, the market-based system, and functioning capital markets), then I don't have any qualms if they say at some point, "I'm sorry, but we can't continue to produce at a profit in this market." Frankly, given the basic bargain on which a market economy is based, telling the markets, shareholders, and workers about the future fortunes of the enterprise is essential to making the market system work.

I think it is also important to say that there are penalties that attach, under our security laws, when a company misleads the markets, shareholders, and employees. In a circumstance like that the system generally forces that information out into the open, no matter how much that company tries to hide it. That said, are there things that we ought to be doing to improve the functioning of our capital markets by ensuring the free flow of accurate information about the prospects of companies offering securities on our markets? Absolutely. Always.

For example, with respect to accounting standards, are there things— since markets are about information—that we can do to reinforce the rules to bring that information to the market sooner? Of course there are, and we should ensure that we are always vigilant about ways in which we can improve the flow of financial information to the markets. But, even then, we will never fully eliminate the risk of a company failing or of persons who might willfully break the law.

Still hypothetically speaking, does such behavior put egg on our face worldwide?

Would I hold up any country or its companies as absolute paragons of virtue? No, of course not. But at the end of the day, the United States comes pretty close in terms of its business ethics and its adherence to the rule of law. In my experience, our system works in most instances to force financial information out into the marketplace where companies and investors can act on it.

Let's take the example provided by recent events. Although there is a great effort under way to find a scandal, the press often overlooks a much more fundamental question. What other country could sustain the failure of its seventh-largest company and have every high-level government official say, "No, that's the way markets work. We're not going to intervene to save a company from mismanagement. The economy can absorb it, and we'll deal with the consequences, including ways to help workers who are affected by the failure. But, we aren't in the business of shoring up failed enterprises."? That's a remarkable statement that, in my experience, I would be very surprised to hear any high-ranking official in any foreign government make.

What it ultimately goes to is the question of trust. President Bush and Department of Commerce Secretary Don Evans have both made crystal clear that one of their primary goals, if not the primary challenge facing us, is to restore the ability of the American public to have faith in its government. That is something that has been squandered in the past and has to be rebuilt.

When all is said and done, that trust depends on people doing the right thing, frequently under very difficult circumstances. To me, that trust depends on the work of people of good faith, good intentions, and trustworthiness at the top levels of the government. If you don't have that, it's the quickest way to slide into trouble. If you do have that, you at least have one strong bulwark against a lot of bad things happening economically.

Let's project three years—if not seven years. What does success look like at the end of the Bush Administration? How will you like to see international trade policy progress by the time boxes are packed?

I would like to see a free and more open world. I mean that both in terms of what goes on within countries, as well as internationally among countries. I would like to think that we took a stand in support of human freedom and made a contribution to expanding the possibilities for individuals to pursue their own dreams. I would like to see us do that here in the United States first, in order to vindicate the dream of our own country as an equal opportunity society, and then extend that light to the world. That would be the strongest statement of who we are as Americans and the best thing we could do both domestically and internationally.

That includes an insistence on taking a stand for what's right. This president is willing to do that in no uncertain terms, and I think that's good, not only for our own society, but also for the world at large. When the United States takes on that leadership role, historically, good things happen.

What are you certain of?

I'm certain that everyone's prediction about the logic and inevitability of globalization is wrong. There have been many times in the past when we've made significant strides in liberalizing trade, liberalizing capital flows, even taking hesitant steps toward liberalizing the movement of labor. In short, to the extent that those are indicia of progress toward human freedom, there have been times, including during the past decade, where we have made considerable progress.

That said, there are many stumbling blocks that get thrown in the way of that progress. There are any number of movements, institutions, and governments that aren't interested in human freedom, which is really what globalization is about. They resist it. As a consequence you find that the progress toward human freedom moves in fits and starts. Although I have a lot of confidence in freedom ultimately prevailing, it's not linear progress by any stretch of the imagination.

It's going to take some goodwill both in establishing relationships between governments and, almost more importantly, among people in private life to maintain the kind of progress we've seen in the decade or so since the fall of the Berlin Wall. And, it's going to take that kind of progress to expand the horizons for future generations and raise the standards of living around the world.

What that means in practical terms for those of us on the trade policy front is pretty simple. If we let governments segment markets, and introduce barriers to trade or communication among the world's peoples, we will not only destroy the efficiencies that we've gained and the productivity increases that are essential to raising standards of living in the United States and elsewhere around the world, but we will forfeit the promise of progress toward the goal of human freedom that is the essence of our American values.

What are you uncertain of?

I'm uncertain about—using a phrase borrowed from Zbigniew Brzezinski— the "arc of crisis" that stretches across Central Asia to western China, and how that will affect the state of the world both politically and economically.

I worry less about the institutions. Some folks worried about the World Trade Organization after the Seattle riots, for example. It took a lot of hard work by an awful lot of people to go from the failure in Seattle—this stain on the international trading system—to the success at Doha in simply launching a new round of trade negotiations. While that is a feat in and of itself, we are still a long way from delivering the end result we're working toward. Having said that, I never actually worried about the institution of the World Trade Organization itself, certainly not as much as I worried about the risk to the larger dynamic of opening markets and expanding the economic future of the next generation.

I'm also worried about the implications of what's going on demographically around the world. In many places around the world, you have aging societies combined with a sclerotic economic system and too much government involvement in the market. The end result is fewer workers trying to support more retirees and a significant social safety net, while operating under significant constraints economically.

Where you have a very expensive social safety net, and fewer workers to pay for it, you're going to have to raise productivity. Given the obstacles to innovation, the lack of flexibility in labor markets, and the relative inefficiency of capital markets in many countries due to overregulation by governments, productivity gains may be hard to come by. In those economies where productivity gains are not strong enough to sustain the existing safety net, they will be looking at a lot of economic dislocation and potential unrest. And all that comes, once again, from governments misleading people about the facts of economic life.

The other demographic problem is that you have the opposite effect in much of the developing world, particularly in the Middle East and Central Asia, where more than half of the population is below the age of 18. You need enough economic growth to be able to absorb that new generation and give it a stake in its own future. Those demographic factors alone will put great pressure on societies that are coming to grips with increasing openness to the rest of the world politically, socially, culturally, and economically.

All those issues have the possibility of blocking progress toward the world we would all prefer to see—one in which markets and societies are open and standards of living are rising around the world.

What is the essential ingredient for resilience?

I'm a big believer that the work of individuals can make a difference. But that dynamic works best in a world that maximizes the freedom of individuals to pursue their own interests both economically and politically. What I can't stress enough in that regard is that economic and political freedom are indivisible. If a nation wants to maximize the future prospects for its own citizens, it has to expand the horizon of human freedom in all its manifold forms.

That is not a purely libertarian prescription. It may be the lawyer in me, but I am a firm believer based on my experience and my reading of history that you have to have a system of rules that reinforces human freedom. In other words, there is a concrete and positive role for government—one that creates an environment that ensures individuals are free to do what they do best, which is to go out and pursue their economic destiny as far as their drive, initiative, and dreams can take them. That's the only way to produce both the economic and political foundation capable of providing for the next generation of Americans and the next generation of citizens around the world.

In short, ignorance is always the enemy, and human freedom is always the answer.

2

John Alexander
President, Center for Creative Leadership

It can be exhausting and frustrating. You can be misunderstood. And there's no room for error, which is particularly true in this new environment. The tolerance for error is narrowing. You may get one chance to try it again and then you're out.

Leaders may be born, or leaders may be made. But all leaders benefit from development and training programs. The Center for Creative Leadership is recognized internationally as one of the leaders in the study and cultivation of leadership itself—as a discipline, as an art, as a business tool, and as a personal philosophy.

One of the largest institutions in the world dedicated solely to the study of leadership, the Center describes itself as "a cross between a university business school and a research institute—serving as a clearinghouse for innovative ideas and techniques for creative leadership development and education."

The Center's president, John Alexander, came to the organization after having already pursued a twenty-year career in journalism. A Rhodes scholar, Alexander received a B.A. in English from Princeton University and an M.A. in Politics, Philosophy, and Economics from Magdalen College, Oxford. In this conversation he discusses the nature of leadership in these high-pressure times:

- Balancing organizational leadership with personal authenticity
- Creating a systemic culture of leadership that transcends the celebrity CEO
- Leading in crises
- Seeking leadership inspiration from throughout the ranks

What does it mean to be a leader today?

You have to be able to balance and manage paradoxes and tensions. For example, you have to be decisive and ready to take rapid action; but you also have to engage others, which can slow things down. You have to engage the whole person who comes to work. If you don't regularly circle back as you lead to meet people where they are, and take the time to coach them along, then you will quickly be seen as out of touch or irrelevant. And you have to engage a wider group of people. You have to not only see what's ahead but also look around you and see who's there at your side and who's supporting you from behind.

Although leadership is a process of interaction between leaders and the people around them, leadership itself begins with the individual. It engages the whole individual—not just the head but also the heart, and then the behaviors the leader exhibits. To be an effective leader, especially in the environment we're in today, you have to know yourself very well.

Leadership is an art form. Too often leaders get trapped in the analytical side of the work they do, which is understandable. It's easier to manipulate numbers and spreadsheets than it is to use other parts of your brain, as well as other parts of your personality. To be effective in this environment you also have to be able to talk in terms of your gut and your instincts, and to be able to draw from your creative side as fluently as you access your analytical side.

Literature and the arts reflect the often suppressed elements of our being that can help us in leadership situations. Leadership is not something you can easily compartmentalize. It engages the person's own career, history, family, and community.

If you're able to play on all those parts of your life, is your ability to sustain energy, focus, and creative thought ratcheted up?

Absolutely. Energy and stamina are among the criteria we use in an assessment process to develop leaders. Leadership can be compared to a marathon. You're running a long race. Yes, there are sprints within the marathon, but you still are on a long journey. You have to be physically, mentally, and emotionally stable.

As an activity, leadership takes greater endurance than sports, actually. An athlete trains and trains, and then only has to go out and perform for an hour or two in the game itself. A leader performs in a fishbowl that is always on display.

And the performance has to vary depending on the audience. It's said that leadership is situational. I would say leadership is more *contextual* than situational. During the tragic events of September 2001, for instance, Rudy Giuliani moved from funerals to press conferences to meetings, and he had to modulate his behavior and his communication to fit the context and the audience he was facing. The performance of leadership is very exacting. The stage set changes practically by the hour or the minute.

Is that especially true given today's circumstances?

Yes, especially when you're talking about the global environment. Leaders are in front of different audiences with different expectations and different cultural backgrounds. You have to communicate with employees, boards, customers, partners, shareholders, and financial analysts. They all want the leader to deliver precisely what they're looking for.

You have to give it to them, but with authenticity. No matter how different contexts may demand different performances, you must be both appropriate to your audience and consistent in your message. Giving mixed or confusing or contradictory messages can get you in more trouble in today's world than anything else. What people want most is integrity. They want someone they can trust. People are going to trust only those leaders who are authentic, honest, straight talking, truthful, and effective.

You have to know yourself. The contextual modulation you then practice is based on a thorough understanding of who you are and what your values are. Within those boundaries there is a lot of room for changing behavior. You have to be aware of your surroundings, and of what you're saying, and the way you come across. It's almost like having a running conversation with yourself even as you're performing. This is a very difficult thing to do. That's why so many top leaders fail or get out of the race.

It can be exhausting and frustrating. You can be misunderstood. And there's no room for error, which is particularly true in this new environment. The tolerance for error is narrowing. You may get one chance to try it again and then you're out.

How can companies cultivate a culture of leadership that is sustained over time, independent of individual personalities?

In a culture of systemic leadership, all the practical and conceptual aspects of leadership are widely shared and discussed. There is a visible and deliberate set of processes and systems to identify, select, and develop leadership talent at *all* levels of the organization. There is also a shared vocabulary—a common understanding, for example, of what leadership and vision mean to the organization as a whole.

Leadership can and should take place in all parts of the organization. It shouldn't be exclusively connected with positions of official authority and hierarchy. Crucial decisions are being made at critical times throughout the ranks. We saw it repeatedly on September 11. People in outlying parts of organizations made critical decisions that saved people's lives. For example, lower-level Verizon employees kept the Pentagon's telephone system from shutting down. They demonstrated extraordinary leadership in a chaotic time. The more people can see themselves as having potential for leadership at all levels, the more likely they are to take charge in a crisis situation or when there isn't time to consult with headquarters or higher-ups.

And because knowledge is much more readily available throughout the ranks, the people on the scene will often be more knowledgeable about the immediate problems and the best possible responses to them.

People have to at least see themselves as capable of acting and performing as a leader would in certain situations. We're seeing that now as airline passengers are emotionally and mentally prepared to overpower hijackers.

And how does a company promote that in a regular, systemic way when there are no crises?

It has to be done deliberately and supported from the top of the organization. It involves a whole range of initiatives: workshops, performance management, and developmental assignments, for instance. Even community volunteering projects will give employees developmental leadership experience. You also have to build in rewards and recognition for the managers to encourage them to provide this development to their direct reports.

How can leaders gain inspiration from those below them on the org chart?

You're making an assumption that people in top leadership are in touch with people several levels down from them. Leaders are easily cut off from that part of the organization. They're isolated, and their own direct reports may be unwilling to tell them the truth about what's going on. One way to be inspired by what people below you are doing is to go out and meet with them in informal settings and listen. Ask people what's going on. Invariably something inspiring will come up. It's amazing what stories you will hear. But you have to have good antennae.

If you think of leadership as a role you step in and out of, that gets you quickly to the perspective that your job is to create an environment where other people can perform at the highest possible level. And your job as a leader is not always to tell everybody *what* to do. Your job is to help people find out what it is that they need to do and give them the tools and systems to get that work done. Today's leadership requirements put you more in a coaching-and-enabling role than a telling-and-doing role.

If you're not in touch with people around you and below you in the organization, you're not doing your job as a leader. Leadership is not a solo act. If it ever was, it certainly isn't anymore.

We are in an era where we're making celebrities out of CEOs more than ever before. What is the function of the celebrity CEO?

That is more a phenomenon in the United States than in other parts of the world. CEOs in Europe and Asia, who in some ways are afforded more authority to act within organizations and attract more reverence, still tend to be lower profile. It's a part of our culture to create celebrities. It's easier to exalt the person on the magazine cover than it is to look at how that person got there. When you do, you'll usually find a team of people behind him or her. The CEOs who increase shareholder value over time are typically modest, self-effacing, and always pointing to others around them. They take a long view and have a strong drive to succeed. But they also believe their objectives can be accomplished only through the efforts and dedication of others.

It's a mistake to turn CEOs into celebrities. We all have egos, and it's nice to be featured in a positive way. But sometimes being a celebrity isn't so beneficial. It overemphasizes the role the CEO plays in the immediate and long-term potential of the company. It makes the company more about the CEO than the other way around. And it could be disempowering to the employees, who won't enjoy watching their achievements being repeatedly claimed by a publicity-hungry leader.

Truly talented and mission-oriented leaders are the first to say, "I didn't do this alone."

When given the chance to blow their own horns, is it generally better for leaders to evangelize their corporate mission instead of celebrating any one person?

It's critical to attach intrinsic meaning to the product. Everyone, especially at a time like this, would like to think he or she works for a higher purpose. The challenge is to find companies that are able to do that in an authentic way. Organizations with a very clear mission and strong values are the ones that are going to do better.

Part of the job of leadership is to show a connection to higher purpose. It's the key motivator for staying engaged when people hear their salaries are being frozen or cut, or when they're being asked to work long hours because of layoffs. What is going to keep those people loyal to the company? There has to be a rallying cry.

Given the wave of patriotism that has swept the country since late 2001, everyone has had a taste of how utterly satisfying it is to be completely and sharply focused on one mission. Is this a permanent shift in the demands made on leadership, or will things get back to where they were before?

The challenges and demands on leadership were accentuated in this situation, but they were already there. For example, political and corporate leaders were trying to respond to the attacks of the antiglobalization movement. It had reached a point where leaders couldn't meet safely without large demonstrations, and even without violence. All kinds of warning signals told us that we need to act and behave differently as leaders if global society is to improve.

Not everything changed then, but I do think leadership needs to be enacted differently. The whole leader has to be engaged in an authentic way.

And whole groups of people have to be engaged in an authentic way. In fact, we're seeing a movement toward shared leadership. We're even seeing co-CEOs more frequently now. More teams of people are sharing decision making at the top. And more organizations are working together through global partnerships and alliances that require new leadership capabilities.

I think to the extent we go back to the linear, strongly bottom-line orientation we had in the 1990s, we do so at our peril. We have to engage all parts of ourselves, bringing together a wider group of people in the leadership process.

What are you certain of?

Good leadership is a key ingredient for success in organizations and societies today. It's the key variable in the equation of building a better world and solving problems. That need will not go away.

What are you uncertain of?

There will be some new types of organizations emerging, and I'm not sure what shape they'll take.

What is the essential ingredient for resilience?

The ability to adapt to, and learn from, change. When we suffer a setback, a lot of people just walk away or go back to an old answer rather than try to deal with it directly. You have to be able to take blows and then get up and analyze them, then move on.

When you embrace change, you have to accept the possibility that you'll make mistakes. That's what real risk is all about. But it's important to recognize that just because things don't turn out as anticipated, that doesn't mean that the effort has failed. We're talking about leadership in a time of turbulence and rapid change. There are no easy answers to begin with. Things are just not obvious. That's the real definition of leadership anyway. It's not doing the stuff that's easy or clear. It's figuring things out when you hit a wall.

3

Charles Barclay

President, American Association of
Airport Executives

In the long run, history shows that transportation creates more wealth and less poverty. And aviation and telecommunications are key to moving people, ideas, and goods over long distances. Aviation contributes to creating global wealth by bringing more people into this economy and into the wealth creation process.

On September 11, 2001, the staff of the American Association of Airport Executives (AAAE) were able to look out their Alexandria, Va., windows and watch the smoke rise from the burning Pentagon. For everyone living, working, and commuting around the Washington, D.C., area (of which Alexandria is a suburb), the Pentagon is more than the military headquarters for the United States. It is the low, solid building representing permanence and security. It is a familiar landmark on the commute of thousands. And it is more than just the place where starched military personnel report for duty; it is also the place where husbands and wives, children and neighbors go to work. More than 180 of them died that day, and AAAE staffers saw the resulting black smoke billowing out into the fall air.

As the leading membership organization for thousands of airport professionals around the United States, AAAE's own course would shift significantly that day. The business side of the organization declined substantially as the lucrative seminars it hosts had to be cancelled one after the other. But more to the point, AAAE had members and friends caught in the World Trade Center towers in New York, and its members coast to coast were looking out their own windows and watching planes coming in to land. When they would take off again, well, on that day, it would be anyone's guess. For the time being, the sky was closed. And airport managers were faced with a day, a week, and a future that was beyond anyone's ability to imagine.

As president of AAAE since 1983, Charles M. (Chip) Barclay has dedicated his career to the development and promotion of aviation in the United States. Before joining the AAAE leadership, he served on the staffs of the Senate Aviation Subcommittee and the Civil Aeronautics Board. He also was elected chairman of the board of directors of Travelers Aid International in June 1996, as well as serving on the National Civil Aviation Review Commission in 1997. Most recently he served on the Rapid Response Team for Airport Security, formed at the request of Department of Transportation Secretary Norman Mineta in response to the September 11 terrorist attacks. In this interview he discusses aviation as an important player in supporting U.S. economic vitality:

- The role of aviation in maintaining a free and open society
- How airports are expected to evolve in response to heightened security requirements
- How aviation can be used to promote a pro-American message throughout the world

How have the events of September 11 changed the role of aviation in this free and open society?

By the time we figured out that, with the second plane, it must be terrorism, it immediately got all of us thinking ahead on security. The public has always demanded a mix of safety, security, low fares, and convenience. If, in July 2001, someone had tried to put in a procedure that would result in two-hour lines at check-in, they would have probably lost their job. The big issue for passengers up until September 11 was convenience and efficiency of the system. That all came with the presumption that we had a handle on the appropriate level of security.

Now we have to start thinking in a military fashion. We've always looked on ourselves as public transportation and as having a reasonable level of security for that type of system. But if a team of special ops types are going to train for years and then come on the plane as suicide pilots, having the crudest of weapons, intent on using the plane as a bomb, that's a threat that nobody prepared our systems to defend against. Now we have a military type threat against us, and we have to respond with near military-defense procedures.

Aviation has always been a leader in the question of where you divide freedom from safety and security in a mass transportation system. In the early 1970s we put in magnetometers in response to the Cuban hijackings. A lot of people said, "Hey, that's an illegal search and seizure! Just because I'm walking in an airport that doesn't give you the right to search me. If I were driving over the 14th Street Bridge going into Washington, you couldn't stop my car and go through it because you felt like it."

But through all the years of arguing in the courts, aviation has been very clear: You're choosing to use the system, so you are going to have to accept a reasonable level of invasion of privacy to ensure other people's safety. It's going to ratchet up again now, obviously.

How important is the aviation industry to the United States?

Aviation is critically important to the United States because it's such a large country. Because of its geographic size, aviation plays a much more important role to our society and the economy than it does in most parts of the developed world. We must have the ability to travel over those great distances and transport our entrepreneurs, resources, and people quickly in a world economy where speed is the key. The irony is that when you're on the airplane in the future, you're going to surrender a certain amount of the very same privacy rights that usually come in an open society. Driving in your car, you're not likely to have your person searched or your bag searched. On an airplane you are. Ironically, by giving up some of those freedoms and rights in order to travel, you're actually increasing the rest of your freedoms.

Obviously we have been focused on security and airlines' economic issues more than on the airports themselves as business entities. What is the role of airports as business partners with their economic communities and how do you see that role changing? Is the American public finally catching on that the airports themselves are an important economic engine?

Airports and the services they bring to their communities have such a broad impact on the local—and global—economies. They provide speed in transportation. And speed continues to add greater value, whether it's in clock cycles on a computer chip or getting to the market with a product more quickly than your competitors. Air transportation is the fastest form of moving anything that's not electrons. If it's made of atoms, air transportation is how it wants to go. If it's made of electrons it's going to go by satellite, the Internet, or land lines. But anything of value that's made of atoms wants to go by air.

The more you're worth, the more it's worth getting you there faster.

The importance of air transportation systems to their communities is getting clearer. We do these airport economic impact statements for communities and always get nice high numbers. Aviation shows up in the 5 percent to 6 percent range of whatever the local gross domestic product is. This is always an impressive number. But the true value is much greater. Try to imagine your local economy without an airport at all. Think of all the businesses that couldn't survive. What are all the things you couldn't do in Atlanta if you didn't have an airport? And if you didn't have air transportation serving Atlanta, what kind of society and community would you have? That's a national question, as well as a local one. When you think about the answers in details that relate directly to your own life, you get a better sense of the positive impacts airports have.

With every major historic event that alters the American way of life, it seems that the smaller communities are left with a little less every time. How will the smaller airports come out of this turn of events? Could they possibly benefit from this?

I doubt it. The key for smaller communities is the continued efficiency of the hub-and-spoke system of air connections. The prevailing wisdom says that if we just put up with a little more inconvenience, we can have the security we want. But what we're really trading off is time. Multiply that "little more time delay" by 700 million passengers a year, and you wind up with huge delays. Building delays into the system will stop the efficient operation of the hubs. If you can only handle fewer flights, the first ones to lose will be the smaller communities.

As networking gets better, information technology improves, and speed goes up, you have the ability to live anywhere you want. You don't have to get people physically together in the same place. That might create a significant incentive for people who don't want to live in large communities and choose to live in smaller communities. That makes the small community air service issue even more important, but you're still constrained by the economics of the airlines' need to fill up planes if they are to continue service to a community.

How are airports the proverbial canary in the mine as a way of measuring economic health?

Air transportation has been a leading indicator, particularly in a downslide. You can often see a downturn in air transportation first. You can see it particularly in looking at air passenger volume. Airports themselves are so fundamental, they can go up and down within a limited range. Even if we had all the airlines file for Chapter 11 as a result of the mess we're in now, the government would have to buy all their assets out of bankruptcy, if there were no other takers. You still wind up having to have airports and an air transportation system in the country. Their fundamental importance in a knowledge economy based on speed does give them the sort of protection a typical canary in a mine doesn't have.

But where you will see the impacts of the downturn is in airport services. Airports make much of their income from parking lot revenues. If no one's flying, no one's driving to the airport. If no one's driving, no one's parking. The local businesses at the airport—the barbershop, the bookstore, or the Cinnabon franchise, for instance—may not be able to sustain a profitable enterprise if passengers and their friends don't come in. But you're going to have air transportation, even if it's by a single national airline, in an extreme example.

If the system continues with 20 percent fewer people traveling, airlines are going to have to increase prices. So then we'll have fewer people traveling at higher prices. That's a different kind of market from the mass market we've had. You won't get to a billion passengers as quickly, because the prices are higher. But you will eventually grow to that point. You will have to readjust all those businesses at the airports for the new economic realities. Fewer people means higher fares and prices if you want to keep the economics going.

Companies all over the country are talking about the importance of being adaptive organizations. And they're looking at their future developments as an evolutionary process. How do you expect

airports will have to adapt, say, over the next five years? How will the airport itself have evolved?

I don't think airports are much different from any other business in those terms. Companies differentiate themselves by how they survive in bad times. They keep investing in their people, and they keep pushing technological improvements. Airport managers are a talented group of people. Actually, they're the most talented they have ever been, with an historically high saturation of professionally trained airport experts with both business acumen and a passion for aviation. They're going to figure out how to adapt. So we'll find a new equilibrium. It may mean added costs. And it will certainly mean added security. But we'll be persistent in making sure we keep airports running.

Do you see airports becoming fortresses for the sake of security, where passengers must endure long waits and long distances from their cars to check-in and then to the gates?

We can't sustain this attitude that security and convenience are mutually exclusive. And technology is how we're going to get at that problem. There are basically three ways to use technology to heighten security: You can look for bad people, you can look for bad things, or you can identify people who are not a threat.

That third way of using technology is easy. We've already envisioned voluntary smart cards that passengers can use to expedite their security screening. Because it would be a strictly voluntary proposition, people who are concerned with privacy rights could opt to not participate.

We can also focus all this technology on looking for bad people and bad things that we don't know anything about. We're not just in public transportation now. We're in an era where a few people can disrupt networks that are very important. Looking for nineteen suicide pilots out of 700 million people isn't easy. Great technology is what's going to let us sort through 700 million people and find the nineteen that we're worried about.

But that puts us in the uncomfortable role of profiling people, doesn't it?

If we're only pulling people out because they have Arab-looking features, we're definitely doing something wrong. On the other hand, we don't go looking for Irish terrorists in the Mexican-American community. We profile all the time. You're only kidding yourself if you say we don't know that a lot of the current threat comes from men who are between certain ages and who have Middle Eastern backgrounds. This is not the same as saying that it's okay to take everyone who fits that description and pull him out only for that reason. But you also don't throw those factors out, in addition to other factors in the threat profile, when you are looking for bad people because you want to pretend those factors don't apply.

It's also important to remember that there are other groups that would bring a plane down if they could. White supremacists may present a significant threat of trying to get a bomb on and then get away. They don't want to commit suicide but they may want to do bad things. Further, passengers are at risk of being used unwittingly by terrorists. Who would have thought to stop a pregnant Irish woman at Heathrow? It's a good thing someone did, because her boyfriend had planted a bomb in her suitcase and she didn't even know it. These different threats require layers of aviation security, but we must use all the information we have on threats to be effective.

You have been in aviation for quite a while. I'm sure that there have been many times when you said to yourself that things will never be the same again. Based on that perspective, what comfort can you offer anyone else for getting beyond this immediate crisis of changes?

Make friends with change; it's coming whether you like it or not. It's coming faster than it ever has before. The whole notion that we're going to keep doing business as usual really has always been wrong. Adapting has always been the key to being successful in business. If you make the love of change part of the culture of your organization, and view change as an opportunity rather than with dread, you'll have a much happier existence.

It's actually fun to be on the leading edge of change, particularly if you choose to regard change as an asset. If you hide in your cave and say, "I hope nothing changes and that I can keep whatever successful program I have going," you will wind up frustrated and unhappy. Upheaval is part of the destructive/reconstructive cycle that is built into our economy. It's both an advantage and a disadvantage at any specific time. You might as well love it because it's not going to change.

In these last several months you have cycled through some changes yourself, starting with being infuriated by the direct attack on the business environment that you've spent so many years developing. There must have been many times when you've taken the attack on American aviation quite personally.

I've spent close to twenty years building this association up, and to be taking it apart again is very painful. We're cutting back our budget by 30 percent for planning purposes. As a result we're taking a huge hit in our programming for next year. Of course, as activity picks up, we'll replace the spending and hopefully build back up to 2001 levels.

After you sit around feeling sorry for yourself for a while, you have to get back to doing something constructive. That's when you get back to the fundamental persistence that makes people successful. People here in Washington know that substance does count for something. It just often doesn't count in the short run. The successful people are the ones who have good ideas and will bang away over and over and over again in order to get them adopted. You just have to keep going.

What good will come out of this?

We're going to be safer on an airplane than anywhere else. The whole notion that we can overcome these kinds of individual threats as a networked society is important. These networks, whether they're telecommunications, power grids, or air transportation are the keys to having a more mobile, open, and free society. With new technology we're going to have a lot of things that are boring and repetitive done by machines. It's going to create more interesting opportunities for human beings. It's an exciting future.

How can aviation neutralize anti-Americanism in the many ways it manifests itself?

Aviation can neutralize anti-Americanism just by doing its job bringing people together globally. You have to be dealing with the rational folks who are the majority out there around the world. You can't spend all your time focused on the few aberrations or you miss the bigger point. In the long run history shows that transportation creates more wealth and less poverty. And aviation and telecommunications are key to moving people, ideas, and goods over long distances. Aviation contributes to creating global wealth by bringing more people into this economy and into the wealth creation process.

What has enduring relevance in an environment of rapidly shifting priorities?

Treating people with respect. Once we learn how to feed and clothe ourselves, we spend our lives in constant search for respect. The world fights wars over the lack of respect people feel. Treat people with the respect they crave, and success will endure.

The ability to understand technology and what it means to us will also be relevant in the future. You don't have to know how to do cold fusion programming. You just have to understand the fundamentals of where communications and computing are going so you can understand what they can and can't do to solve your business problems.

What are you certain of?

The importance of information technology in the long run.

What are you uncertain of?

I'm uncertain of the timing of the shifts of important technology. When people consider technology they tend to overestimate the short-term impact and underestimate the long-term impact.

What is the essential ingredient for resilience?

Persistence in the face of failure. Failure always makes you mad. Some people get discouraged and give up. Others get mad and just try harder.

4

Curtis R. Carlson
CEO and President, SRI International

But the truth is, if you don't find people who are committed to doing something important, it just doesn't work—especially over the long term. Doing truly world-changing work takes a long time.

The future not only has to begin sometime, it also has to begin somewhere. And it's no overstatement to say that much of the future begins in California's Silicon Valley, where scientists, entrepreneurs, futurists, engineers, and venture capitalists know that they can find each other at boardroom tables in offices lining Stevens Creek Boulevard or over a plate of quesadillas at the unlikely Buck's Restaurant on Woodside Road.

It's also no hyperbole to say that of all the lights burning day and night up and down there are few companies in the Valley—indeed the world—that contribute to the future in the variety of ways that SRI International does. The name Microsoft may be more familiar to consumers, but SRI's innovations and research touch on almost every aspect of our lives. It invented the computer mouse; the modem; an easy-clean oven surface; airline luggage containers capable of withstanding a blast of plastic explosives; those visible pieces at the very end of jet wings that discharge static electricity; and new drugs for treating cancer, malaria, and cardiovascular diseases. SRI developed the earliest technologies necessary for what would become wireless networks and the Internet, automatic check processing, and the concept of on-line help. It even conducted the first feasibility study for Disneyland. With a mandate to discover and apply "science and technology for knowledge, commerce, prosperity, and peace," SRI leads with ideas.

As CEO and president of SRI since 1998, Curtis Carlson is one of Silicon Valley's extraordinary thought leaders who are able to marry business and technological problems and create solutions that not only serve to improve the human condition but also create extraordinary business opportunities. For Carlson (the recipient of fifteen patents himself) and his staff, vision, mission, enterprise, and technological breakthroughs are the necessary ingredients for creating a deliberate future. In this interview, he discusses leading a cutting-edge, futuristic organization in an environment charged with possibilities:

- Motivating supremely intelligent and gifted staff through mission and purpose

- Staying focused on the important questions rather than being distracted by interesting ones

- Finding the essential ingredients for creating a workplace environment that promotes breakthrough creativity

- Creating revolutionary innovation in a marketplace that values rapid innovation

When Gerald Levin retired as CEO of AOL Time Warner in late 2001, he said, "There's a human being locked inside. I want the poetry back in my life." How can leaders drive results-oriented, innovative organizations without sacrificing either their own careers or that divine spark that they are seeking now that they are retired?

I don't think there should be a contradiction. The human side of the equation is becoming more important, not less important. I'm a scientist, and there's no contradiction between what we do and our humanity. If you want to get the best from all of us, you need to tap into our humanity in a fundamental way.

At SRI we're blessed to have an organization that's devoted to helping our people do important, good things in the world. If you can find projects for people to work on that inspire them and if you can help them make a positive contribution to the world, you're appealing to one of their fundamental motivations. Most people want to make a contribution to the world. It's an important part of who we are. Helping people make that contribution through their work fulfills an important part of what it means to be alive. It encourages them to bring their best to the workplace.

And you can do that in the context of a for-profit corporate world?

There are many opportunities in this world for people to be engaged in important work to make the world a better place. If you want to think of a really important, but horrible, problem it's the AIDS situation in Africa. We have a whole continent right now that is in terrible trouble. We have people here at SRI who are working on drugs and vaccines to make a contribution to solving that tragedy. To have the privilege of being able to work on a problem of that importance is both daunting and inspiring.

These principles apply to most companies. Money isn't a terribly compelling motivator. Money has to be there, of course. But the truth is, if you don't find people who are committed to doing something important, it just doesn't work—especially over the long term. Doing truly world-changing work takes a long time. If you're not passionately committed to it, frankly you won't have the patience and endurance to get there.

There is increasing pressure to shorten that length of time. How can the typical company resist that ongoing pressure from Wall Street to move technology around and get it out on the street ever faster?

It's not Wall Street that is creating this pressure. It's the knowledge economy, where improvements happen increasingly rapidly. Wall Street is just responding to the world we're in. We, like everyone else, have to respond to that. Say, for example, you put together a business plan that requires five years to become profitable. With the world moving at the rate it is, that is too long in many markets. You probably won't be successful.

All of us have to reinvent how we work together. We must take the real issues and problems of the day much more seriously. This is why the human part of the organizational equation is so important. Everything that happens in the knowledge economy is based on people—their individual abilities and the inherent genius of teams. If you don't treat your people properly, given how rapidly the world is moving, they can destroy a project. All you need is one unhappy person to threaten everything you've been working for. One cynical, negative person can bring a project to a halt. Cynics are really damaging in an organization. They do enormous harm.

You can't pretend to ignore those sorts of issues anymore if you want to survive. This is where the real pressure to perform comes from. Not from Wall Street.

So a company must maintain a kind of youthful naiveté to stay per-petually new and filled with potential?

Right. Naiveté is an interesting word. In the sense that it means remaining open, being willing to explore new opportunities, and being willing to move forward, yes, companies should retain some naiveté. If you don't have those characteristics in today's world, you'll be run over by the tsunami of rapid innovation that will be invisible to you.

As a society we have fallen in love with the prospects of technology, holding it up as the answer. But are we asking the best questions?

Technology isn't the answer to every question. Terrorism, for example, shows us how technology can be used against us. In every significant technological discovery there are possibilities for new threats. Certainly the Internet creates issues about information security. Our new under-standing of the human genome opens up the possibility of serious bio-terrorism.

Even benign uses of technology should compel us to think hard about how we use technology. Take the issues of biodiversity. If we had an agri-cultural monoculture, for example, and someone were to attack it, they could do enormous damage to the United States and to the world. Genetic diversity must be ensured as we make genetic improvements in crops and livestock. Are we asking ourselves the right questions that will result in a robust environment? It's not enough to manipulate the DNA of wheat to, say, double our production capacity. We have to have enough diversity so that if a bioterrorist, or a natural disease, hits that crop, it won't be wiped out completely.

Are you saying that it's absolutely our responsibility to make sure we engineer our future using the principles of natural evolution as well as the breakthroughs of science?

It definitely has to be part of the whole thought process, or else we could create a dangerous situation for the world. We're still in the early days of understanding how to think about these issues. For example, how should we think about the trade-off between the potential loss of genetic diversity in crops and the ability to save the lives of millions of people. If we proceed too aggressively we could become vulnerable to diseases, terrorists, or other enemies. On the other hand, if we do not proceed with improved crops we ignore the desperate needs of millions of people. These issues apply to crops and farm animals today. They will apply eventually to us.

We are in the horse-and-buggy days of biotechnology. But just as important as understanding the promise of technologies is the ability to anticipate their implications in terms of what effect they're going to have on our lives and humanity. These are not trivial issues. I have faith we will work our way through them, but it will be difficult.

Is it as much about always knowing what questions to anticipate, or is it knowing how to stay aware of questions as they arise?

I'm sure both. We need to have an open environment in which to ask questions, where debate is uninhibited, and where the full genius and knowledge of the world is included. Good questions will probably get you good answers. It's been my experience that the answers that come back to good questions are often incredible, far exceeding your expectations. People are capable of remarkable things if the proper environment is set up to tap into their full capabilities.

How can you intentionally set up such an environment?

In many different ways. To start with, your values and strategy must be written down and shared. For example, all SRI employees are given a wallet-sized card to carry that summarizes our strategy and values. It says that we are people with integrity, with passion to make a difference, with freedom to create, with interdisciplinary talent, and with technical and managerial excellence. We treat others with respect, we empower champions, we team productively.

The two foundation concepts are *integrity* and *treating others with respect*. Respect and integrity are the basis for trust. If we're going to work on a really hard project, where we need to commit ourselves totally to it, if we don't have trust we won't commit. We would always be sitting back and wondering, "should I commit myself or should I not?"

The whole management philosophy we've built at SRI is based on the principle that you want to be free to tap into people's abilities wherever they reside in the organization—or in the world for that matter. If you can open people up—without undo constraints—to tap into their genius, you can do remarkable things.

You must have organizational alignment around these basic ideas. The organization must be open, transparent, and the reward system must be consistent with your stated values. All these things must be in place if you want to tap into the genius and resilience of your people.

Most people want to do a good job, and they are capable of achieving remarkable results if you create an environment that supports them. There's a real need for people to do a terrific job. It drives them forward in ways you can never force on them managerially. It's when you create an organization that taps into that need that you find people who are incredibly resilient. They'll work incredible hours. They'll wake up in the morning thinking about their work. They'll suffer a hundred defeats because they see the opportunity to make a significant impact.

Much of what we do in creating technical innovation is really a series of incremental failures. We fail, and we fail, and we fail until we finally succeed. You see it here at SRI all the time. People will pursue their dreams for years and years and be incredibly resilient. But when the critical organizational ingredients are in place, it's remarkable how often they'll eventually succeed.

Can U.S. companies take those same principles abroad to neutralize whatever anti-Americanism there may be?

When we bring these values to the countries where we work around the world and help solve important problems for the people in those countries, we feel we make a contribution to making the world a better place. In turn we hope to make people feel better about America. We have many positive examples around the world to point to over the company's fifty-five-year history.

But we can never rest on our laurels. As soon as you start thinking you're really good, you're probably in trouble. You have to accept that you're just at a certain point and you need to get better.

Do you think America is too naive about the preciousness of our technology, how it can be either stolen by other interests or used against us?

The answer is probably yes. But in today's world if you want to keep on the exponential curve of innovation, you must tap into the genius of people around the world. And to have that kind of access, you also have to be willing to share. Bill Joy of Sun Microsystems has said, "No matter how smart the people are in your company, most of the smartest people in the world are outside your company." You have literally hundreds of thousands of brilliant scientists throughout the world. If you don't tap into that intellectual wealth, then who loses? You do.

The Soviet Union built an "Iron Curtain," and eventually its economy declined to the point where it couldn't keep up with us. If we build a "Silicon Curtain" around the United States, the one thing we can be sure of is that we will decline intellectually.

But we also risk losing our competitive advantage as private industry if we allow a country to tell us, "Sure you can set up shop here provided we get your technology." And then we end up having other countries' subsidized companies competing against us using our own technology. That's the argument, in any case.

There's always some truth to that argument. And there have been situations when people make the wrong judgment in specific cases and lose their competitive advantage.

But it's important to remember that we're all under constant pressure to develop new technologies and business ideas. Because of this ongoing need to innovate, by the time someone has gotten around to copying your current products, you should be well on your way to creating your next ones. We all need to stay ahead of the exponential curve of innovation in our business areas if we want to survive. That's the only guaranteed path to success. That would be true even if it was just U.S. companies competing against each other.

What does "investing in the future" mean to you?

It means spending time and resources working on the important problems, as opposed to the interesting ones. Personal computers, for instance, will continue to survive and grow through the next century. The reason is that they still can't do very much compared with what we dream about. They can't speak to us, they can't see, they can't think. They have a fraction of the computational power of a human being. They're still very primitive objects.

Obviously there's a need there, where computers can benefit a lot of people. It is a huge market today, but it is still just beginning.

Finding a cure for AIDS is another important problem. Working on breast cancer cures is another. Educational tools to improve K-12 education are important. Developing airplane luggage containers that can withstand bomb explosions is another current example.

You do not have to sacrifice doing interesting things by focusing on the important questions. You can pick any number of important problems and the beautiful thing about them is that they're usually both important and interesting. In fact, the important questions are generally more interesting. If you solve the kinds of problems we listed earlier, it's also going to make you feel good about your life when you go to the retirement home.

What you need to do in an organization is create an environment where people think hard about these issues. You can't be casually thinking about them. You have to really work at it. I'm not the person at SRI who selects the important problems we work on. Far from it. The ideas come from our staff. But we talk about them all the time. Are we doing the most important thing in this field? Is this the time to solve this problem? Do we have a breakthrough idea? You really have to open yourself up to work in an environment where these kinds of questions are part of the culture. It requires a lot of vulnerability. It goes back to your naiveté observation. You have to be a little naive about the world and open to what it offers and how you're going to interact with it. That's not easy.

What are you certain of?

I am certain of increasingly rapid rates of change. I call it the *Exponential Economy*. Performance must improve at an increasingly rapid, exponential-like, rate. The classic example is Moore's Law for computers. If you don't improve your performance by a factor of two every eighteen months you're out of business. But that's becoming a general rule for many businesses. It used to be that medicine improved in tiny increments every year. But now, with the decoding of the genome, medicine has its own version of Moore's Law. Content on the Web doubles every six to nine months. Communication speed doubles every nine to twelve months. What I'm certain of is that this trend toward exponential improvement in many businesses is going to continue. It says a lot about how we must rethink and improve our management practices.

I'm also certain that the fundamental business principles will continue to apply even though two years ago, during the dot-com hysteria, we tried to pretend they didn't apply anymore.

What are you uncertain of?

I'm uncertain about how the continuing waves of technology will change the world. One of our brilliant people, Pat Lincoln, calls them "colliding exponentials." For example, when computing and communications collided, they created the Internet. This changed the world in both predictable and unpredictable ways. Now information technology is colliding with biology. Some of the consequences of this are obvious, others not so. There will be many additional colliding exponentials in the future that will open up new business opportunities, one right after another. It's really hard to predict most of them. But you have to keep your eyes open for them. That's part of the joy of my job.

I'm uncertain about terrorism. That can change everything. It will happen, but how? In California we're also uncertain about earthquakes. They will happen, but when? They can change everything here, too.

What is the essential ingredient for resilience?

The ability to know which problems are important ones. And then you need people who have a passionate commitment to solving them. If you don't, then you can't keep up. You also need to have a process inside the organization dedicated to creating compelling value for your clients. Creating client value does not happen by accident. It takes a disciplined process. Finally you need to address the human imperatives of your people. How you motivate, train, and help your people has always been fundamental to organizational success. But in this world it has become even more important. If you don't do these things well, you won't survive.

5

Michael P. C. Carns
General (retired), U.S. Air Force

If your standard is good enough, the risk of losing absolutely skyrockets because of bounding uncertainty and risk. When you lose, not only is the price intolerable, but rematches are not always available. And even if you get one, the result is often the same.

Invest to win and aim to win smart. Every time.

Like many high-profile, mission-driven organizations, the U.S. military has moved in and out of the U.S. public's favor over the decades during and since the Vietnam War. Still, its mission-critical objective remains the same and is non-negotiable: the security of the United States of America. These days it is fashionable to draw parallels between the management of the U.S. military and the management of U.S. enterprise. But in a conversation separate from this interview, General Michael Carns had this to say:

"Business is competition and creating the winning margin. The military is not in the business of shaving it to the margin. The military mission says that when you're betting the security of the nation, you don't go in on the cheap. You want to win decisively. You want to be the monopoly survivor."

Still, there are legitimate parallels to be drawn and lessons to be learned from the military model—and from Carns' experiences directly. A member of the U.S. Air Force Academy's first graduating class in 1959, and equipped with a degree from the Harvard Business School, he has had extensive experience in the leadership, direction, and management of complex organizations—including managing the Air Force's annual budget ($60 billion worth of projects). He served as the Vice Chief of Staff, U.S. Air Force, from 1991 to 1994; as Director of the Joint Staff, Joint Chiefs of Staff, during the Gulf War and the Panama invasion (1989 to 1991); as Deputy Commander in Chief, U.S. Pacific Forces in the late 1980s; and as Com-

mander of the l3th Air Force, Republic of the Philippines, during the Philip-
pine government crisis, from 1986 to 1987. He also has had extensive
strategic planning and resource allocation experience in a variety of senior
military staff appointments in the United States, Europe, and the Pacific.

As a career fighter pilot, he flew 200 combat missions in the F-4
Phantom II fighter in Southeast Asia during the Vietnam War and was
awarded the nation's third highest combat decoration for valor, the Silver
Star. He has also been awarded senior decorations by the governments of
the Philippines, South Korea, and Thailand.

Retired from the U.S. Air Force since 1994, he serves on the board of
advisers for the National Security Agency and the Naval Post-Graduate
School, among many other high-level organizations dedicated to national
security issues. He is also on the board of directors for several companies, including Rockwell Collins, Mykrolis Corporation, Dyncorp, Armed
Forces Services Corporation, and Burdeshaw Associates.

In this interview, Carns discusses the business management principles he has learned throughout the four decades he dedicated to the mission of national security:

- Leading in an environment of uncertainty and ambiguity
- The value of competition in promoting marketplace vitality
- Learning from past global crises
- Discipline as a positive force for innovation

**Modern history is full of changes and emergencies, where every-
thing seems so intense, so life and death. Then the issue gets
resolved and all that intensity is dissipated. How do you put into
proper perspective the importance, that sense of urgency, when you
know from experience several years down the road it will all be forgotten, and Americans will be focusing on something else?**

The world is never free of stresses of one sort or another…and too many of
them bad. Interestingly enough—and ironically enough—we may eventu-

ally decide that the Cold War against the USSR and the Warsaw Pact, which seemed so daunting and demanding at the time, was perhaps one of the most stable periods in recent history. We knew the potential adversaries. They were big enough to see from a distance. Over time we were able to develop a relationship with them. And without openly saying so, we saw them as rational adversaries who could be dealt with. We developed understandings that were truly unprecedented. We had arms agreements, we had military relationships, we had rules of engagement. And for the most part, we had understandings—some in writing—that in the air and on the sea, we wouldn't engage in shooting incidents.

Today is different. We don't have such understandings or agreements with the North Koreans, Iraqis, or other non-state adversaries that we've been dealing with in recent years. Moreover, they and others see the United States as all-powerful in the military sense with no possible way to materially confront us in conventional ways. That sense of impotency in advancing their agenda drives them to approaches that most societies and cultures have agreed to renounce. So, people boarding airplanes with box cutters is an understandable choice of tactics to end-run accepted conventions, striking terror and fear into the hearts of the vulnerable. In the face of this kind of outlaw warfare, it's very easy indeed to keep a sustained sense of urgency. There is no temptation to become complacent simply because we've prevailed in the past.

There is an interesting parallel between the dedicated guerrilla fighter using available technology against the large governmental being and the dedicated entrepreneur using whatever technology may be available to take on the large corporate competitor. We have historically viewed the corporate world as really being the indomitable force, and all things must be processed through the large corporate entity. Now we're seeing the small scrappies taking them down. Has the assumption of might and indomitability changed?

It's a popular perspective that large corporations dominated and little guys were not successful. But I'm skeptical. If you look at the one hundred largest businesses in 1850 or 1900, or even 1950, you'd find few repeaters today. There was no Hewlett Packard in 1950, no Microsoft in 1975.

Large corporations become vulnerable because they calcify over time. This calcification occurs for many reasons, but one key problem is that the development and selection of leaders often changes for the worse over time. The hard-bitten, market-steeled entrepreneurs who started companies build teams that conform, not challenge. Advancement becomes a case of being able to work through the bureaucratic politic to the top, rather than showing great promise, individuality, and inspiration. Therefore, over time, those moving to the top bring expertise based on how it was done yesterday. It's a rare corporation that has highly innovative leadership development and selection programs.

The innovators, however, are seen as threatening to the power structure because they are interpreted as questioning leadership. Large, old-line corporations, including the military, have a habit of snipping off those people because they don't conform.

On the other hand—and to be fair—a great strength of big companies is the rigor and discipline of its processes. They can take—or buy—an idea, and through its well-organized process, bring new ideas to the market. If it is successful, erosion sets in—burdened with supervision taking over and exposing the new market to potential new entrants. I recall the case of the USAF's effort to develop a new long-range air-to-air missile. One manufacturer worked on it for years—and the price only went up, year to year. In exasperation, the USAF bought the proprietary plans from the original developer and gave them to a second producer. We then told both companies that we would vary our buy between 40 percent and 60 percent, year to year, based on their submissions of price and quality. Since that time, the price has stabilized (and in some years decreased), and the quality has soared. The forced introduction of competition resulted in dramatic price reductions and quality improvements—confirmation of the importance of competition in all markets, military as well as commercial.

Constant competitive pressure in the marketplace produces quality, excellence, and value for the customer—and in the defense context, mandatory dominance in the battlespace and the vital national security edge, which is the crucial foreign policy responsibility—the core deliverable—for the nation and its citizenry.

There are some companies where *good enough* is good enough to maintain a presence in the marketplace. But for other companies—as well as for those of us in uniform—losing is an unacceptable outcome. If your standard is good enough, the risk of losing absolutely skyrockets because of bounding uncertainty and risk. When you lose, not only is the price intolerable, but rematches are not always available. And even if you get one, the result is often the same.

Invest to win and aim to win smart. Every time.

American civilians tend to shudder at the word "discipline" as a punishing, bad thing. As someone who spent his career in the military, how do you view discipline?

Discipline gets a bad name because it is not properly understood. Discipline is an ordered commitment to purpose. We all have discipline in our lives. We structure our daily lives to accomplish mundane and repetitive activities efficiently so that we devote time to do more important things. Business has its own disciplines—policies, processes, procedures—which, if not followed, will result in trouble.

In American culture, discipline is thought of as mindless regimentation, which absolutely it is not. It is enlightened order and rigor to accomplish purpose efficiently. In business, as in the military, you expect extraordinary discipline at the operating level. That is, you need to have high confidence that your people are subject matter experts in what they do, that they do it in a very ordered matter to extract best efficiency. Along with that, the business must have management processes in place that encourage innovation—the essence of the "best practices" philosophy now in broadened use in U.S. industry in those processes.

The trick is to decide who can innovate and how. Regardless of how good an innovation may be, if everyone is innovating without discipline, it can destroy a process. An inspired leader establishes pathways for people to propose change in an orderly and disciplined fashion. That marriage between discipline—ordered practices—and seeking "best practices" is leadership's unerring pathway not only to efficiency and quality but also to a motivated workforce.

How important is knowing how to deal with ambiguity in the making of great leadership?

Critical. Leaders are required to make Solomonic judgments, as well as small ones. The pathway to good judgment is learning from bad experience. If you're not being constantly challenged out there to assess, assess, assess, to judge, judge, judge, and then decide, you're not going to learn to be a better and better leader. It is being critically challenged to reason clearly and assess correctly that results in eventually making better judgments and becoming a better leader.

A key responsibility of a leader is to deal with uncertainty. Leaders make risk judgments and decisions about unknowns or as yet unknowables. If everything was certain, you wouldn't need a leader. And, very importantly, by their behavior, leaders inspire confidence in people who can't decide themselves.

Does the force of competition sharpen your own saw, not only in terms of improving your decision-making processes but also in terms of improving your deliverables to the marketplace?

This is the major essence of competitive capitalism. It is competition that brings better products to the market. I'm hard pressed to think of any other single characteristic that causes a business to change its behavior in the marketplace more than competition. There is a cost in the short run, but a major benefit in the long. Competition is expensive in the sense you have to invest in improving your product—a cost that could be avoided if one froze the design. Competition makes sure that the market never rests by pressing for innovation on the one hand and cost reduction on the other. If you discover an industry that has no competition, you won't find much in the way of innovation either.

In America, competition gives us choice as consumers. We take the kinds of choices we have for granted, and they are very much a part of our daily lives. But when people who aren't used to the American "way" come here, we realize that choice can also be a heavy burden.

For instance, when the pilot Viktor Belenko defected from the Soviet Union in the late 1970s, he underwent rigorous and exhausting debriefings from U.S. intelligence officers. Eventually Belenko was provided some break time, and he was escorted to Potomac Mills (an outlet mall south of Washington, D.C.) to look around. He was immediately skeptical and said, "I know what you're doing to me. This is just one of your Potemkin Villages. You're just trying to prove that America's system is better so you've brought me to this government facility where only privileged people can buy." To dissuade him of that particular perspective, they took him out to other malls around Washington. But he wouldn't be swayed. "This is Washington, you've got lots of these places out here," he told them.

Nine months into his stay, his contacts at the CIA and the Air Force said, "Here's a map of the entire United States, we'll take you anywhere you want to go." And so, while initially doubtful, he was eventually convinced that the American competitive capitalist system provides for so much choice.

Later, I had the chance to ask him, once he was settled into his new life: "What troubles you most about America?" His answer was immediate: "It's so hard to make choices. If I go into a food store, I just can't go in and buy cereal, I have to choose among fifty choices. If I go in to buy soap I have to make ten choices. I have to read all the labels to figure out which one is the right one for me. I hate so many choices."

He was just bowled over by the competitive market and the fact it was incumbent upon him to make the choices. In the Russian marketplace, if he wanted to buy soap, there was just one soap. However, he has come to appreciate that competition brings not only alternatives and choices but also superior products.

And is it that surfeit of choices that feeds into that feeling of uncertainty? If we only had one choice we wouldn't have to concern ourselves with certainty versus uncertainty. And we have only ourselves to blame if it goes wrong.

We learn early in life to make thousands of choices and judgments every day and don't even realize it. The burden has been put on us rather than on the state to make those choices. In Russia, Viktor could do his shopping in no time flat, poor as the products were. Here, he finds it daunting to have to deal with this problem every day. For him, it's a problem. For us, it's an expectation.

We have seen the cycles of patriotism in this country. Do you think the current fervor of flag-waving will stick?

A founding principle this country was the right to voice divergent beliefs but not the right to impose your views on others. The government has a sort of "deal" with its citizens: It looks after the nation's security and regulates its well-being; the citizens are free to pursue economic activity and happiness; and the state stays out of running one's daily life and the marketplace.

When you no longer feel safe, your refuge is overt patriotism—a community exhortation to the state to take necessary actions to make you feel safe again. This only shows its bright face when people feel threatened. The patriotic passion that we've seen since September 11 is a collective reflection of fear, yet resolve. The strong outpouring tells me the state is doing its job. It is getting involved when it should—being asked to restore conditions that make America feel safe so that people can again take full charge of their individual lives.

Over recent decades, the government has also recognized that part of the pursuit of happiness is not killing our kids in the pursuit of security. World War I was a watershed. Dying for your country lost its "glory"—"the old lie," as Wilfred Owen bitterly characterized it. In retrospect, it is difficult to understand why cultures thought that way. Why should you have to die? It's a defeat of purpose; you don't get to enjoy the fruits of your victory. Patton popularized the new thinking with his exhortation to "…make the other bastard die for his country."

In the latter half of the twentieth century, we took extraordinary measures to achieve decisive military victory with minimum loss of U.S. and coalition lives. Our approach is to insure that our people feel you are committed to them, that you are giving them the best means available, the most enlightened training, and the structure and the equipment to do the job. They do not disappoint; taking care of the people means that they take care of the mission. This enlightened military approach—of using "best practices," inspiring them, and supplying them, vis-à-vis the old approach of mindless attack, of substituting intellect and firepower for massed manpower—has yielded stunning successes by our soldiers, sailors, airmen, and marines. This continues today as we see our prosecution of the war on terrorism in Afghanistan unfold.

It's been said that greatness comes from the choices we make, not the circumstances we find ourselves in. What kinds of choices facilitate greatness as a function of leadership?

The statement is too strong for me. Greatness is at least a function of circumstance, especially when called upon to overcome great uncertainty and adversity. At a different time, Winston Churchill would not have been judged a great prime minister. At a different time, Rudy Giuliani would not have been judged a great mayor. Circumstance allows greatness to emerge because of the way leaders have prepared themselves to deal with it. Circumstance has a hell of a lot to do with greatness.

Obviously greatness also comes from making the right choices. I certainly believe that Rudy Giuliani could have made some conscious choices that would not have made him great. But, make no mistake, it was the circumstance that offered him the chance to make some incredibly good choices and now be lauded as "great."

One important feature of greatness is to be ready for the challenge when it comes. If you have not very carefully prepared the battlefield, when your time comes, you will not be great. If you have not organized, trained, disciplined, and equipped your people, when the emergency comes you are doomed to fail. In military history terms, many names come to mind: MacArthur, Eisenhower, Marshall, Patton, Powell.

Is part of preparing the battlefield demonstrating your trustworthiness as a leader in small increments up to that moment?

Yes, as well as making significant accomplishments. Giuliani spent years building up his teams and altering the city's processes and procedures, from getting tough on crime to delivering better public services. He took on all sorts of fights where the city, especially the press, bitterly criticized him. Eventually he got his arms around the city and got key subordinate leaders in key places in various important functional areas. And when the crisis came, the leader and the team were organized, trained, and ready. The results speak for themselves. He was great because he was ready when the crisis arose and because he had developed good judgment as circumstances presented themselves, not just in the final big crisis.

So the conscious choices that Giuliani had set up in advance included the choice not to be swayed so much by public opinion at the moment? His choice was to be focused and utterly committed to the long-term mission?

That's absolutely right.

What other conscious choices would facilitate greatness in leadership?

The choices to be committed to selfless purpose, to be orderly and disciplined in approach, to build and mentor the team, to be accountable for one's actions, and to be decisive in execution. Through all of this, one must communicate constantly to gain the mission-critical element of trust among one's team. That's essential, especially here in the United States where public image is so important. In our bottom-up political system, creating an image of competence is necessary to maintain the support of the people, without which you will not be able to prevail in the long term. People may have loved hating Giuliani but they trusted him—he produced when the chips were down. And New Yorkers knew that.

How can leaders gain inspiration from those below them on the organizational chart?

Although leaders need to provide the vision and set the agenda, they also need communicate that they have great confidence and respect for the contributions of the sectoral parts that compose the whole—the team. Leaders don't hold themselves up as the smartest. It's absolutely not the leader's job to be the smartest. The leader's job is to be able to focus, integrate, orchestrate, and harmonize the efforts of all the expertise structured beneath him. And so long as those subject matter experts feel recognized for their contributions, it creates great inspiration, teamwork, and loyalty within the organization. This is leadership at its best.

One of the most inspiring developments that immediately came out of the September 11 attacks was the worldwide coalition against terrorism that George Bush assembled within just a few days. What can business draw from the model of disparate groups joining for one specific common cause?

Voluntary combinations and associations—coalitions and alliances in political-military terms, strategic alliances and joint ventures in business terms—are one of the powerful new developments in modern history. These alliance structures voluntarily come together for a common purpose that benefits all parties. And, to be successful—militarily or economically—they are increasingly necessary to keep up with technology and market changes. As developments move faster and faster, all entities are stressed to cope because their intelligence and operating base is hard pressed to adapt as fast as technology and competitive markets are moving. When a company feels particularly deficient in a particular area, it can now go out and temporarily associate rather than permanently buy the capability it needs. This gives business—and the military—a whole new way of dealing with change by assembling partners for common purpose as the market or situation demands.

And that serves to make your former enemies—or competitors—your current partners?

You used the word *current,* and that's important to keep in mind. These kinds of coalitions can make your competitors *temporarily* cooperative members of a team. But competition is dynamic and changing—and so must you be as well. One makes these temporary arrangements for an intended purpose and then one devises new combinations and alliances to face the next challenge, ever keeping in mind that today's adversary may be tomorrow's partner. So, ongoing diplomacy among competitors is very important; you never know when you're going to need today's competitor to shift his weight a little bit to become your friend, even if only temporarily.

Business relationships are extraordinarily cordial for that reason. No one speaks badly about anyone else. In fact they are disingenuous to the extreme. No one is going to start the fight. They are very complimentary and tell each other how wonderful they are. But in their minds they're thinking, "How can I use this person in my next operation?"

How can companies help neutralize anti-Americanism abroad?

This is a problem that is as much corporate as it is interpersonal. Americans are very parochial in their understanding of the rest of the world. Americans think that our way is the right way. And the media powerfully reinforces that message as to how superior we are. In our insularity, we then go abroad with a misunderstanding and insensitivity to the pride and self-esteem of other cultures—business as well as interpersonal.

The successful overseas military or commercial operation looks very carefully at the culture it intends to operate in and tunes its practices—as best it can—in a socially advantageous way for that particular culture without violating U.S. law. You don't go over and preach to them. You show respect for their culture, and you lead by example. But you don't voice your views of their lifestyle. If you're tuned in you can be very successful.

What are you certain of?

I am certain of uncertainty. But I'm also certain that inspired leadership is the best way to deal with uncertainty. I'm convinced that leadership without inspiration will not succeed. Leadership is what gives mission meaning. It fuses people with purpose.

I don't think you can be certain of much of anything.

What are you uncertain of?

Since I am certain about uncertainty, it's hard to be certain about anything else. The world is by its very nature uncertain, and it's important to recognize that. If you're certain about something, you're likely to be wrong.

What is the essential ingredient for resilience?

Commitment to purpose. There has to be a total belief in what you're trying to accomplish. That belief needs to be rooted in your own value system. And when it is, you're willing to be resilient in its pursuit, to overcome adversities, to mitigate risks, and assess potential costs of failure. You just have to say, "I'm committed to this, no matter what. I believe it's the right thing. If we don't do this, the alternatives are worse. I'm responsible for it, I'm accountable for it, and I've just got to see this thing through." This is service over self. There is no limit to what a selfless person can accomplish.

6

Peggy Conlon

CEO and President, the Ad Council

I didn't think this group could work any harder because they have always been truly dedicated. But here we are, all working so much harder, and we feel good about it. We're at war, this is what's required, and what we're doing is important.

For days after the September 11 attacks, television was filled with all news all the time. But television is expensive, and bills must be paid. So inevitably commercials began to creep back on the air—most notably, and most frequently, car commercials with such exploitative slogans as "Keep America Rolling." But not too far behind was a commercial featuring a gentle series of faces of many races and ethnic groups, all proudly declaring, "I am an American." This commercial does what all commercials do: It sends its viewer into action. But instead of the message being, "go out and buy this," the message was, "remember that this is a nation that takes pride in its ethnic, racial, and cultural diversity." As reports of hate crimes started to come into newsrooms coast to coast, this message was promoting a valuable product: tolerance.

This commercial, distributed by the Ad Council, typifies the Ad Council's primary mission: telling Americans to take action to improve their lives. Americans everywhere know its messages: "buckle up for safety," "take a bite out of crime," "only you can prevent forest fires," "friends don't let friends drive drunk," "the mind is a terrible thing to waste." Currently the organization is distributing humorous commercials reminding you to get those pesky polyps under control before they develop into full-blown colon cancer. And, as this book is being written, a new series of commercials is airing, backed by Aaron Copland's stirring *Appalachian Spring,* telling Americans to battle terrorism by living their lives to the fullest. This is part of the Ad Council's war campaign to give civilians inspiration and information about fighting the battle at home.

As president of the Ad Council, Peggy Conlon mobilizes yearly more than $1.5 billion of advertising time and space, the creative services of more than forty major advertising agencies, and related financial support from hundreds of corporations. She also serves on the board of directors of the Partnership for a Drug Free America (PDFA) and sits on the Harvard School of Public Health's Health and Social Behavior Advisory Committee.

In this interview, Conlon talks about the days immediately following the attack and the management lessons she drew from them:

- Having the nerve and mission focus to depart from procedure for the sake of necessary responsiveness
- Transitioning back to "business as usual"
- Keeping staff and volunteers inspired and mission driven

Although most Americans are aware of at least one Ad Council-sponsored message, it seemed as though just days after September 11, most Americans became aware of the Ad Council itself—most notably through the "I am an American" campaign and then through the small feature about you on CNN Headline News. How was it that your organization figured so prominently in the immediate aftermath and recovery post–September 11?

We have gone back to the war footing that we were on when we were founded. The Ad Council was originally called the War Ad Council and was founded by the leaders of advertising industry and President Roosevelt just weeks after the 1941 attack on Pearl Harbor. At a time like this communication is critically important.

But it also has caused us to change our whole model as to how we do business day-to-day. In order to be responsive to this new set of circumstances, we had to telescope down our campaign development process, which had evolved since World War II to take up to nine months from start to finish. It's a very precise process involving a campaign proposal stage and creative approval stages as the issue is accepted and the creative team progresses. It's a process that has worked for us in relatively peaceful times.

But we don't have that kind of time now. The special crisis response team we've put together after the September 11 attacks has reduced the process down to just days.

When the attack happened, our senior staff got together the very next day and said, "Clearly, this is not business as usual. How do we respond?" We began by reaching out to all of the rescue organizations, like the Red Cross and United Way, and we told them, "Even though you're not a campaign of ours right now, get us your crisis-related public service message and we'll take it from there." They got us the messages and we made sure they were distributed to the media outlets and broadcast on donated time.

We knew the White House (specifically the First Lady's office) wanted to tell parents to comfort their children. So we went down to Washington eight days after the attack to film the First Lady. A pro bono agency edited it overnight, we had tapes made, and an Ad Council team ran the tapes all over New York City to broadcast on cable networks and local stations the minute they came out of the duplicating house. We were on the air forty-eight hours from the time we filmed the First Lady—and only ten days after the attack.

An agency in Austin, GSD&M, created a spot called "I am an American," and we also had that on the air ten days after the attack.

From the very beginning we decided to throw the rulebook out and act instinctively. The board of directors applauded that and appreciated it. Desperate times call for desperate measures, as they say. They were pleased with the fact that we didn't ask for permission, because that would have taken too much time. We just did what needed to be done.

How did you transition from the immediate crisis of the first few days and weeks to more of a "crisis business as usual" mode—still retaining that sense of urgency but hitting a more deliberate stride and doable pace?

Ten days after the attack we brought together representatives of the whole industry: trade associations that represent the advertising agencies, major advertisers, and media outlets, who are also members of our board. By this time we already had several messages on the air, so our main question was how do we go forward proactively, rather than continuing in the reactive mode we'd been in.

We want this to ultimately be a cohesive campaign, and we want the entire advertising community to support it. How do we do this? First, the industry reaffirmed that in this war effort the Ad Council, just as it had in World War II, would continue to speak for the entire industry.

Then we put together a special crisis response team, which developed the communications strategy that informs all of the work developed in response to 9/11. Our mission is to develop public service messages that inform, involve, and inspire Americans to do something in this war against terrorism. According to the research we did up front, Americans were feeling out of control. The very goal of terrorism is to commit random acts that create immobilizing fear. The best way people can overcome that fear is to take action.

We certainly saw that in New York after the towers came down. People couldn't find enough things to do: giving blood, giving money, giving food, volunteering. Not coincidentally, this was the nature of our communications during World War II, urging people to buy war bonds, plant victory gardens, conserve energy, watch what they say (our "Loose Lips Sink Ships" campaign), and recruiting millions of women into what were traditionally men's jobs (our "Rosie the Riveter" campaign). These were all things individual Americans could do to support the war effort back then. We just had to figure out what Americans could do now to support the war effort.

If the purpose of terrorism is to rob us of our way of life, the way to fight terrorism is to go back to doing what you were doing before the attack. One of our campaigns for the Live Brave Coalition says, "I will fight terrorism by going to my best friend's wedding, I will fight terrorism by going back to work, I will fight terrorism by going out to dinner with a friend." It's really giving people an understanding that it's not only *okay* in terms of giving people permission to go back to business as usual but it's also *vital* in terms of fighting terrorism directly.

After this crisis passes, what will have changed in the long run as far as the Ad Council is concerned, and as far as you're concerned?

Some of those old, time-consuming, institutionalized procedures will change as a result. One of the steps that had bogged the process down was the bi-monthly creative review committee meeting to approve these campaigns as they developed. Now we're e-mailing work to the committee and we're getting feedback on a real-time basis.

Every one of these messages that you're putting out there to inspire America must be inspiring your own staff tremendously.

We have a really tight staff, but we're even more motivated and committed now. We see the relevance and the importance of the messages we're putting out there in this war on terrorism. Based on economic realities, we are not adding to staff. Therefore, we are all doing our regular jobs in addition to this overlay of crisis-related work. It's given us a tremendous sense of confidence that we can do it. I didn't think this group could work any harder because they have always been truly dedicated. But here we are, all working much harder, and we feel good about it. We're at war, this is what's required, and what we're doing is important.

The advertising industry is notorious for being high ego, highly competitive, even cutthroat at times. How do you bring all these people together under one mission when, after they leave your offices, they're back at it tooth and claw?

We really are the conscience of the industry. I can't tell you how many creative teams I've worked with that at some point in the process stop and say, "Boy, this sure beats the hell out of selling soap."

They all love the Ad Council because they see it as an opportunity to take the talents that they bring to commercial products and put them to work for the benefit of the American people. When the Ad Council was founded, it was envisioned as "advertising's gift to America." When people think about pro bono work, they usually think about medicine and the legal profession. They don't think about the advertising industry as one that does a tremendous body of pro bono work on behalf of the country. And yet it does.

You were dealing with a changing industry long before September 11. What are the ongoing change issues that you're dealing with and how are you addressing them?

The major challenges are coming from the fragmentation of the media industry. Fifteen years ago, if the three networks accepted your work, you'd get 95 percent of the country. Today, as you know, that's not the case. We actually distribute our materials to 26,000 media outlets. That represents a tremendous cost in duplication and distribution costs.

Then there is the issue of persuading all those outlets to donate free air and space time for our messages. That requires a special type of outreach function that's different from conventional advertising agencies. They have media departments that are responsible for *purchasing* time and space. Our media department is responsible for, in effect, *selling* our messages to outlets so that they will donate time and space.

When I got here our media department had been significantly cut back. But it's a very competitive environment to get donated time and space, so we've been growing that department aggressively. We actually reached more than $1.5 billion of donated media last year on behalf of our campaigns. So this investment is paying off.

We're also getting very smart about how we're using technology, including using e-mail to reach out to media public service directors. They may not take your call, but they are more likely to read an e-mail—they may even open an attachment to preview a spot and order it online. We can do a lot of things electronically. And where possible we use digital distribution.

We're also being more proactive in seeking out campaigns. Rather than just sitting here and picking from organizations that come to us, we've turned that model around. We have a big commitment to children, for instance, and 80 percent of our campaign docket concerns the welfare of children. When I first came onboard we looked at the line-up of campaigns, and we noticed that there were some areas that needed to be there if we were going to address the well-being of children—not the least of which was childhood hunger. And it took us a year, but we found someone to underwrite the campaign.

Finally, we're trying to find more and more ways to support our operating costs and wean ourselves off such tremendous dependence on fund-raising. We have a $9 million operating budget that we have to raise each year, starting from scratch. We are now at the point where 50 percent of our operating revenue comes from fees and indirect charges related to campaign production. Still, about half of our funding comes from donations. But that's way down from what it was three years ago.

How do you keep your key contributors at the table during such a stressful time in their own business?

Since I joined the Ad Council, we have been building up our corporate development activities. We have a base of approximately 300 contributors.

Before I joined, only a handful of our donors had received personal sales calls from Ad Council staff. We had been cultivating those relationships primarily through our board members—which is still very important—and through direct mail and phone. But our supporters deserve more from us. By the end of the first year, we had personally called on 75 percent of our contributors, and that effort continues. We are now broadening and trying to bring in new companies as well.

When it comes to fund-raising, probably the single most important element is the work that our board of directors does. Our 85-person board is made up of three different groups: media companies, advertising agency executives, and advertisers. Those people are very, very influential. We are not shy, and neither are they, about putting the touch on others for donations. It's a very, very powerful group. When you think about the influence that those three groups wield, it's phenomenal.

They would all love to do more in the area of public service. If they can't physically get out and do it, at least they know we're doing it in their name. We never have any trouble recruiting agencies do the work pro bono—and they have to find time to do the work in addition to their billable workload. Our funders and volunteers are committed to supporting the Ad Council, which serves the American people.

Do you expect that when this particular emergency subsides, there might be a deflation of passion?

There was a natural spike right after September 11 that caused people to do things that even today you couldn't get them to do anymore. But that was quite natural. We were all shocked and horrified. When we reached out to all the organizations and told them, "Let us do the distribution and outreach for all of your campaigns," we frankly didn't know how we were going to pay for it. Our approach was: Let's do the right thing now and figure out how to pay for it later. Fortunately, all of our vendors—the duplicators, the printers, the mailing houses—all said, "Hey, don't worry about it. We'll do it for free." We had $300,000 worth of services donated to us the first week after the attack.

What does that say to you?

It makes me proud to be a human being, proud to be an American, and proud to be in advertising. We have more people who have reached out to volun-

teer to do things than we know what to do with. One of my biggest problems
right now is that I don't have enough assignments to go around.

**Do you think you'll ever be able to fully return to those simple
everyday campaigns, such as "Friends Don't Let Friends
Drive Drunk"?**

Our strategy will be to continue to embrace the other messages we have
done all along. For instance, we do the McGruff "Take a Bite Out of Crime"
campaign for the National Crime Prevention Council. Just a week after the
attack the team was in here for a meeting. We asked ourselves, "What
should the message be now?" The message was basically the same but with
a topical twist: People need things to do. So our strategy is to give them specific suggestions and specific actions they can take to keep themselves safe,
their communities safe, their country safe. People are looking for things to
do to keep their country strong.

So with all of our traditional peacetime messages—whether it's mentoring children, stopping friends from driving drunk, participating in after-
school programs, or whatever it is—the core message is the same: We're
caring for one another as a country. Out of that comes the strength and
resolve we need to get through what the country's going to have to get
through over the next few years in this war on terrorism.

**How can American business use communications to combat terror-
ism and anti-Americanism abroad?**

One of the most important things, obviously, is that we sustain an economy
that stays strong. And advertising has a positive impact on our economy. We
have to continue to stimulate business and keep people employed so that the
economy can continue to function properly. Having said that, there are a lot
of corporations that have tried to tie their communications to the war effort
and they have been criticized for it. Even though their intentions may have
been pure, they were seen to be capitalizing on the tragedy to promote their
company and build brand awareness.

This is nothing new. It happened right after Pearl Harbor as well. Many
companies were putting war messages into their paid advertising. And I
think it was Eisenhower who complained, "You would have thought it was
the brands who won the war and not the military."

When it comes to tying your external message to the war effort, there's a very fine line between good and bad taste.

What have you learned about yourself during this time?

I've learned to trust myself. When the terrorists attacked, there was no time to engage our board for advice on what to do. Indeed, many of them couldn't be reached due to travel and communications difficulties. So, I just followed my instincts and relied on experience and plain common sense. I believe we accomplished some very important things in those first few weeks. But, whether what we did was exactly right was not as important as the fact that we leapt into action. Our staff and our community were looking for leadership. And that put all our activities into a very favorable light.

A lot of people have said to me, "You've got the best job in the business. What you're doing helps a lot of people and is contributing to creating a positive social change." To me that's huge. I have the luxury of heading up the organization that harnesses the incredible power of advertising and can change the public mindset to create a better way of life in the United States. What we're doing is motivating Americans to take specific actions that will strengthen this country.

What are you certain of?

I have a much broader definition of what our product should be. There are several new areas beyond the definition of traditional advertising that we want move into as a natural direction of our growth. How soon and to what degree we can extend our influence, I'm not sure. But it has to go beyond advertising. We are looking at expanding our entertainment media outreach in the Hollywood community to influence content that appears on television and in movies. We are also expanding services to our clients, such as building Web sites, public relations, and publicity and direct mail services.

What are you uncertain of?

We're going to be facing a continuing financial challenge. The major advertising agencies, media companies, and major advertisers are in very aggressive cost cutting modes. Ad agencies are laying off 20 percent of their workforce. That makes it more difficult for us to go to them and say, "I need $25,000 in operating expenses."

They're all public companies now, so they have to worry about their share prices as well. Therefore, it is critical to keep them engaged, on the board, doing pro bono work, and serving on the committees. In this way, they will sustain their passion about the work we're doing.

Another area of uncertainty is the increasingly fragmenting media universe. We have to work harder than ever to get donated media support from a broader number of media outlets that have a shrinking audience. The ability to reach a mass audience will continue to challenge us.

What is the essential ingredient for resilience?

Having a purpose.

7

Leo A. Daly, III
Chairman and President, Leo A Daly

Cultural traditions and behaviors may be changing more slowly in some countries than in others, but we're all changing. And we have to be sensitive to this. If we're not, we're not going to have a successful relationship or a successful design. This also means that we must remember to honor tradition.

Although the Leo A Daly firm did not design the Twin Towers themselves, when the towers collapsed, several Leo A Daly–designed interiors fell with them. When President George W. Bush rushed to Offutt Air Force Base on that day, he was heading for the headquarters of the Strategic Air Command—designed by Leo A Daly. When the Joint Chiefs of Staff meet, they convene at the National Military Command Center in the Pentagon, designed by Leo A Daly.

Since its founding in 1915, from command centers to cathedrals to commercial complexes to campuses throughout the world, Leo A Daly has designed the sites of many historic events. Incidentally, the Liberace Museum in Las Vegas is another Leo A Daly design.

Today, the man, Leo A. Daly, III is the third generation leading one of the world's largest architectural and engineering firms, building not only landmarks around the world but also thousands of architecture careers of young professionals from almost every nation. In this interview, Daly discusses the issues surrounding safety in architecture and the influence of American culture and values around the world:

- What architects, engineers, and building owners are learning from the collapse of the World Trade Center Twin Towers

- How American firms can influence the future of professionalism in their fields around the world

- The value of cross-functional strategic alliances
- How prestigious office buildings will be transformed in the face of fear and for the sake of safety

After the attacks of September 11, architects must be asking themselves new questions about the vulnerability of buildings and even their appropriate use. I was surprised, for instance, to realize that wheelchair-bound employees could not get down. Given the loss of elevator service, they were stuck. What are architects doing to solve this problem, which had such tragic consequences?

When, as a society, we prevent discrimination against workers with disabilities by passing legislation such as the ADA, we must also make sure we can keep these workers safe in our buildings. The World Trade Center was built in 1973 before the ADA was made into law. However, although ADA has greatly improved accessibility standards in the workplace, it has not solved the problem of how to safely evacuate disabled workers from high-rise buildings if the elevators are inoperable. Architects and engineers are still wrestling with this problem.

I'm working right now with a committee sponsored by the American Institute of Architects to come up with a national building code for high-rise buildings. One of the chief drivers on this is, of course, emergency access and egress. The loss of disabled employees because they can't use the stairs to get out of a high-rise is a tragedy that must not be repeated.

It's possible to build a safe skyscraper. There's some research being done in the United States and abroad on concrete materials that are going to be better than steel. If we can somehow protect the core of high-rise buildings, they're going to be a lot safer. The airplanes on September 11 penetrated the cores of the Twin Towers. Because the towers were designed to be flexible at the top to withstand strong winds, they were also more lightweight. And so those planes went right through. What most people didn't realize was how quickly the towers would collapse. The building engineers themselves only expected the towers to hold up for a half hour, and were surprised they stood for so long. We're going to devise ways of making high-rises safer. But there will be a price tag to that. And even then wheelchair-bound employees may have to be on the lower floors.

If wheelchair-bound employees are required to work on lower floors, does that mean we're going to have to change our emotional attachment to the prestige of being on higher floors?

In a way that has already been happening. There have been relatively few high-rise buildings done in the last ten years. The emphasis has been on the design of campus complexes. There will continue to be high-rise buildings built in certain venues, but there are some very prestigious campuses around the country that are only three or four stories high.

But they require open space. How do you see the evolution of architecture affecting the life of the downtown area, given what has happened?

There will continue to be high-rise buildings, only they might not be reaching for the sky as much. They're talking about replacing the World Trade Center towers with fifty-story buildings—which just happens to be the height at which you can have rigid cores in most locations, except for earthquake areas such as San Francisco. The new signature tower that my firm has designed for the First National Bank of Omaha, which will be the focal point of Omaha's downtown renaissance, is, for instance, forty stories high.

There will be a lot of corporations who will question the importance of extremely tall skyscrapers—and many will continue to want them. But it all comes back to the comfort level of the user, doesn't it? The employees may be safe, but are they going to *feel* safe? You can make a hundred-story building that is safe, and you can tell people that it is safe. But if no one uses those top forty floors, it's no good.

What old rules and expectations are no longer valid for you and your work? What has taken their place?

In our business the old rules can't be thrown out. You have to respect the old rules and be very selective about integrating new solutions. Everything we do is based on historic precedence. We then apply innovation, combining it with existing experience and knowledge.

Every time we do an urban plan, for example, we look to other urban plans for inspiration. When creating architecture, we often use a combination of long-standing guidelines for proportion and scale, including the "golden mean" and the "double cube." These classical rules give us a systemized approach to scale and proportion to follow, whether we are designing a door, an interior space, or the façade of a building. And the result is very pleasing to the eye. Every time I see an architect deviate from these well-tested rules I feel that the design is not quite as successful.

How has multicultural sensitivity evolved in recent years, either in the way you do business or design buildings?

The basics are the same: communication, listening, and being very, very conscious of personal needs of the people who are going to occupy our buildings. We're getting better at it. We have to create buildings that are not only safer and offer a better quality of life, but they also have to be more client-centric.

People all over the world want some American innovation in their buildings. But they want it in terms of their own cultural background. We have to be sensitive to that. Now, in order to do that, we deal with all these different cultures in their own environments. So we set up offices in those countries. We've been in Hong Kong since 1967. That office is a Chinese office, with Chinese architects, engineers, and planners. It has a Leo A Daly system but in the context of the client's culture.

And we have to remember that the client's culture is also going through drastic changes. America isn't the only country that's undergoing a metamorphosis. Take, for instance, Spain, where for centuries the tradition of a two-hour midday siesta has been a deeply ingrained part of the way they work and live. Now, though, many of the younger professionals and their companies want to work through that siesta time. That way the employees can spend the evening with their families, and the companies can be globally competitive.

So how can we, as an American company, architecturally help client companies support that shift in a deeply rooted tradition? By designing into our buildings in Spain an environment in which the employees will want to stay at work the full eight hours. We're designing the Spanish power company Repsol's new research and development headquarters just south of Madrid for 400 researchers and scientists. And we've built into the design a grand avenue straight down the middle of the building, with the labs and workspaces off to the sides. That grand avenue serves the same function as the urban plazas where people like to congregate and socialize. With this design, employees can take shorter breaks just steps away from their work areas and relax and brainstorm with their colleagues, while staying on the premises.

Cultural traditions and behaviors may be changing more slowly in some countries than in others, but we're all changing. And we have to be sensitive to this. If we're not, we're not going to have a successful relationship or a successful design. This also means that we must remember to honor tradition in even the most modern, technologically advanced projects we're working on.

We just finished a tremendous building next to the Bank of China for a very prosperous Hong Kong businessman. He wanted a state-of-the-art, seventy-story building, incorporating all the latest building materials, engineering, and digital technology. He wanted an international design, but he also wanted to include Chinese influence as well. So we consulted his Feng Shui Master throughout the design process. The building was fully leased right away, and our client credits part of that to our sensitivity to Chinese tradition and culture. Naturally, he is very pleased!

How does the U.S. company such as yours develop a "citizen of the world" reputation among such disparate clients in such diverse cultures?

We run an extensive training program in-house—which we call the "Leo A Daly University"—where we educate our people in certain aspects of our business, including cultural sensitivity. One thing we talk about is how to improve the image of American multinational business through our own practices and behaviors. Our people can be ambassadors to the world.

I enjoyed a thirty-year relationship with King Hussein of Jordan, and during that time I learned a lot about the Jordanian culture and problems. Sometimes there weren't even signed contracts. He'd call me and say, "I have an idea. The next time you're in Jordan, stop in so we can have a visit." And naturally, I'd arrange to be in Jordan the next week. I would walk in and he'd say, "You know, we have this piece of land, I'd like to build a college. Would you help me with that?" And then we'd get started.

We would get paid right on time every time, but there would be no contract. It was a cultural thing combined with trust. There's no way you would ask someone like that to sign a piece of paper; you wouldn't need anything more than his word. We had to adapt to that culture.

We've been doing work around the world for a very long time, so it's part of our culture—even domestically. In the Washington, D.C., office alone, we have 150 professionals representing seventeen different nationalities and speaking forty different languages and dialects.

How do you see your role as mentor for future generations of different nationalities that may eventually leave Leo A Daly and open up practices of their own abroad? Do you see yourself as creating a legacy of standards that will carry on long after your employees have left their relationship with your firm?

Absolutely. I can't tell you how gratifying it is to travel through the Middle East or Asia and meet someone who says, "I'm now the chief of architecture for this government agency or company. I had wonderful years training at your company." In Saudi Arabia we actually had the assignment to train almost 400 professionals during the late 1970s and early 1980s. At that time there were no Saudi-owned architectural firms in which young engineers who had come out of American and British schools at the top of their class could get their early professional experience. So we trained them in the business of architecture. The whole society is now full of our graduates. And now that they're in their forties, they're all senior professionals in their country.

Back home in Omaha, where we have our domestic headquarters, almost every architect in that city at one time has worked for our firm. I get a great pleasure seeing how people develop. To the extent that we can do that, it's wonderful.

What light can you shed on the question of elevating customer relationships and strategic alliances and developing a working team spirit among all parties to move projects forward?

We have always had a policy of interdependence, inside our firm, and outside with our contractors, consultants, and clients. And we use this policy as a strategic advantage. Clients who retain us know that we insist on a collaborative relationship with everyone concerned, and that translates into an excellent, cost-effective, and timely project.

Leo A Daly has 900 professionals spread throughout the world. We're fostering this kind of approach in every office. The strategic alliance ensures that all the parties are totally committed to the process through the same goals, same attitudes, same total commitment to the schedule and budget, the same definition of responsibilities and what it means to be involved.

We're very careful that the partnerships we create are very committed to this philosophy of interdependence and we make it part of our selection process. This understanding has to be balanced and shared among all the participants on a project. If one side—the building contractor, consultant, or owner—backs off, it's not going to work. We need to make sure up-front that everyone is genuinely committed to this principle. We've devised a series of partnering briefings, and we get everyone in one room and we talk about this. If there are individuals in the corporations who aren't ready to sign on to this approach, we explain the need for total collaboration and request replacement players.

How important is it to evaluate the philosophical positioning of the client? Have you turned clients down who seem to be at odds with your approach?

They self-select. We accept commissions only when we know there is going to be a powerful, collaborative relationship between the client and ourselves. When we were planning the Pope John Paul II Cultural Center in Washington, I met with the Holy Father several times in Rome. He shared his vision with me, I then came back and we set about to design this building, which is very contemporary for the Catholic Church. There were people on the committees who would have liked a miniature version of St. Peter's, complete with domes! This is a very advanced symbol of the future of the Catholic Church. It's been a fantastic success. But it needed total commitment from everyone in order to become this extraordinarily modern and technologically advanced statement of what the Catholic Church wants to represent in today's world.

How important is high-quality competition for keeping your own saw sharpened?

Leo A Daly plays in the big leagues, and we enjoy vigorous competition all over the world. We have to compete with many international firms on their turf, and it's tough. We have to understand their culture. We have to be sympathetic and good listeners. In the United States it's the same thing. We compete. We win sometimes; we lose sometimes. Without this competition we wouldn't keep improving. To excel and be competitive, we have to keep improving ourselves and our product.

To stay competitive we regularly ask ourselves a series of questions: How different are we from those other firms? What is our unique value proposition? Is our idea creation powerful enough? Are we getting our talented people to push themselves and stretch? Are we as informed on the current issues around these cities as we should be? Are we as informed on the issues that affect our clients as we should be? What can we do to be more compassionate? Do our actions reflect our compassion? Where do we really expect to be in three to five years? Are we listening well enough to our clients? How can we become more strategically effective in ways that foster communication and collaboration with others?

What are you learning about the emotional resonance between the built space and its users?

What we try to do is create places where people feel very good and have a sense of well-being. It's hard to put into words, but that's the power of architecture. We need to design office buildings from the inside out with the inhabitants' needs in mind. We can create space that directly affects people's attitudes, spirits, and emotions. And that's what we strive for.

The power of architecture is amazing! Design really can enhance our future. We can help people, make them feel safe, and give them shelter. But architecture, throughout the ages, has also had the power to elevate humanity. From Stonehenge to those Gothic-inspired columns on the World Trade Center plaza, which captured your eye and drew your attention skyward, the fundamental message of architecture is, "Look! See the possibilities! We have made a space for you to create the future and to implement your dreams."

The architect's, engineer's, or designer's challenge, whether creating a home or an office space—perhaps on the 102nd floor overlooking one of the most powerful cities of the world—is to create a place where people can safely and comfortably turn their dreams into reality.

That's one of the rules of architecture that will never change.

What do you think should be done with the World Trade Center site?

I really think that it is too soon after the tragedy of September 11 to rush into a decision about what should be done with the site. Whatever the final decision is, I think it should be made slowly and with great care.

Personally, I believe that those who died in the tragedy should be honored and commemorated at the World Trade Center site; however, I also think that we should rebuild. I envision a new complex of office buildings—probably several shorter towers (fifty stories or so)—as I think it is vital for the financial health of New York City, and for everyone involved, that lower Manhattan returns to be the dynamic center of commerce that it once was.

However, I would also like to see a small, but beautiful park built in memory of the victims, one that can be shared by the victims' families as well as those who live and work in the area. My hope is that we will create an oasis, a small but lush garden, that encourages reflection of the events of September 11 and that inspires all who visit.

What are you certain of?

I'm certain that I'm uncertain. We should all have a little bit of uncertainty. We know there's going to be change. In our profession, that's what it's all about. We're looking out into the future. We may have a lot of background and a lot of experience, but we have to create new solutions for the future every day. There's going to be change, and there's going to be uncertainty. But we feel very confident that we can deal with that uncertainty.

What are you uncertain of?

I'm uncertain of the timing of these changes and how radical they will be. We're constantly developing scenarios to anticipate the future, using a range between best case and worst case situations. We're prepared, but we're still uncertain about where in the range we will be.

What is the essential ingredient for resilience?

We have to have faith in the future. We're confident we can deal with the future. You have to be an optimist, and architects are optimists by nature—we are constantly anticipating the future in our work.

8

Ronald E. Daly
President, R.R. Donnelley Print Solutions

A lot of American businesses can't grow in the United States. They're in markets that are mature. So you reach outside for other markets with growth opportunities. That has made the American corporation more stable, and at the same time you're bringing in a new standard of living to people around the world.

Pick up any phone book in China, the U.K., Brazil, Poland, India, Chile, or the United States (among other countries), and you've already entered the R.R. Donnelley world. Read a magazine, and you're likely to be handling R.R. Donnelley printing. Open a book, and it was probably printed by R.R. Donnelley. Sift through the Sunday newspaper looking for coupons and the other inserts. Those are R.R. Donnelley–printed pieces you're looking for. With 33,000 people working in fifty-two manufacturing plants around the world, R.R. Donnelley brings home the written—and printed—word.

Ronald E. Daly began his relationship with R.R Donnelley at age 17, when he took a job as an entry-level employee. Since then he has built a distinguished career with this single company, all the while building his education, culminating with an M.B.A. from Loyola University. He has served on the boards of Leadership Greater Chicago and the Chicago Symphony Orchestra, and he is also a member of the National Black MBA Association and the Conference Board Council of Operating Executives.

In this interview, Daly discusses the major contemporary issues attendant to positioning a gigantic U.S. corporation for future growth:

- The roles and responsibilities business must bear in developing a literate workforce

- Considerations involved in opening a corporate presence in China

- The corporate role in fighting against terrorism and for global hope

∼

What do you see as the biggest change and challenge facing American business today?

The deficiency of our school systems to prepare our young people with the rapid transition that we're going to be experiencing from now on. We've already seen it happen. In Silicon Valley we didn't have enough skilled labor to fill those positions the New Economy generated, so we had to reach around the world to get those people. The fact is there aren't enough people coming out of our schools who understand mathematics and sciences.

Our government is incapable of teaching people what they need to know to live in the future world. Since the business world depends on the availability of qualified workers, it's going to have to take more responsibility in making sure our workers are qualified to get the job done.

Not all education should go through business, though. The liberal arts piece definitely should go through the schools. When it comes to highly technical, business-focused education, probably business will have to take over the responsibility for it. Government either can't or won't.

Business is going to have to take a bigger role in education. Particularly along the lines of worker preparedness. And we're going to have to do the one thing that schools aren't doing: teach people how to read.

The alternative is to let American business just slide. China is doing everything to train its people and make them as smart as they can be.

So, we're going to constantly get an influx of new generations of Americans who don't know how to do what we need them to do. If the schools don't train them, business is going to have to. It's in our own self-interest. We're going to have to take over a larger role in education, because the school system is blowing it.

Taking this theme and pulling back even more, what's the role of American companies in global economic development?

A lot of companies have gone to international locations and failed miserably. They either don't understand the culture, or they let cultural differences stop them from performing. Or they were never perceived by the government to be looking out for that country's best interest. If you're going to really succeed in a foreign land, you have to become a partner to the culture, even to the government.

If you look like you're just trying to take a buck out of that country and bring it back to the United States, you're going to have a problem. But if you bring something of lasting value to them—and I'm not saying you can't make money in the process, you're not going to do this for free—then you've got a deal.

Sometimes it takes longer to establish that belief in their minds. We've been in China since 1993, and in the beginning it was hard. We had all types of government restrictions about what we could produce. For instance, we had to produce 40 percent of all our printed volume for export.

We weren't getting anywhere for a few years. We tried to sell directory printing, which was an evolving business in China, and we started holding small seminars to explain the directory business. It was new to them and they didn't understand the marketplace and how the financial model works for the telephone directory industry. The Chinese thought you make phone books and you sell them to people. Nobody buys a telephone directory—they're free. They didn't understand any of that.

So, our R.R. Donnelley Chinese sales director and a sales executive from the United States were doing a flip-chart presentation in Mandarin about the dynamics of the directory business in the United States. And when our people were done with the presentation, they took the sheets off the flip chart, wadded them up, and threw them away.

We learned afterward that the audience pulled them out of the garbage. It became for them a primer on how to do business. Our folks said, "Wait a minute, we're not selling printing here, we're selling knowledge. Let's sell knowledge. Let's teach them what they don't know and the printing will flow."

And it did.

So the next year we held another seminar and invited publishers from all over China to come. And they did—130 people. We had our own marketing people who really understood the directory business very well and we also brought some of our customers over from the United States to give presentations.

The next year the China Telephone Company, which is the umbrella organization, called us up and said, "We'd like to partner with you in the seminar." Instead of doing it in the south near our plant, we do it in Shanghai.

There's a big audience and a huge production. And we're bringing them something they don't have: knowledge about the industry. Within a short time we were printing the lion's share of the telephone directories in China. And that's a small number. Probably no more than the telephone directories of four American cities. But the fact is we're helping them grow their business, and we're growing along with them.

We bring education, and they like us for it. The Chinese government has lifted its restrictions on us. We've been chosen a friend of the state. The government in Shanghai that wanted a world-class printing plant came to R.R. Donnelley and said, "We would like to joint venture with you on building a state-of-art printing plant in Shanghai." It's about job creation and it's about provincialism. They're tired of having all their magazines printed in the south where the economic zone is. They want to print in Shanghai. It's a pride thing. And they picked R.R. Donnelley.

They have to go to the Beijing government to get approval for this. But they get that approval, and it's the first joint venture of its type to be done in China.

Why did they do that with us? We brought them something. We stayed the course. We showed we were interested in the Chinese people. We showed them we were interested in spending our money to educate them on the ways to grow their business.

In 1996 we signed a contract to print the Shanghai telephone directories. At the time, Shanghai, a city of 13 million people, had only 250,000 telephone directories distributed. Within three years they were distributing 4 million directories. Why? We also signed a marketing services agreement with them and we gave them ideas. We showed them how to market their product and sell advertising.

So not only is knowledge power but the ability to help people generate ideas is also power.

Yes. When you bring people something that they don't have, they embrace you. The best example of that principle is Motorola. It recognized right away that there was a knowledge gap in cellular technology when it went to China. So it opened up Motorola U, where they trained Chinese engineers. They brought quality practices to their supply base. They lifted up an entire segment of the Chinese economy. There were already businesses in China that made plastics and wires; so they had a good supply chain. Motorola helped its supply chain learn and grow so it could make a good cell phone in China. Now Motorola is a multibillion-dollar market leader in cellular phones in China.

But Motorola's relationship with China didn't just stop with cell phones. When the Chinese wanted to launch their first credit card in China, to whom did they turn to partner in this? They came to Motorola. Motorola demonstrated beyond doubt that their presence would benefit China far beyond the single cell-phone business venture. They were bringing knowledge with them.

As a leader is it more effective to rally the troops for something or against something?

They both can be effective but it's more positive to be for something. Pick a course, strive to achieve what you're working for, and then celebrate the wins along the way. That's much more powerful than, "I hate the enemy, let's kill him." You have to be focused on the competition. You can't be blind to the competition. But you have to be focused on where you have to go and what you have to do to get there. That's a much better course.

In the New Economy much was written about the "first mover advantage." What's the marketplace advantage now?

Understand the marketplace. Those guys had technology, and they created products and then tried to go out and sell them. There was a lot of hype about what they had. But still action on the part of the consumer means something. People still had to buy, and they just didn't come in the numbers that were necessary to carry the business. The Internet isn't dead. There are some great business-to-business products being developed and used out there. Under the surface, it's becoming the infrastructure for America.

Over the last couple of years we saw e-books try to emerge in the marketplace. Are they threatening to you?

We thought they were. Donnelley's response to e-books was to convert our customers' content to e-book formats, and we partnered with the e-book manufacturer early on.

We also thought the Internet was threatening us. The world was being convinced that print was dead. Not true. In fact, one of the biggest things that came out of the Internet was Internet-focused magazines: *Wired, Internet Magazine, PC Weekly, Computer Shopper, Yahoo!, Red Herring*. People are still buying books. You still cuddle up in bed with your book every night. America still sells a lot of newspapers. I just don't see print being dead. It's part of our cultural coding.

Information available on the Internet and on CDs will have a place. Certainly the encyclopedia is used more now on line than it will ever be in book form again. Research material and reference books work well on a computer. Maybe even some college textbooks. There may be a time when a professor will teach with a customized textbook, printing off just in time for forty students three chapters from one book, three chapters from another book, and four chapters from a third book. And the student won't have to buy three or four books. But it will still be printed by somebody. It may be printed in a different form on a different kind of press. That's possible. But it will still be printed.

If I had said something like this during the Internet boom, people would have said that I was archaic, out of step, and just didn't get it. And now they would say, "You make a lot of sense."

It's not to say we didn't focus on the Internet. Any threat to our business also poses an opportunity. Clayton Christianson, a Harvard Business School professor, has said that there are disruptive technologies that will come along and eat your business alive. Who's better to eat your business alive than you are? If you see these disruptive business technologies, cannibalize your own business and then grow with the new technology.

We did look at the Internet big time. When I was running the telecommunications business for R.R. Donnelley, I had four individual Internet start-ups in the works.

What is the corporate role for fighting against terrorism and fighting for global hope?

Bringing knowledge and education to other parts of the world.

Doesn't that make the established power structure nervous when we do things like that?

Nationally, we know we are as strong as our weakest link. I have to look at the world this same way. When I see all these protests against globalism, I think, "You people just don't get it." Globalism is a good thing. If you can export knowledge and education and wealth to these impoverished nations, maybe then you can stop the hate and the killing.

How can you do that without imposing your values on them?

I don't have to impose my value structure on you. You want to make money doing business? I can show you how to do that. I don't culturally have to dictate how you do it. I can just show you how. If I have a printing press, it doesn't care what language it's printing in. The manufacturer has a rated speed for it. If you run that press with the quality that's rated and in the speed that's rated, culturally I don't care how you do it. You have customers to serve, and they have expectations. Just do it.

There have been many strong criticisms about doing business in China and economically supporting its Communist political structure. Can joining the community of world commerce really benefit the Chinese individual? And can we realistically expect human rights violations to dissolve in the face of financial incentive?

If we don't trade with China, we're not hurting the Chinese government, we're hurting the Chinese people. They need a place to sell what they make. They need to have access to foreign capital and they need to have access to foreign goods. We stand a better chance of helping China through economics than we ever will through being morally superior.

I believe in capitalism. It's worked well for us. We feed people a lot better with this system. We tend to accumulate wealth a lot better. I challenge anybody to lay down a map of the world and pick a place in the Third World where they'd rather live than the United States of America.

What we've got is pretty good. If we can export that, it is a wonderful thing.

So if you could round up all those World Trade Organization protesters in one big auditorium, what would you say to them?

I'd tell them they're terribly misguided. Globalism is not a bad thing. Where it's happened, we've seen peoples' standard of living increase. They ought to look at facts. My plant in China employs a thousand people who are a lot better off than if we weren't there.

I read an article the other day that said the United States is ranked 19th in reading, 14th in science, and 15th in math, compared with other nations. Why aren't we first, first, and first? Let those people protest that.

Are those jobs that could have gone to American workers here? Where we have almost a million people laid off this year alone?

No, not necessarily. If we want to compete in China, do you think we should create everything here and ship it over there? It's not cost effective to do that. I've got customers in the United States who go into Asia to buy printing all the time. Do I allow them to do that, or do I go into Asia and sell them printing myself? They're going to buy from Asia anyway. Why not from an American company in Asia? We print the Chinese telephone directories. Do we really think we're going to produce them in the United States and ship them to China?

So it's marketplace-appropriate commerce?

Growth is a good thing. A lot of American businesses can't grow in the United States. They're in markets that are mature. So you reach outside for other markets with growth opportunities. That has made the American corporation more stable, and at the same time you're bringing in a new standard of living to people around the world. That's a benefit.

Theoretically, it should also come the other way. It certainly has with the Japanese, hasn't it? They make cars and appliances in the United States. And they employ Americans. That's the way it ought to work; it ought to work both ways.

What is the future role of the CEO?

The CEO has to continue to be a leader, not a manager. And the CEO is going to continue to adapt to change at a rapid pace.

Does the CEO have to worry about the celebrity factor?

No. Recent research is showing that the most effective CEOs in the long term aren't celebrities at all. They're quiet, unassuming, and they just get it done. Celebrity status certainly can boost your stock in tough times. But being a leader, understanding the winds of change, being able to connect with your people and get them focused on the direction in which you want to go is absolutely essential.

A CEO has to be nimble and quick and willing to take a risk. But the CEO doesn't have to be a celebrity in order to do that. The truth is if he does it often enough he'll be a celebrity whether he wants to be or not.

CEOs of the future are going to have to focus on their investment in human capital. There are a lot of people who work to have a job. And then there are the lucky people who work because they enjoy exactly what it is they do. If you can get everyone to really like what they do, the energy they would create would be awesome.

Can an entire industry be electrified by a greater sense of purpose?

The world was ignorant before Gutenberg invented moveable type. Because of that the world became educated. Can you imagine being in a craft that does that? The American Revolution wasn't influenced by anything as much as by Thomas Payne's *Common Sense*. Just a little book that people read and got fired up about their liberties. So I see us being right in the middle of what is great about this country.

If there is to be a revolution in communications, we ought to lead the charge. We've got to quit thinking about being a rust-belt industry and get our people thinking about what it is that we do. The press operator has to understand the value of this thing he printed, what it's place in America is, and what its place in America is because he printed it. We have a purpose. Our purpose is to enrich lives by connecting people with the power of words and images.

What are you certain of?

Every day of my life I'm going to see some facet of change. And it's going to come faster and faster. Most companies in America like a steady state. They want to be able to predict tomorrow. And it's not going to be that way. The winners will be those people who can respond to change quickly, who can be decisive, and have a good way of gathering information about future changes. And they have to listen to the marketplace well.

What are you uncertain of?

I'm uncertain of this country's ability to generate the level of people we need to deal with the future world. I'm concerned about our ability to keep workers prepared for what comes, given the world that I've just described. I don't know how well a lot of us will cope. We're going to have a permanent underclass in this country unless we can prepare the disadvantaged for the rapid changing future. I don't see anything in process. I'm uncertain of our resolve to solve that problem as a nation.

What is the essential ingredient for resilience?

A belief in oneself and a set of values. And liking what you do certainly helps. I've been in the printing business thirty-seven years. One of the reasons why I never left is the fact I get really emotional about what we do. I'm passionate about it. We educate the masses. We store the wisdom and knowledge of the ages in books. That's what we do.

9

Ralph Dickerson
President, United Way of New York City

Now that we've hired the very best and brightest people, how do we keep them inspired with the highest level of self-esteem? How do we keep them equipped with the highest ability to develop the best business models that are going to help us become a better organization and help us achieve what we need to achieve?

When the hijacked planes struck their intended targets on September 11, two questions were asked by millions of individuals throughout the United States—indeed the world: "How could this happen?" and "How can I help?"

It will take years for investigators to discover all the answers to the first question. But the United Way of New York City provided an answer to the second by the close of business that very day, with the establishment of the September 11th Fund, which it set up in cooperation with the New York Community Trust. As of December 31, 2001, the September 11th Fund received $404 million in 1.7 million contributions from individuals, corporations, and foundations in all fifty states, three U.S. protectorates, and 150 countries. This total includes $112 million raised through the "America: Tribute to Heroes" telethon, broadcast September 21, 2001, on all major television networks and designated specifically to help victims and families.

A career United Way leader for thirty years, Ralph Dickerson has been the president of the United Way of New York City since 1988, transforming it into the largest private funder of health and human services in New York City—before the events of September 11. He has also developed the organization into the largest United Way in the United States. Before taking the New York City United Way post, he held key executive positions in other local United Ways, including St. Louis, Madison, Cleveland, and Pittsburgh.

> In this interview, Dickerson discusses the changing role of corporate philanthropy:
>
> ■ The synergistic relationship between corporations and philan-
> thropic organizations
>
> ■ Benefits of pro bono work in employee development
>
> ■ The individual drive to make a difference in the lives of others

How should a corporation regard its philanthropic role in these uncertain times?

Philanthropy should be treated as one of a corporation's top priorities. In the last ten years corporate philanthropic interest rarely came up on the radar screen at shareholders' meetings. It's all been about earnings per share, marketability, market position, and new product development. And now our pendulum has swung the other way. The one thing that September 11 has brought to us is the recognition that we need to maintain a balance of ambition and community citizenship. Part of the balance for a corporation is to continue to be a success. But it also needs to focus on the people who are helping them be successful. That includes both their employees and the people in the community around them.

Corporations have resources that, if used effectively, can change the landscape for individuals, families, and communities around the world. That measurement of success can be as strong as the ability to measure your chances of improving market share of your product from 37 percent to 39 percent in the next two years.

What's in it for the corporation to take that point of view?

The first thing to consider is the value to its employees. An employee who is entirely devoted to trying to move the market share from 37 percent to 39 percent is not the most productive employee. No matter how much creativ-ity and ingenuity you invest in moving from 37 percent to 39 percent, it's just not really compelling in a person's life. If you can expose employees to nonbusiness problems, they can be just as creative and enthusiastic about solving those problems and benefiting humanity outside the corporate world. When they come back to the core business problem, they bring fresh insights and experiences to their work.

So you're inviting the employees to take the same set of skills that they've been using to drive the business to new levels and apply them to different kinds of business problems. When they return to the company their skills sets have been honed by the added experience and understanding that came from their philanthropic efforts.

The consulting firms McKinsey and Bain have both learned that when they take their best and brightest and put them on client projects, of course they're going to be successful. But when they keep putting those same consultants on one project after another after another after another, they become burned out. The companies have learned that putting them on a pro bono project after several business projects ignites a fire in them like nothing else. It gives the consultants the opportunity to learn new things, try new skills, and meet people in the corporation that they wouldn't have met in their daily work. The added experience gives them a more global perspective. And ultimately they come to see familiar client problems in entirely different ways.

Do they also have a heightened self-esteem when they see how their skills sets can directly benefit others?

These people already know they're good when they're working with top levels of the client organization on high-stakes problems. But now they really see how valuable they can be when they use the same skills and knowledge, for instance, to help a drug addiction agency figure out a better way of serving clients. Why wouldn't this additional experience be advantageous to the intellectual capital of the company—which is really the only thing a company has? The questions companies should really be asking themselves are, "Now that we've hired the very best and brightest people, how do we keep them inspired with the highest level of self-esteem? How do we keep them equipped with the highest ability to develop the best business models that are going to help us become a better organization and help us achieve what we need to achieve?"

Philanthropy in a corporation is more than just another unit. It's more than just good will for the corporation, it's more than just sending out checks, it's more than trying to match philanthropy with marketing to prove that it has bottom line value. It is the intellectual capital future of the organization. It is the only thing that is going to keep the individual inspired over the long haul. I don't care who they are. I don't care how good an IT person it is. I don't care how good a marketing person it is. After working in a business environment so long, if they haven't been exposed to nonbusiness environment opportunities, they're not going to be prepared to drive the company forward to the future.

Now that we have the employees covered, let's look at the other side of the philanthropy relationship. Why is it important for companies to care about the recipients of philanthropy?

If American Express decides it wants to support the construction of housing, the beneficiaries may be inspired to improve their lives in additional ways, such as going to retraining to renew or rebuild their skills. Maybe they might ultimately go to work at American Express as an entry-level employee. Maybe they will one day be inspired to go forward and get a degree—maybe ultimately becoming qualified to be Gold Card members. Is it a long shot? Yes, it's a long shot. But in today's environment, customers come in all kinds of forms. Just the encouragement of helping to put decent homes within their reach can change peoples' lives.

Corporations have got to see that just because people may be indigent today, that doesn't mean they're going to be indigent tomorrow. True, not everyone living in Habitat for Humanity homes is going to become a Gold Card member one day. But there could be many more people who might qualify for a green card. Or they'll be in a position to take advantage of other kinds of opportunities because now they're in the self-help mode.

Do you have an abiding faith that people really do want to make a difference beyond their own immediate circle of influence?

People always want to rise to the challenge. They always want to come through for themselves and others when things aren't going well. People do want get into the mix and make a contribution.

I hear so many people say, "I want to make a difference." But sometimes the difference people make is incremental, and they may not have the satisfaction of seeing the end result. Or sometimes the contribution that someone makes is just the ability to analyze a familiar problem in a fresh way and develop a different approach to it.

We need that additional intellectual capability. The ingenuity that volunteers bring to a situation far outstrips anything our organization can develop from within. Often, when you're close to the problem—when you've been studying it for years, have been reading about it and writing about it, and are considered to be the expert on it—you need the lifeline of someone else who sees it for the first time.

What are you certain of?

Well, I know what we *should* be certain of. We should be certain of the skills and knowledge base that make us individually and organizationally successful. We should be very certain about our own ambitions of what we want to achieve. And we should be certain that none of us can do it by ourselves.

We should be certain that any time we take a project on, it's all about only one thing. And it's not vision. It's about execution. Vision is nothing without the ability to make it happen.

We should be certain of being able to listen to our soul, of being able to understand that inside each of us is a greater driving force that will help us achieve, even when we don't think we can. I see so many people accomplish things, not because they're working any harder, or have more knowledge than the people around them. The most important thing is that they understand the soul of who they are. They understand that when they're in really tough times they can respond more quickly than others. Or that when their family or others are in crisis situations, they can do things that others can't. Maybe they have the ability to be extremely compassionate when others are coarse or have an edge to them. Or they have the ability to drive right through a problem when others are frozen. That self-awareness is a part of the soul that helps people understand the importance of who they are and how they fit into a greater plan.

What are you uncertain of?

The thing I'm uncertain of, obviously, is what's going to happen tomorrow. I'm uncertain about people's prognostications of what the market is going to do. I'm uncertain about whether an organization is going to have the ability to survive. I'm uncertain of the changing needs for services and products. I'm uncertain of people's ability to not be selfish.

What is the essential ingredient for resilience?

The personal desire to go through "the wall." My son is a marathon runner, and in the Boston Marathon he experienced what the runners call "the wall" at about the 19-mile mark. He tells me, "Dad, you have to run through the wall." Resiliency is the ability to take yourself through the wall. You don't hit the wall. And you don't avoid the wall. You go *through* the wall. You have to be able to visualize yourself beyond the wall—to transcend it.

Resiliency also comes from an anatomical, spiritual, and psychological preparedness that you have as a result of the experiences you've already had. You already know yourself in the context of a variety of situations, and you know how you can use those experiences to help others. We lost our daughter in a plane crash in 1994. And now when there's trouble in our family, people come to us first for support. That's because the very worst thing in the world has already happened to us. So we have the resilience that allows us to take what we have suffered and transform it to help other people.

10

Gerald FitzGerald

President, PB Aviation

Heroic acts happen all the time at work. And likely as not it won't be the manager in a suit who will take charge and save the day.

On February 26, 1993, a few minutes after noon, a bomb exploded in the basement of the World Trade Center. In addition to causing devastating structural damage, the blast also knocked out the emergency lighting and filled the escape routes—the towers' complicated configuration of stairwells—with smoke. More than a thousand were injured, and six people were killed. As director of aviation for the Port Authority of New York and New Jersey, in charge of three of the nation's busiest airports, Jerry FitzGerald was among the 50,000 World Trade Center workers who made their way out of the damaged building onto the snowy streets.

Today he is well into his second career as president of PB Aviation, a Parsons Brinckerhoff company known for its expertise in transportation-oriented planning, engineering, design, and construction projects worldwide. PB Aviation airport clients have recently included Reagan National and Dulles International airports, serving the Washington, D.C., area; Miami International; Greater Pittsburgh International; San Jose International; Hong Kong International; Madrid-Barajas; Calgary International; Heathrow International; and, of course, New York's JFK International and La Guardia airports.

In this interview, FitzGerald discusses the lessons he learned both before and since surviving the World Trade Center bombing in 1993:

- The power of the human spirit to prevail in the face of devastation
- True leadership as it is manifested throughout the organization
- Anticipating and meeting the needs of a suddenly transformed marketplace
- Growing a global company by operating locally

~

As an individual, how do you go through such a devastating experience as a building being bombed and come out of it at a higher level of understanding?

There's always growth in everything that you do. But growth occurs when you look back, not necessarily as you are going through it. Growth takes place even when you experience tragedies. You try to somehow allow them come into your life but not dominate it.

When September 11 happened, I of course flashed back to the bombing in 1993. I had been telling people that I had put the memory in the proverbial basement closet. When September 11 occurred it flew back up into my living room again. I had to grab hold of it and put it back down in the basement and close the door. It doesn't go away, but you want to contain it, and not allow it to be in your everyday existence. When it flies back up again you need to come to grips with your own emotions, what you felt, what you did, and how you finally coped with it again.

Looking back to 1993, that experience gave me an increased understanding of the nature of human commonality, human values, and how those values are shared worldwide. In the stairwells as we made our way down, it was people from many nations, races, and socio-economic groups helping each other, reaching out into the darkness, grabbing someone's shoulder, saying "I got you," when fear began to rise. When you were in the stairwell it didn't matter where you lived, what car you drove, what job you had. I remember passing groups of people huddled in the dark corners and wondering what that was all about. It turns out they were all asthmatics sharing each others' medicine.

There was a blind guy I rode up in the elevator with every morning, and I especially worried about what happened to him and his dog. He had been out of the building when the bomb exploded, but he had left his dog behind, leashed to his desk. Now you know those dogs are trained to never leave the place where their master leaves them. So when the people on his floor evacuated, the dog refused to go with them. So they gathered up this huge golden retriever in their arms and carried him down more than 60 floors. And they were able to deliver the dog to his frantic master who was stuck behind the barricades. I saw that same guy and his dog again in the newspaper the other day. They survived this one too.

On September 11, I was in Montreal attending an international airports conference and saw the whole thing happen on television. When I watched the buildings go down, I thought, "All my friends are gone." In 1993, it had taken me three-and-a-half hours to go down the stairs from the 65th floor, and these people only had an hour to evacuate from the time the first plane hit to when the first building collapsed. I was convinced they were all dead.

But, while the Port Authority lost more than 70 people, many many more survived. And as my friends described to me what it was like this time, I realized, "They're repeating the same stories. Different people, some of them, different circumstances, but the same reactions. People reaching out to help each other. That is the commonality of the human spirit. What more evidence do you need than that?

What does that tell you about humanity from a leader's perspective?

As soon as you look for and find the common traits that unify humanity, you become more aware that we have more things in common with each other than not. At PB, we have a diverse workforce, with 9,000 employees. And 40 percent of them are outside the country. All over the world people are motivated by the same things; they respond similarly to the big issues of work and life.

Sure, culture to culture, we may respond differently to criticism. And we respond differently to certain ideas. But there are a lot of similarities. People generally want to get along. They are generally well intended. They all come to work with a shared reason for coming. And this creates a level of intention that for the most part, if managed right, produces a good product.

It's very easy to think we have few opportunities to be heroes in our ordinary, everyday lives. Is there any way leaders can capture that spark of selflessness and humanity you saw in 1993 and use it to benefit not only the organization but also the individuals working in the day to day?

Heroic acts happen all the time at work. And likely as not it won't be the manager in a suit who will take charge and save the day. I remember one time when I was at JFK International Airport and we had a huge, sudden snowstorm. I went out with a group of our maintenance men onto the roads to check the cars that had been abandoned there, in case there might be people trapped. When we opened up the door to one car we found a man inside in a wheelchair. The maintenance guy I was with said, "I'll go get the bucket truck, you wait here." I may have been the one wearing the tie, but this guy was the one who took charge. So I waited right there with the man in the car. We soon pulled him out and drove him back to the terminal, where everyone else who was stranded was waiting out the storm in pretty high spirits considering. We likely saved this guy's life. Not too far away three people got trapped in their car when snow fell off a bus and covered it. They died of asphyxiation.

The maintenance guy who stepped up and said, "I'll go do this and you wait," was the leader in that situation. We didn't sit around and say, "Let's have a little management discussion about this." Organizationally, I may have been the official manager, but I was the helper in this situation. The human spirit is going to bring out the leader in whatever situation there might be. It's going to pop up when and where you least expect it. To me, that's true leadership.

As head of an American company with facilities all over the world, how do you handle whatever anti-Americanism that you might face?

We have just developed our new strategic plan in which we're emphasizing more than we have in the past our responsibility for supporting the communities we have a presence in. It's unusual for a corporate strategic plan to identify that community service is an important element. But it's crucial to us. We think if a representative of PB is in the local community, PB should be standing up and helping with local needs and issues. With 150 offices worldwide, our strategy is to be local globally. This includes an obligation for members of local offices to be involved in their communities; to join local clubs; to be involved in community activities. It's not just good to do, it's expected. When managers are asked about their local offices, they will be asked about their community service. We want PB to be viewed as a firm that is concerned with all the communities it has a presence in.

Additionally, we never undertake any endeavor without partnering with local firms. We always try to have a balance between Americans on the job and locals. This isn't to say that the name of PB doesn't draw a certain amount of criticism and anti-Americanism abroad. But there's a reason why we have successful projects even in areas that have a vocal anti-American population: We have a strong philosophy of transferring our skills and knowledge to our local partners. That's one of the reasons why we're able to do the Cairo metro and Kuwait power company. We are a global engineering firm recognized first for our expertise and then for our philosophy of passing it on. We train our local partners and help them improve their skills so that maybe the next time they will be able to compete without us—or even against us. That's seen as a benefit locally. And, in the future, perhaps we'll all recombine and work again as a team. And they would be glad to because we treated them so nicely the first time.

In a global market, be as local as you can. And in that local market, don't walk alone.

Almost every major airport manager has mentioned security-related terminal redesign as the most immediate priority for project funding. So while the economy is suffering in so many other sectors, airport-related construction and engineering are looking forward to expanded work. How do you expect to handle a huge growth in business?

We've developed an approach to fast-tracking projects. We can give a potential client five examples of similar projects and show where we have cut the time by 60 percent. Our value in the marketplace is implementation and allowing the client to get it done more quickly. Typically, many of these infrastructure projects take far too long to implement. It shouldn't take four years from start to finish. It should take two years, maybe even less. So we will say to a client, "Let's step back and look at how things are being done. Let's understand why it takes so long and then figure out how to change it." We can help airports cut the time from master planning to final construction. And consequently we can move our own business along more efficiently.

So we're talking about responsiveness to need as a form of customer service?

That's exactly right. Fast tracking is a very important part of the aviation business now because we have to have time to catch up with demand for more capacity, renovation, and updating at airports. With passenger traffic down temporarily, we can take advantage of this little pause to go ahead and build in more capacity and security. The traffic will come back eventually. And unless airports take advantage of this lull now they are going to be in the same spot when passenger traffic returns to its pre-September 11 levels: No capacity. And with the fast-tracking program we can help them complete projects in the fraction of the time it traditionally takes.

How has September 11 changed your business in terms of how you position yourself to serve airports' needs?

We immediately put an exclusive marketing agreement together with the number-one blast design engineering firm in the United States. They're not working with any other firm. Then we secured nonexclusive marketing agreements with the best baggage system engineering firm in the United States and two top security firms.

We also studied the planning implications of terrorism for every mode of transportation in the United States. Then we developed a report and sent out 900 copies for free. Our philosophy is that no matter whether you're a PB client or not, we think we can be helpful.

Give it out. That's what I mean when I say you have to be responsive in the marketplace. You'll get it back in some way. I have gotten calls from people saying, "I'm just calling to thank you. I had to brief my board the day after I received your report and I used your report. We're not sure what to do in this environment. Can you come in and talk to us?" So I would call our local office and tell them to go see the airport director. That's being responsive. We send the message, "Look, we're here. If you want to call us, call us. And by the way, maybe this will help you."

It's worked pretty well.

It's been said that old rules and assumptions are no longer valid. What is no longer valid for you, and what has taken their place?

I've always believed old rules and old assumptions have to be discarded on a regular basis. To anyone who says now, "We finally have to get rid of old rules and assumptions," I would say they're not getting their share of the market. Probably for some time now. You can't be burdened by old rules and assumptions. Before September 11, I wouldn't have gone out and gotten a blast consultant and a baggage consultant and put them together. I wouldn't have sent 900 letters out. But I did just that after September 11. You have to respond to the marketplace.

When you say "respond to the marketplace," is it more accurate to say "anticipate the marketplace"—to know what they need before they know it themselves?

Yes, Anticipate it and having your eye focused on growth. You have to have a profit objective but you can't ignore the growth objective. Growth means new work.

What have you discovered about yourself in recent months?

My feeling is that the older you get, the more you realize life really is a journey. It's a cliche precisely because it's true. You absorb a little bit of everything that you experience, and you try to learn from it. A lot of good things have happened because of September 11. Maybe the human spirit is coming out more, and we're recognizing our dependence on each other. People are more aware of others around them; we're talking to each other more. I've watched it happening here in the subways and walking down the streets. We're recognizing that we may be trapped in a stairwell someplace someday, so maybe I could talk to you on the street or in the subway now.

You're going to die, and I'm going to die. When the time comes we're all going to have our questions answered. I truly believe there's a purpose to all of this, and we're going to find out what it is.

What are you certain about?

I'm certain that the global aviation structure has to continue. It's the most important part of global commerce second only to the Internet. It's here and it's not going away.

I'm confident that we're going to keep doing what we've been doing. The aviation business is going to continue. We're going to have to be smarter, more market responsive, more flexible, and more willing to team with others both locally and nationally. I feel positive about it.

What are you uncertain of?

This is the most uncertain market I've ever seen. There's a lot of work that's pending. How it's implemented and who pays for it are the questions. I'm not sure anyone knows the cost of the security we're putting in. And until the airports figure out their source of funds, it's hard to say how much of their plans will be going forward now. Will it be phased? Will they pre-fer doing it in three phases rather than all at once?

It's not clear when the passenger traffic will return. And I'm uncertain about the overall cost of security and what will have to be done.

What is the essential ingredient for resilience?

The ability to sense the marketplace and then respond to its needs. We do not accept the continuation of the status quo as an objective.

11

Joe Galli
President and CEO, Newell Rubbermaid

Our role as a corporation is to build the most successful and effective company we possibly can and be as competitive as possible in the global arena. And that is the best way we can contribute to the economy and hence the country.

In the course of just a few short years, Joe Galli moved from his role as longtime, loyal high-potential employee of Black & Decker through a brief spurt of a variety leadership experiments—including a year as president of Amazon—and now back to the so-called Old Economy world of durable everyday consumer goods. Only this time he's not in drill bits and small household appliances. He's now in trashcans, strollers, Sharpie pens, Rolodex files, high-end pens, and cookware.

Joe Galli, whom *Forbes* magazine in a recent cover story called "the Sultan of Sizzle," just may be on the cusp of becoming a celebrity CEO. His vision for revitalizing humdrum household products and refreshing Newell Rubbermaid's worn relationships with major retailers could put the sizzle back in the company's name on Wall Street as well.

Known as much for his Old Economy, nineteen-year loyalty to Black & Decker as he is for what happened immediately after his abrupt departure—accepting the position of Amazom.com president just hours after saying yes to the offer to head Frito-Lay North America and then a year later moving to VerticalNet, where he lasted only 167 days—Galli says he is now dug in at Newell Rubbermaid. He has even begun persuading some of his old Black & Decker contacts to pull up stakes and move to Illinois to join him in this new adventure.

In this interview, Galli discusses what it takes to revive an old, established consumer goods company serving the mass market:

■ Recruiting and working with high-potential college graduates

- The real difference between New Economy companies and Old Economy companies
- The role of CEOs as celebrity leaders
- Keeping the overall business plan on course under pressure from Wall Street

We have gone through an emotional and economic roller-coaster ride in the last five years. Is there anything lasting and of value we can take away from this period?

Yes, our country has been through period of unprecedented prosperity. It's great that in this country great ideas, entrepreneurs, and innovations can be rewarded. But we got to an ugly extreme where even bad ideas that had no hope of ever achieving profitability were rewarded by the investment community.

Now the requirement for leaders is to create an environment where we can get back to what has made the country great and what makes great people great—which is all about graduating from college, applying yourself, and developing your full potential. There aren't going to be any more lottery tickets passed out to twenty-two-year-olds on college campuses. That's over. But this is a great time for people who really want to apply themselves and maximize their potential. There's an opportunity now for them to move into the workforce, dig in, and roll up their sleeves.

Do you think they'll stand out because so many of their peers are still buying the "what can you do for me" ethic?

We're past the "what can you do for me" idea. The New Economy fostered an unbelievable me-oriented environment where people focused on their stock option grants and their vesting periods. Development of the enterprise took a back seat. You had managers, employees, even leaders watch the stock price every hour, as opposed to watching the relevant business issues or getting out of the office and building the company.

Now we're in a whole different place. It can be a real opportunity or a real issue. We view it as a real opportunity at Newell Rubbermaid. We're hiring hundreds of fresh college graduates and giving them an opportunity to maximize their potential. But it's not easy. We're very picky, we look at a hundred people for every one we hire. They work very, very hard. The first two years in your career make up the foundation time. This is when you build your skill set and when you develop your basic perspective in business. So it's very healthy for people to work very hard in that phase in their lives.

How does using young people reflect overall growth philosophy for the company?

We're developing future leaders of the company. This is the next generation of vice presidents, presidents, group presidents. This is the next generation of our leadership. It's actually the most important thing we're doing for the company. We have great brands. But the truth is, great people build great companies. We're being incredibly selective and will only hire outstanding graduates.

We look for people who are leaders first, who are overachievers, who are team players, who want to be part of something special, who have the ability to communicate and a passion about what they're doing in their lives. Their grade point average is an interesting fun fact, but we look at those other attributes first. Those are where we have the most success. And we look for energy level. We want people with the energy to go out and create excitement and get it done. In three years we can develop a fresh graduate into a very effective manager.

We're also committed to diversity. In the past year 68 percent of the people were female, 20 percent were trilingual, including some who speak Mandarin, German, and Portuguese. All these languages are relevant in our future because we're very global.

This is how we fuel the company, by creating an infusion of all this energy, talent, and potential. Then we nurture it and develop it by creating an environment where these folks know no limits. A lot of companies go through the motions of creating an environment where they hire a lot of people off the campus. But the people who eventually run the company all come from elite M.B.A. programs. While we love the elite M.B.A. programs, we treat those people exactly the same as those people from state universities. We put all those people in the same program, choose the best people—not based on their pedigree or what prep schools they went to, but on their abilities and their results.

That's why so many people flock to our company. They know it's equal opportunity no matter where they're from, no matter where they went to school. If they're good, they'll have the chance to achieve their potential. If they're not good, they won't make it here.

How have recent events changed your role as a corporate leader and the role of Newell Rubbermaid as an American company with a huge global presence?

This country is as strong as the economy. And the economy is as strong as the companies that comprise the economy. Our role as a corporation is to build the most successful and effective company we possibly can and be as competitive as possible in the global arena. And that is the best way we can contribute to the economy and hence the country. It's even more important now that we have a strong economic environment here. The backbone of America is its defense system, and we pay for that based on the tax base that comes from the economy. If the economy were to drift, that would be an unthinkable tragedy. We're a $7 billion corporation that employs 50,000 people all over the world, but we are an American company. And our contribution to society is to build a great thriving economy that generates a growing array of innovative new products that make people's lives more productive in some fashion.

It's been said, "This is our time to lead." What does that mean to you? And what business practices or attitudes retained from an earlier time should we change right away?

The worst thing that can happen to our economic environment is the notion of easy money. The best thing is the restoration of a values system that says that effort will be rewarded in the long term. Great achievements don't come easily, but great achievements can still be very much a part of our economic environment. They just take a lot of effort. We have to get back to reading, studying, applying ourselves, taking care of ourselves physically, and trying to become the best we can be.

When we get back to that, we can perpetuate a great society.

Do you think the so-called New Economy companies are going to run the risk of becoming stagnant like their 1970s and 1980s predecessors?

I don't think there are New Economy companies. There were companies formed in the 1980s and 1990s that are well managed. And companies formed in the 1980s and 1990s that aren't well managed. There are companies formed fifty years ago that continue to be well managed. Look at a company like Colgate-Palmolive, which has been around a long time. It's an incredibly well-managed company. And innovative and successful.

There's nothing good or bad that goes along with being New Economy or Old Economy. The differentiator is whether you are innovative or resistant to change. Are you obsessed with hiring and developing great people? Or does your company have a culture of complacency and entitlement where people know their job security is based on tenure and not on results?

How important is it for leaders to actively model and communicate their values and ethics during times of crisis?

It's extremely important at any time. Leaders should always be highly visible and repetitive in communicating their values, direction, and strategy. Leaders should be compulsive about communicating the success of heroes in the company. They should build the energy of the company. And they should always be close to people in the company—not reclusive, isolated, stuck back in mahogany-laden offices where they're away from what's happening.

In a crisis time, people are more apt to seek out their leaders. In a time of crisis leaders are sought after and expected to do more. But that doesn't mean that in easy times leaders should sit back and relax in the office. The effective leader always has to be very visible.

Do you think it's appropriate for your employees to know Joe the man as well as Joe the leader?

There are many different styles of leaders that can be very effective. Some leaders have more charisma and the ability to build relationships. But that doesn't necessarily mean that leaders who don't have some personality won't also be effective. They must practice the right leadership attributes when it counts.

Informality is a plus for a leader. People want to know and understand their leaders. On the other hand, I think people want to look up to them and respect them. Too high a level of informality can reduce some of the cachet and the importance of the leader's office and role.

What is the U.S. corporation's new role as corporate citizen?

First and foremost the corporation has to be highly successful. The successful, vibrant, thriving company is hiring more people, generating more tax revenues for the government, consuming more products from suppliers, and building more jobs. The most important thing for me is to foster a strong economy and employ people.

If you have a company that is poorly managed and losing market share, that company can still communicate corporate citizenship. But the fact is if you're laying people off and closing factories, if your volumes are shrinking, and if you're buying less from suppliers, you're not contributing to the country. In the end that's more harmful to the country than anything you can do. The company's first responsibility is to be highly successful.

That said, great companies support their communities. And great people find ways to volunteer and help in all kinds of worthy causes. But you can't lose sight of the sequence of events. The company has to be highly successful before the people in the company can devote an increasing amount of time to other contributions in society.

In the New Economy much was written about the "first mover advantage." What's the marketplace advantage now?

There are highly successful companies that are built on a first mover advantage, like e-Bay. On the other hand, there are many companies that are fast followers, that are designed to be nimble, quick, and able to move into emerging markets—even in better ways than first movers. I don't think the first mover advantage creates any guarantee whatsoever in success. And there is absolutely no correlation between first mover advantage and ultimate success ten years down the road.

A highly successful company is the company that is tuned into its customers. It listens to feedback from a broad base of customers in a real-time way, and it is able to convert that input into successful products and services. And then when those products and services are launched and are successful, the company goes back and gets more input and makes those products and services even better. You don't have to be a first mover to do that. When you do move you have to move in a very thoughtful way based on a close alignment with what consumers want from your products.

You didn't mention investors. Do you care about what investors want quarter by quarter?

I care about investors a lot. Investors own the company, and they are critical stakeholders in any scenario. But I care mostly about long-term investor success. A company that manages quarter to quarter without a long-term perspective can run into a lot of problems.

On the other hand, there has to be a duality of purpose. You have to be able to communicate a long-term vision to investors (and then they can decide whether they want to be in or not). And then you have to make each quarter achieve meaningful progress toward those ultimate goals. You can't just say you care about the long term and that you're not obsessed with delivering results on a quarter-to-quarter basis.

There has to be a concurrent focus of the company. Companies that only worry about the quarters and don't have a three-, five-, and ten-year outlook will underachieve long term. Companies that only talk about the long term and don't rigorously deliver quarterly results will underachieve as well.

So is that the solution to standing up to investors who are looking for impressive numbers on a quarterly basis?

I don't feel it's an issue at all. Investors have the right to expect progress in companies they invest in. I never feel any real burden or pressure here. What companies need to do is communicate in a very direct way what their long-term plans are and the pace in which they will move toward achieving those plans. Investors can self-select. Investors should buy stock in those companies where they agree with the leadership philosophy and strategy of the company. And what the company should do is make a real effort to eliminate any ambiguities surrounding these strategies, approach, and culture. To me it's a healthy approach. I love investors. They're very pure, and over the long haul smart ones are rewarded richly because they sift out short-term versus long-term issues. They invest in companies based on being aligned with that company's direction.

So short-term progress doesn't have to be measured necessarily in terms of dollars?

You have to measure long-term progress in a company. If you only measure short-term progress, you're going to make a very big mistake. Some companies have demonstrated spurts of short-term progress only to be later discovered as companies that were robbing the future for short-term results. And that's what investors have to watch out for.

Investors should be looking for those companies who are building quarter after quarter. Those are results marching toward the future. There are many, many examples of companies that have tried to take the shortcut at the expense of the future. And this is bad.

What are you certain of?

We can control destiny. If we do the right things, then good things will happen. I'm certain it's futile to worry about things that are beyond our control.

What are you uncertain of?

I'm uncertain of the global political environment over the next twenty years. It will dictate many of the investment and strategic decisions we make as a company. Judgment is the key. Not all decisions we make as leaders will be the right decisions. But when you have very talented people as advisers, and you have the willingness to make a decision based on judgment, you should be right more often than wrong.

What is the essential ingredient for resilience?

Mental discipline. The ability to stick to your course in good times and bad times. When bad things happen—and they always do—when unpleasant surprises happen, if you're disciplined mentally and you stick to your course, and don't get disrupted, no matter how tough things are, to me, that's resilience. Don't get disrupted by fear, insecurity, paranoia, trauma, grief, or failure. Resilience is an essential quality of leadership and the function of being able to blast through whatever happens to your company, to you individually. You can't get into bad moods, get depressed, or get into slumps, if you're in a position of leadership. You don't have that luxury. That's the burden of leadership.

12

Stephen G. Harrison

President, Lee Hecht Harrison

In leadership, charisma is fine, but it had better be accompanied with other, more practical things like competency, credibility, results orientation, collaboration, and effective communication. Leadership creates hope by galvanizing diverse talents and helping people win. Hope and leadership...you can no longer separate the two.

For millions of Americans, hope is challenged when they receive the news that they have lost their jobs. Whether the employers plan to lay off only one or an entire division, they often turn to such outplacement firms as Lee Hecht Harrison to help the departing employees manage their transition and, ideally, emerge from the experience with both greater self-awareness, better careers, and an enduring positive attitude toward their previous employer.

A global company with more than 150 offices worldwide, Lee Hecht Harrison is no stranger to sudden loss itself. On September 11, Lee Hecht Harrison lost one of its contract employees, Jasper Baxter, who was conducting a public seminar on the ninety-third floor of Tower Two in the World Trade Center. Additionally, its own 13,000 square foot office on the twenty-first floor was demolished, but everyone—staffers and clients alike—were able to escape before the tower fell.

As president of Lee Hecht Harrison, Stephen Harrison has invested his entire career in the mission of linking organizational objectives with individual fulfillment. After fourteen years at Tenneco, where he specialized in labor relations and human resource management, he became a partner with the Center for Diagnostic Medicine in New York, which provided executive and occupational health services for major corporations. Associated with Lee Hecht Harrison since 1982, he has helped grow this outplacement services firm to one of the top companies in its field in the world.

In this interview, Harrison discusses the relationship of hope, work, and business in this time of uncertainty:

- The true meaning of leadership and greatness
- Engaging survivors in a time of drastic corporate cutbacks
- Staffing lessons of the most recent expansion/contraction cycle

~

In 2001, well over a million people were laid off from their jobs. It's been devastating for everyone concerned, including the people who remain employed with the companies doing the layoffs. But businesses must continue to function. How can they proactively establish a post-layoff workplace environment that continues to engage the survivors?

Employees' accessibility to top management is probably the single most important thing that employers can provide to begin to reinstill a sense of engagement among the staff. Sometimes being visible and communicative isn't management's style, but it's their job to rise above their own natural reticence for the sake of their employees and the company. Rudy Giuliani is a model for what I mean. Up until September 11 he was the man New Yorkers loved to hate. But when September 11 happened, he emerged from whatever controversies he had been dealing with the day before as the most engaging, accessible, regular guy you could imagine. He kept talking, talking, talking. And I listened to him endlessly, which I found to be very therapeutic.

The message that leaders deliver must be the unvarnished truth. And it must be consistent from the entire top management team. Granted, some of that message has to be prepared and rehearsed, which means some loss of spontaneity. But a truthful, consistent message is essential for regaining employee confidence. So it will require top management sitting down together and running through "what if" scenarios. It's important that top management sing from the same hymnal. And whatever you have to do to get to that place, you have to do.

Companies in post-survival mode must also be absolutely, desperately sure that there's nothing going on in the company environment that can engender cynicism. Employees will have a keen eye peeled on subtle and not-too-subtle evidence of hypocrisy or mixed messages. All your dots have to connect. For instance, if you've just laid off several thousand employees for financial reasons, you had better remember to cancel that new shipment of high-end office furniture.

A lot of companies in post-survival mode are hiring and firing at same time. That's to be expected; many companies have to radically change their product priorities to protect their profitability. But you should explain this development to the employees so they can see this action as careful business management. People will understand that.

You must also remember that there is still a pipeline between the survivors and the people whom you have laid off. This is actually to your benefit because you still want to retain these people, either as consumers of your product or as members of the future pool of potential candidates that you will want to draw from again when times improve. But that pipeline can get corroded if you don't take very good care of it.

What does that mean in practical terms? Take excellent care of the people who are leaving—or who have already left. If you can't afford fully individualized outplacement for your employees, create career centers for them. You can even do this as a joint venture with your competitors—as we did with ours after September 11, to help the New Yorkers who were suddenly out of work because of the attacks.

When you must speak about departed employees, use only terms of utmost respect. What you say may or may not get back to the former employees. But, more to the point, you will be demonstrating to your current employees that they are working in an environment that honors the individuals who are or ever have been associated with the company.

The little things and the big things that you do will make all the difference in reconstituting a mission-driven organization after a layoff.

The words *purpose, passion,* and *meaning* are on everyone's lips these days. How can companies help survivors return to that loftier purpose of the business? How can you ask that person to invest heart, soul, and passion in a function when that employee is sitting next to an empty cubicle that had once been occupied by someone else who had invested his heart, soul, and passion in his work?

You can't. That's why the distinction of *engaging* your employees rather than *committing* them is so important. All you can hope to do is help them start the process of reengagement, which means communicating your company's mission and asking them to rededicate their efforts toward it. Recommitment—in which employees may dedicate themselves to the company itself—will likely happen by itself over time, if you want it to happen. Most highly evolved companies and employees alike prefer a relationship of engagement, where they are partners in the mutual mission for however long it takes to achieve that purpose. Commitment to the company itself invites a certain kind of blind loyalty that creates an unhealthy, one-sided benefit that is short lived.

What staffing lessons can we learn from this recent era of drastic expansion and then sudden contraction?

These cycles of staffing and then downsizing are like the binge-and-purge eating disorder. Their effects are enormously stressful, enormously expensive, and enormously destructive. Unfortunately, as companies we tend to jump on bandwagons. When things are bad, we divest ourselves of talented people. And when things are good, we recruit more and more and more. I'd like to hope that recruiters will soon become perspicacious enough to understand that there's a bigger game here—sustainability for both the employer and the employees. Therefore, recruiters shouldn't be just hiring people for their specific skill sets to match specific jobs that are open in the immediate term. The total human being brings so much more to the company, and the more the employer recognizes all that each candidate brings, the better off that employer will be. And the more likely the employer is to have a resilient employee who will help the company change as it needs to.

What are you learning as the leader of your own company during these times of expansion and contraction?

This has been a very busy time for us. And we're trying to be artful around the mix of retaining full-time employees versus the part-time people we retain to help us meet demand. Just as importantly, however, is our customer service. We have been very careful to continue serving those customers who have been with us for many years before there was the sudden growth of demand for our services. When things recover we don't want to end up scrambling to fix the pipeline and say to people who have been wonderful to us for many years, "I hope you haven't felt neglected." That would be completely unacceptable.

How has the definition of great leadership changed? What does greatness mean to you now?

Great leadership is manifested or articulated by people who know how to understate it. There is leadership value in humility—the leadership that comes from putting other people in the limelight, not yourself. We're also getting lessons in great leadership from people who never sought that role—all kinds of people from all kinds of circumstances. There is no question that much of the inspiration we have gotten since September 11 has been from the most unlikely corners—a remote field in Pennsylvania, for example—from people who would never have sought out that responsibility. Look at Lisa Beamer, for example, and how we have all taken strength and inspiration from her understated dignity.

The people on Flight 93 are still leading us! If it wasn't for their example, I doubt that the passengers on the Miami flight from Paris would have been so aggressive in taking down that guy who tried to light his shoes.

Great leadership comes from entirely unexpected places. It's understatement, it's dignity, it's service, it's selflessness. We're seeing that everywhere in America today. Business has a lot to learn from the average American.

So business organizations are seeing that leadership is not a function and privilege of the hierarchy?

A lot of people who teach leadership have been saying that for a long time. But when it comes to actual practice, that principle has only been given lip service. And in most companies, only the high-potential fast trackers get the budget to go to the leadership training programs. But now we have proof that leadership comes from literally everywhere. I'll be interested to see how that learning plays out in the way companies make leadership training available throughout the ranks.

I've long been fascinated by the subject of leadership. How do you get feedback on being a leader? It's not as if I can pass people in the hallway and they say, "Hey Steve, good morning, and by the way, you're a great leader." How do you cultivate leadership deep inside an organization? Are leaders born? Can they be developed? Is charisma vital or is it just value added? What about management versus leadership? Is one bad and the other good? Can they coexist in the same person? Should they coexist in the same function? Can individual leadership be effective in today's collaborative team-driven organization? How do you lead the round table? If there are so many wonderful ways good leaders are described—visionary, collaborative, integrity—why is it that the SOBs win so often?

And how does leadership relate to hope? I'd like to think that leadership is what gives feet to hope. That with leadership hope has its feet on the ground and can then go places. In leadership, charisma is fine, but it had better be accompanied with other, more practical things like competency, credibility, results orientation, collaboration, and effective communication. Leadership creates hope by galvanizing diverse talents and helping people win.

Hope and leadership...you can no longer separate the two.

What are you certain of?

The legacy of American resiliency puts me squarely in the camp of those who are certain that we will survive and thrive. I have already spent many years in the world of work, and I've seen thousands of examples of amazing power to recover as individuals regain their spirit and sense of purpose. And then, of course, we've had a couple of hundred years of historical perspective in this country. This doesn't automatically make me a cockeyed optimist, but I refuse to be a cynic.

With recovery will come Americans who have a unique talent to repress their self-doubts and whatever feelings of defeat they may be feeling now.

What are you uncertain of?

I'm very uncertain of the enduring nature of the lessons we've learned. Many of these young people who were making so much money during the New Economy and who are now forced out of work are going through the adventure of self-examination to discover for themselves what kinds of careers will give them lasting meaning and fulfillment. Even though their new careers might offer them substantially less income, many of them are finding work grounded in better business values that can also offer them a healthier, more well-rounded life. I'm concerned that when the economy turns around again they might abandon the meaningful work they're creating for themselves now for the sake of the greater financial reward again.

It's an American characteristic to have a dangerously short memory. In recent years, we had been incredibly riveted to the notion that success is built on intense, individual competitiveness. Right now we're very community spirited, and we've seen examples of generosity and selflessness everywhere. I hope that we will remember that spirit when things get good again.

What is the essential ingredient for resilience?

Experience. You have to have walked in a few moccasins to be resilient. The fact that you have been knocked around before and survived will give you the self-assurance you need to continue. It's the coming back from the bad experience that builds your resilience. Only experience can do that.

13

Chester D. Haskell

President, Monterey Institute for International Studies

If you're really interested in the security of the United States, you ought not to be talking about how we should restrict international students. You ought to be talking about how we can encourage more students to come here. In the long term that's how you build the understanding and the leadership of other countries in the future.

As investigators began identifying the likely participants of the September 11 terrorist attacks, it became very clear very early that many of the nineteen hijackers had been living in the United States on student visas. As a result, new scrutiny has been placed on the role of international education in the United States and whether its value outweighs the risks inherent in bringing thousands of students from all over the world inside U.S. borders. In the corridors of Congress, academia, and the Immigration and Naturalization Service, the question has been asked in a variety of ways: Does the ideal of global understanding truly justify taking the risk of allowing entry to a handful of individuals who would try to bring down an entire nation?

So far, at the Monterey Institute of International Studies, the answer is yes. More than half of the school's 650 students come from more than fifty countries around the world; its alumni come from—or are now located—all over the planet. Although everyone speaks English, as well as at least one other language, additional language classes are offered in Chinese, English, French, German, Japanese, Korean, Russian, and Spanish. The Monterey Institute of International Studies is the home of programs on international policy studies, international environmental policy, commercial diplomacy, and—not coincidentally—the Center for Nonproliferation Studies, the world's largest program researching issues related to weapons of mass destruction.

Chester "Chet" D. Haskell is the president of the Monterey Institute of International Studies. Prior to joining the Institute, Haskell was the executive director of the Harvard Academy for International and Area Studies at Harvard University for thirteen years. He has also served as dean of the College of Arts and Sciences and Professional Studies at Simmons College.

In this interview, Haskell talks about how international education will lead the way toward corporate globalism in the future:

- How international education promotes global awareness and peace
- The ways diplomacy and business skills enhance each other
- Doing business with nations whose human rights principles are in conflict with those of the United States

How does international education play a role in developing future enterprise, especially in the face of terrorism and hair-trigger uncertainty?

I don't think the world changed on September 11. I think the world is exactly the same as it was on September 10. Our *awareness* of certain things has changed. The fundamental issues about the world and the future are not the war on terrorism. They have to do with poverty, the absence of democratic governments in certain countries, and issues of that sort. Those are issues that existed long before September 11, and they will exist long after all the terrorists have been taken care of.

The role that education has in this is paramount on a variety of levels. If you're interested in building societies in other countries so that people don't resort to terrorism, then education is the key. If you're interested in building friends for the United States, education is the key. Virtually all of the foreign students who study here return to their countries, and they usually go back to their countries thinking the United States is a pretty terrific place. If you're really interested in the security of the United States, you ought not to be talking about how you should restrict international students. You ought to be talking about how we can encourage *more* students to come here. In the long term that's how you build the understanding and the leadership of other countries in the future.

We've taken a very narrow view of that because of the September 11 incident. I'm not saying we shouldn't have better INS tracking of people. But we should be seeing investment in international education as a very important thing for the U.S. future. There are ways to do this.

In terms of campus life itself, is this a practical laboratory for individuals from all over the world to experience what it is like to work toward the same objectives with people from a wide variety of backgrounds?

The educational experience they have with each other is extraordinary. Students learn as much or more from each other than from any other part of the educational process. Here at the Monterey Institute, all of our American students have lived outside the United States. Half of our students are foreign nationals. Everyone speaks one additional language besides English. They're all older. You want to have diversity in the classroom, not just because it's a good thing in a moral sense (which it is) but because it means better education for everyone there. If you have a group of students who all look the same and who have the exact same experiences in their background, they're not going to learn as much as a more diverse group of students. This is a well-known principle in educational circles.

If you're concerned about broadening the experience of students—especially U.S. students—one of the best things you can do is to have more international students in the classroom who have different perspectives and different backgrounds. At the same time, those students are being influenced by the U.S. students. That happens everywhere in higher education. It's an essential part of high education and one that we should be doing more to promote.

What are the business skills that will be necessary for the advancement of world peace?

You have to be able to communicate, which means being able to both listen *and* get your message across. You have to be able to operate in settings that are multilateral, where you must function in both a collaborative and cooperative way. The use of language and the ability to communicate across cultures is a set of tools that are essential to do those things.

What are the diplomatic skills that are essential for the advancement of global business?

It is the same thing. The lines among business and government and education are increasingly blurred in lots of ways. When you look at people who are successful in international business, they also have the same skill set as successful diplomats. The diplomats may not have the same financial background or the M.B.A.s that a lot of the business people have, so it's harder to go the other way. But the general sense of being able to talk to other people, get through to other people, listen to other people, and understand other people—it's the same thing.

How has the face of American businesses operating abroad been changed by and since September 11?

There are some obvious changes about security that are not inconsequential. One of the things we tend to forget here in the United States is that our European friends have been dealing with terrorism for years. There's nothing new; it's just here now. During the week before September 11, one of my best friends who lives in Madrid just missed being blown up by a car bomb while walking through a parking lot. The Brits have been experiencing this with the IRA for a long time. This is not news. In fact, they lost more in the World Trade Center incident themselves than in any other single terrorist incident in British history.

The attack has made for some strange bedfellows. It created opportunities for alliances with some surprising people.

Yes. It makes you sort out what your priorities are. I was in China back in November 2001. Beijing is very excited about two things: the World Trade Organization and the Olympics. In every meeting I attended, they all expressed condolences about September 11. In the next breath they would say, "We welcome you to the war on terrorism because we know about terrorism ourselves." Now you can argue about their view of terrorism. But it does create some different alliances and gets us focused on different sets of issues—like who really are our friends in the long run?

When we talk about increased globalism of economies and the fact that we're all going to have to do business with countries that have a history of human rights abuses, how do we reconcile this basic conflict of American principles in order to transact with them?

American hands aren't clean either. We tend to forget some of the things that have happened in American history. Look at the history of California and what happened to the Chinese, Japanese, and Native Americans. We are an advanced industrial nation and we went through that history in order to get to where we are now. Other countries that aren't as advanced are going through history that will get them to something that's different down the road. We must be very careful with absolutes in these settings. Again, human rights is a very gray area. You have to accept the fact that you don't go from an underdeveloped society to a free market democratic society overnight. It just doesn't happen.

Throughout the world, in fact, capitalism has already won out and will continue to win out. But that's going to mean different things in different places. From a business perspective it doesn't matter as long as you're selling whatever you're selling. On the other hand the conditions for selling whatever you're selling might be very different. There are lots of companies that are very upright about their stands about these things, but when you get into their local operations in various countries you'll discover that they're sometimes involved in corruption. Otherwise you wouldn't get anything done. So who's got the clean hands there?

The United States is not going to be able to run roughshod over every other culture. The way to get to a more enlightened view throughout the world is to build other societies. As countries become wealthier they become more democratic, and they become more enlightened in terms of human values.

So if you really want to help things get better in other places, you ought to be thinking about how to improve opportunities for jobs in other countries. How do you improve market opportunities in those countries? How do you improve educational opportunities in those countries?

How do you do these things without lining the pockets of the oppressors?

The oppressors of the world are in very difficult straits. They can't isolate their societies from the rest of the world. For instance, if Castro dies tomorrow Cuba becomes, in effect, the 51st state. The Communist society, such as it is in Cuba, is being held together by the charisma of one man. When he leaves the scene there's hardly any scenario that anyone has come up with where it survives for very long. If the United States were truly interested in promoting capitalism in Cuba, then we would be doing things to *increase* interaction with Cuba as opposed to maintaining the sanctions that we still have.

What about China?

China is one of the most interesting places right now. The Chinese are very sophisticated, and they have a huge problem on their hands. If the Communist party is to stay in power, the country has to become wealthy economically. They've gone way down that road. They have a lot of things going for them economically. At some point they're not going to be able to continue doing the things they have to do economically and still have the same governmental structure. It's going to have to change in one way or the other, and they know it. What they're going to try to do is a transition that's gradual so they don't have the same kind of downfall of their society that the Soviet Union had. And they won't have the chaos at the end of it either.

How do you see the human rights side of the story evolving in China?

Gradually over time, and sooner rather than later, that will be dampened down considerably. Part of the problem in China is that they have not historically had a national legal system, which they're trying to build now. The only way they've been able to deal with internal criminal problems is through severe measures, including executions. Well, we have executions, too, and the Europeans are horrified at our death penalty. They call that a human rights issue.

As far as the political human rights kinds of questions are concerned, the Chinese will gradually figure out better ways of dealing with them. They've not been at this very long in terms of being open to the world. What they're worried most about are those things they perceive as threatening to the political control of the party, but they know that change is necessary.

So you believe that becoming part of the overall economic community will fund the transition to a new way, as opposed to funding the entrenchment of the old way?

Absolutely. If your goal is to undermine the Communist Party of China, the best way to do that is to get the country more interconnected with the rest of the world.

What does investing in the future mean now to you?

People. And that means education—no matter what your goal is in the future, be it in business or government. It's going to be more complicated, and it's going to require skills that you can only get through the educational processes.

What are you certain of?

I'm certain there's going to be a lot of change. And change is going to lead us toward greater heterogeneity, greater interconnectedness, and greater internationalization. I'm certain that the world is going to look different from the world today.

What are you uncertain of?

How we in the United States will be able to deal with the change. There is a real set of issues, and September 11 has an impact on how we prioritize our issues. The only way any of us is going to make progress in the world of the future is in a way that's more cooperative, collaborative, and multilateral. It doesn't mean we must or will give up on a particular set of issues or that national sovereignty is going to go away. But we're still a very insular place. Those of us who are in international higher education see it all the time. There are falling numbers of people who speak foreign languages and falling numbers of people who have lived in a foreign country. It's stunning.

What is the essential ingredient for resilience?

You have to be clear about what your principles are, and you have to be clear about where you're going. If you can't see what your main direction is, it's really easy to get buffeted off course by all those unexpected things out there. And there are going to be many unexpected things.

14

Sunir Kapoor
Founder, E-Stamp

The reason the economy is in the situation it's in now isn't totally borne out by technology, or the Internet, or the so-called New Economy. The fact is, if you look around today, the New Economy has changed the world as we know it. And it's changed by and large for the better.

Before launching his historic E-Stamp business, the first company in seventy-six years to receive approval to print U.S. postage and the first worldwide approval to print Internet postage, Sunir Kapoor had already developed a lengthy curriculum vitae working for such giants as Novell, Oracle, and Microsoft, where he was part of the team that opened Microsoft's European headquarters. In 1996, he began E-Stamp. By the time it went public in October 1999, the company had received thirty-three worldwide patents for its innovative technology that would allow customers to download their postage off the Web, thereby avoiding lengthy lines at the post office.

In 2000, Kapoor began another company, Tsola (Mandarin for "Let's go!"), which was founded to develop the software necessary to enable the "next generation of wireless data services." By early 2001, however, the once hopeful telecommunications sector began to show signs of decline, and by June 2001, he was forced to close the company. But as one of the leading proponents of the economic promise of technology and innovation, Kapoor has not abandoned the long-term view of technology's role in shaping the future.

In this interview, Kapoor talks about the lessons learned from his experiences launching two high-tech start-ups during the New Economy boom era:

- The nature of entrepreneurial optimism
- The enduring value of innovation as a market advantage in a cyclical economy

■ The global reputation of the United States during discouraging economic times

What is the essential ingredient for resilience?

An optimistic outlook on life. The way you are, your personality, your view on life in general really does impact how you approach business. And from there you can put things into perspective. All these things that happen from time to time, however tragic they are, are events. Although they can be very serious events, they do have a beginning, an end, and a finite depth. When you put that in the perspective of your own life, you carefully question why you do what you do and the amount of time you spend on what you do.

And you relate what's happening in your present with things that happened in your past. Personally, with respect to the two core issues of the day, which are economy and terrorism, they go back to when I was growing up in Britain. The story of the day was another car bombing, another letter bomb, a post office blowing up in London, and pictures of British soldiers fighting against various factions in Northern Ireland.

My parents were average middle-class parents who went through economic upturns and downturns and all the other socio-political changes of the 1960s. But they kept our home life constant. And my father had yet another perspective based on his youth: He had seen and lived through the partition of India by the British. He has stories of ethnic and racial hatred in a country that had already survived thousands of years as a heterogeneous society. People of all faiths who had been living quite happily with each other suddenly started killing each other.

When you put what has been happening now in the perspective of the history of humankind, then you can really put it in perspective. Things like this will happen in the future, as they have happened in the past. All you can do is review your priorities.

I'm fairly realistic generally, but I like to look at the good side of the coin rather than the negative side.

Can optimists be made, or are they born?

I think they're made. You're essentially born with a blank mind. Although genetics play a part in basic elements of who you are, whether you are good at leading other people, foreseeing trends in industry, or whether you are an optimist or a pessimist, that is all based on what you've been exposed to in life. If my father hadn't been optimistic about people, despite some of the things he's seen with his own eyes, I wouldn't be as optimistic as I am.

It is interesting, though, how events form people's long-term perspective on life and perhaps on business. When you go through the experience of having to close down a business and think about the people who worked for you and their families, it isn't something that you ever forget. I'd like to think it's something that makes you stronger. It has to make you a better manager in business and hopefully a more humane person individually.

Except for Tsola, I hadn't encountered a situation where I hadn't succeeded or overcome and turned everything around positively. There was a happy ending to almost everything I had done. You don't worry about things you can't control.

How did you avoid taking the unexpected outcome of Tsola personally?

I did take it personally. Tsola was a situation I couldn't recover from no matter what I did. The telecommunications market for future wireless data services just disappeared. But the closing of Tsola had very personal impacts on thirty-seven employees, their families, and all the people associated with them. Although I personally did what I could to help them, it does make an impact. I have coped by seriously analyzing what could have been different.

What would I have done differently given the information I knew at any given point in time? In hindsight, obviously, I would have done things differently. But when you can look back on it and honestly consider all the things that happened and what you might have done differently knowing only what you knew then, and you can honestly say you did what you could with what you knew at the time, that's the most you can ask of yourself.

Knowing what you know now, what would you have done differently?

I would have focused on a different market altogether. I wouldn't have focused on wireless carriers. We (the board of directors and I) would have operated the company at a different tempo. The pressure was that there was a window of opportunity and we were going after that window of opportunity. We spent most of our money on engineering and building the product. The yardsticks used by the board were "how quickly can you hire" and "how quickly can you secure beta customers." Again it comes back to pace. We would have re-paced ourselves to be more appropriate for the change in environment. With E-Stamp it was a marathon. It was three years, seven months, and twenty-six days from taking the company from my kitchen table to NASDAQ. And we paced ourselves accordingly. Now with Tsola, it was a 400-meter race, we felt—and everyone on the planet seemed to concur—that there was a small window, a lot of companies were getting funded to deliver information to people while they're mobile, via cell phones and personal digital assistants, and we were under pressure to get a product out. And we did, based on the timeline we had developed. Everything has a finite momentum and takes time.

What made it very unusual compared to earlier economic downturns has been the rate of decline. Unfortunately for Tsola, the principal market we were going after, the telecommunications carriers, was the one that led the economic downturn in the technology market. It was impossible to turn on a dime and change markets.

Technology markets seem to be driven so much by innovation, opportunity, and demand. Is there a place in the technology employment discussion for personal meaning and purpose?

Absolutely. When you're hiring people you're looking for what I like to call the "impedance match," borrowing from the vocabulary of physics. When you change a fuse, you need to replace the old one with a new one that will be compatible with the electrical circuit. That's impedance matching. In business you're also looking for a match, in business acumen, experience, or personal values between two people. You're looking for a hook you both can relate to.

Everyone is looking for a role in life. It's not stock options or employee benefit plans. What really drives people is the search for meaning in their role in the bigger picture of what this group of individuals has set out to do. Can they find a fulfilling role for themselves in that mission? If you can find that as a manager and communicate that to the person who has come aboard to join the mission, then you've got one of the most loyal employees you'll ever recruit.

What's the role of innovation in driving business toward creating a more deliberate future?

The future will happen whether or not you have innovation. But likewise, innovation is inevitable. You can't decide whether or not there will be innovation. You may wish that innovation will happen faster or slower. But innovation will happen. And good ideas will come to the fore. The only thing you can control is where you set the bar on innovation.

You can enable less innovative ideas to bear fruit, grow, prosper, and ultimately fail, because they're lower innovation ideas. Or you can raise the bar and have the greatest of the greatest ideas. There are always people who will want to participate in creating the future and improving its potential with better and better innovations.

So all the trouble that Silicon Valley as suffered over the last two years hasn't disenchanted you about the potential of innovation?

If anything, events like this raise the bar on all the other things that need to happen to take innovation to business success. From investors to board members to partners to customers, everyone's more conservative and more wary. But that serves to raise the bar on what actually succeeds now. The real innovators are looking toward the future as creatively as they ever were. Nothing's changed for them. Entrepreneurs' behavior is driven by the priorities of their investors. If your investors seek a short-term return on their investment, your priorities as a CEO are set accordingly. If they are interested to build a company on the other hand, then you have the ability to grow steadily. The recent downturn will enable more of the latter.

Clearly more of them will be disappointed because the bar has been raised. But that doesn't mean that innovation won't happen. It just may not happen this year. But what I am finding is there's as much of an opportunity as there ever was.

At any point in time you always have an equilibrium among various factors in life and business. That equilibrium may not be what you want, but it's still an equilibrium. Today, even though you have a greater scarcity of capital, conversely you have a greater availability of human resources. There certainly are plenty of very smart people around, a number of whom are free to invent our future, which wasn't the case even a year ago.

Also, the amount of capital you need to raise has decreased. The cost of real estate, for instance, in the valley has come down hugely. Customers haven't stopped spending. They've just changed their priorities on what they want to buy. So what they're spending on now is dictated by shorter-term benefits rather than longer-term goals. That's a good thing if you happen to provide technology solutions for shorter-term problems. Companies that build security software or data storage solutions, for instance—those vendors are benefiting hugely right now.

So it's a matter of being at the right place at the right time?

However successful they are, very few people will admit the role that luck had to do with it. Think about the companies out there now that are in the security business. Clearly they never set out to anticipate what was going to happen. And in business in general, it's exactly the same thing. It's very easy to take credit for things and not to point out that there are many great ideas that have everything going for them that never make it. And conversely there are less revolutionary ideas that make it by some metric. Luck has a big part to play in the success or failure of a venture.

The New Economy has been used as a whipping boy. What's your response to the popular conclusion that the economic trouble we're in right now is all the New Economy's fault?

Quite frankly I think it's absurd. The reason the economy is in the situation it's in now isn't totally borne out by technology, or the Internet, or the so-called New Economy. The fact is, if you look around today, the New Economy has changed the world as we know it. And it's changed by and large for the better. Any technological advance has its downsides as well as its upsides. The fact is that people's lives have changed through the communications revolution— look at the cellular phone or the Internet—as well as through impacting the supply chains of all industries, making American business more productive.

People who blame the New Economy should go back and look at the contribution to the gross domestic product and the contribution of new companies over the last five years to new employment in the United States. Consider how the United States has dominated the new technology economy, the jobs it's created, and the wealth it's generated. Blaming the New Economy for the disappointments we're suffering now is very shortsighted. Where are the jobs going to come from in the future? Where is the economic growth going to come from to take the country out of the situation it's in? It isn't through increasing steel, coal, or oil production. It is actually the New Economy that's going to get us out of the situation that we're in now.

In the last thirty years it is estimated that 7.9 million jobs were created in the United States by start-ups. By the end of 2000, more than $1.3 trillion in revenue came from $273.3 billion provided by venture capital funded companies. Look at some of the leading companies that represent the New Economy. Cisco, for example. It's one of the most highly capitalized companies in the world with more than 38,000 employees.

There are many, many examples where the New Economy has actually contributed net positive and should not be viewed as net negative. That's just too shortsighted. And it's too easy to blame one thing. The reason why we are where we are is due to a number of things. Whether it's the New Economy or not, economies go in cycles. They don't continue in a meteoric rise.

What buzz are you hearing from foreign nationals about whether America is still considered the "Land of Promise"? Has that changed?

The factors that make the United States an attractive environment for entrepreneurs haven't changed at all. There are three factors in the United States that continue to indicate a more opportunistic environment for entrepreneurs worldwide: First, the mindset of society in this country that encourages risk and reward— it's not considered mediocre to work for a no-name company (read: start-up) here as it still is in Europe. Second, the availability of capital. Although it's more difficult, it's still here. And third, the relationship between academia and industry, epitomized here by Berkeley and Stanford, of course. It is also true that for a given capital investment the business value that can be created here is much greater than in other countries.

What happened in the last five years were the excesses of the changing expectations of the risk/return ratio and over what time frame that return should come, both on the part of venture investors and public investors. But that's still very much a U.S. phenomenon. NASDAQ and the ability to get public liquidity and support for start-up companies still exist in the United States.

Generally foreign nationals are optimistic about the United States. None of that has changed.

How are U.S. companies with international locations regarded in their host countries now?

It's more about what the U.S. company represents in terms of the way it does business, as opposed to the fact that it's simply American. But if you go to Microsoft or Oracle subsidiaries, what you find is a new recipe that is a mixture of French or British or German culture with American. At least in the technology industry it really is the best of both worlds. You get French wine in the company cafeterias, but you'll have a management-by-objectives approach as well, which is very much a U.S. export. So you really do end up with a positive blend of the best of both cultures. In many ways, the way U.S. subsidiary companies do business abroad is a lot more interesting for employees than working in a U.S. company over here or a European or Asian company over there. You end up with a much more positive, and unique, environment.

I think you'll find that, given the choice, a number of American employees would prefer to work for a U.S. company—but actually overseas, at least for a period of time.

Much has been written about the "first mover advantage." What's the marketplace advantage now?

Even in historic businesses, those who were first had a meaningful advantage. Ford is still a major business in the field that it innovated. In pharmaceuticals, first mover advantage is critical in the commercial exploitation of new drugs. In technology, first mover advantage continues to be important. But it doesn't replace good execution, which my experience with E-Stamp as a public company vividly illustrated.

So it's possible to be the second comer and prevail over the first mover if better systems are in place?

Yes. Long-term success depends on processes, infrastructure, and people. True, E-Stamp conceived and created the Internet postage marketplace. The game was E-Stamp's to lose and they lost it. Stamps.com had superior execution. It came from behind, bought our patents, and through superior management execution prevailed. That example doesn't eliminate the theory of first-mover advantage. It just reinforces the importance of execution by boards and management on par with innovation and the right idea.

Innovation on its own is insufficient. You really need the complete team. Investors, management, board members, staff—they must all be aligned. But eventually we had that misalignment where we had individual venture investors who, despite lacking operating experience, felt overconfident that the company was on a path that couldn't fail. They brought in executive management from a large corporation. When I decided to leave E-Stamp, the company had many things configured correctly around it: Investors included Microsoft and Compaq, and partners such as Yahoo and Sunbeam. We had thirty-three patents; we had cash in the bank. This momentum enabled the company to undertake a successful IPO—$125 million was raised. It couldn't fail.

The theory was that the worst that could happen was that it would be a two-horse race. But once investors interfered, it created an inflection point that resulted in the company's going down a path to failure. One of the things I learned is that you do business with people who share your values and vision. Ultimately that's the founders' responsibility. It's amazing that here is a company that has a unique intellectual property that locks up a market segment, that is the first company in that space for seventy-six years, that innovates with a solution that millions of customers around the world want, and that impacts an American institution, the U.S. Postal Service— and it still fails despite having the business ecosystem created and financial assets of almost $155 million.

What are you certain of?

I'm certain that the economy will improve. I'm certain that for better or for worse, people will move on with their lives, even after the horror of September 11, and go back to business. We should never lose sight of the fact that things will get better again, but we should never forget what happened either.

Economic recoveries have a beginning and an end. Every recession has a boom. A lot has been written about some substantial companies that were formed in economic downturns. I'm sure that the next great companies and new business ideas are being conceived now during this economic downturn. That has to make you optimistic about the future.

I'm very certain that the Internet will become even more relevant in people's day-to-day lives.

What are you uncertain of?

Anything we have no control over. How quickly the economic recovery will happen, for instance. When there will be a rebound in the economy. Even if you try to create the next Microsoft now, the reality is you don't know if this is the best time for new products to be accepted by the marketplace. If you knew when the economy will bounce back you would do things at a certain pace. Certainly the biggest challenge for any company is knowing when to do things. Not just what are the things that need to be done.

Having a generally positive outlook on life, I think you shouldn't focus on uncertainties. You don't worry about the things you can't control in business. You try and frame the likelihood of certain things happening through the practice of risk analysis. You focus on the things you can control and then figure out the pace in which to do them. Actually, that's what life is, right?

15

Christopher Komisarjevsky

CEO Worldwide and President Burson-Marsteller

The statements that are made by companies that speak of the right values in a time like this resonate for a long time. The ones that don't are very badly received, and people don't forget them either.

Both the September 11 attack and the stumbling economy have left businesses with many questions. Beside the most pressing question, "What do we do about it?" there is also the question, "What do we say about it?" It is the ways companies have chosen to answer that second question—especially in the aftermath of September 11—that has set businesses apart from one another. With eighty-five offices in forty-five countries, the public relations firm Burson-Marsteller's job has been to help clients say the right thing for almost sixty years.

As CEO Worldwide and president of Burson-Marsteller, Chris Komisarjevsky is headquartered in the company's New York office. He had just come to work and started his day when the events of September 11 played out both down the street outside his window and in front of him as he watched on television. He also lives in an expansive but tightly knit Long Island community largely made up of New York's firefighters. It would suffer a second tragedy two months later on November 12, 2001, with the crash of American Airline 587.

In this interview he talks about finding a new meaning and heightened sense of purpose through managing impassioned, dedicated staff during a time of crisis:

■ The changing role of the CEO

- Taking inspiration from employees
- The best approach for corporate public relations during tragedy
- The power of unwaivering values in the face of upheaval

We have been through some events that have shifted the ground under us—the September 11 attacks, the resulting damage to the economy, the reminders that we're not unquestioningly admired among all nations and religions. How can these events be used as an opportunity for American companies to reassert themselves as citizens of a larger community—as members of the more global Family of Man, so to speak?

Companies need to first consider their social responsibility philosophy. There's no question that as an economic institution a business has a responsibility to return to shareholders, to make money, to make a profit, and to have a margin that is respectable within the industry. The needs of the investment community must not be forgotten.

But I don't think that people consider that to be enough today. How the company behaves, how its people behave, is also important. And it may contribute to the bottom line in ways that are intangible or perhaps less direct. People expect companies to demonstrate that they are not only good as businesses in producing the bottom line, but they are also good as corporate citizens in doing what's right in the way that they behave: ethically, supportive of human rights, environmentally responsible, and permitting employees to not only have good careers but also learn and grow in the process.

Our research has shown that the CEOs' behavior is also supremely important in their companies' reputation. The most important characteristic of a chief executive—who embodies the corporation as the most visible element other than the product itself—is that he or she must be believable.

What's interesting is that our survey was done before September 11, and even then the importance of being believable (which is being someone the public can trust and have confidence in) was number one. But it wasn't number one either two years ago or two years prior to that. Now it is.

The second important characteristic today is that the CEO demands high ethical standards. In 1999, that was number 4 in importance.

So now you have two qualities that are being focused on that don't speak to producing a financial result, but speak to what some people may call the "softer side" of the business—the values, the ethics, the trust. Those kinds of concepts.

What do you suppose accounted for this shift?

The study was done in the latter portion of 2000–2001, and people had already become tired and disillusioned about the false promises that came out of some of the start-up, highly funded businesses built around the Internet. What we really are looking for is something that is durable, with some real substance to it. People have begun say, "Hey, wait a minute, let's go back to the things that stand the test of time." In my way of thinking, it's the values that stand the test of time.

You can have a great quarter or a tough quarter from a financial perspective. But values stand the test of time.

What have you been learning about your employees during this test of time?

These kinds of tough situations provide a backdrop on which you can again appreciate the strength of individuals. When they have the opportunity to challenge their thinking and it's constructive, there are enormous things that they can do. What we've seen is energy that has been channeled to help out. It's not only the money that has been raised, which has been extraordinary. It has also been not only the time and effort that people spend caring about friends, relatives, and neighbors who have been personally affected by this tragedy, but also what they did to reach out to people they didn't know.

I think the strength of the human spirit is remarkable. You are reminded of these kinds of things when you go through these difficult times.

Has your role as a manager and leader changed?

I'm reminded of the value of giving people an opportunity to have a say in what they do, creating teams, and involving people who might not otherwise have been involved in the past; it is a much stronger way to go. What has been happening reminds you how important teamwork is. You get some good ideas and energy from other people. It also reminds you that there needs to be someone standing up in front who is willing to make the decisions, provide the leadership from out in front, and help channel and focus people's energies.

If you do both of those then the corporation will grow.

You walk away saying the human spirit is very strong, that it's remarkable in many ways. And unfortunately it takes tough times sometimes for it to be revealed.

I would imagine that for a lot of organizational leaders to witness this kind of mass heroism, it has to be a reminder that we're dealing with adults who have truly intrinsic motivation to make a difference in the world.

It makes such a strong statement about people's ability to do the right thing. And it is a challenge for leadership of companies to make sure they channel it and give voice to it. Unfortunately, companies feel that when you give voice to it you're also giving voice to so many differing opinions. And it's hard to create consensus and move things forward. But the fact is that strength comes from giving everyone the opportunity to voice their own opinions, come to agreement among themselves, and then move forward together. And then do what needs to be done.

We know we're going to make mistakes. We know we're going to have problems. But if we can't encourage people to solve those problems and move beyond their mistakes, how can we have a company that is filled with strong, excited people who are going to try different things, and develop new products and ideas?

Sure, that's hard to do. It's very hard to do. It opens up a boss to new ideas and different ways of thinking, which can be threatening. But that's how you connect with people who have good ideas and who are looking for ways to share those good ideas.

I'm tempted to say that's especially important in a company like yours, which is especially dependent on creativity. But the fact is that today every company is creativity dependent.

I don't see how you can get away from it. The intangibles of the business are far more important than the tangibles—the machinery, the assembly lines, the hardware stuff. That's not what makes a business successful today. It's the *intangibles:* the human capital, the ideas. It is the intangible assets that make a difference in terms of the way the company is viewed by the financial marketplace. Everywhere in the world, the market cap for intellectually driven companies is higher than for those companies that are hardware driven.

We saw some disastrous attempts by companies to continue with their publicity campaigns in the immediate aftermath of September 11. There were some that even seemed to exploit certain related themes, such as tragedy and heroism. How has the field of public relations moved forward as a result of this experience?

Right away we began discussing with our clients what should be done, what shouldn't be done, and what would be proper. Our advice and guidance to clients was that you should be seen at this point as doing everything necessary for recovery. You should not be seen as doing anything that could be perceived as cheap, exploitative, or insubstantial. Again it comes back to the values.

I drive in from Long Island every morning, and there is a billboard at the entrance to Manhattan, right before you get to the Queens Midtown Tunnel. The words read: "Welcome to the city of heroes." And it's signed *Perry Ellis.* That is the kind of thing that says more about a company than what many other companies have done. There aren't a lot of words, but the message of support and pride is loud and clear.

The statements that are made by companies that speak of the right values in a time like this resonate for a long time. The ones that don't are very badly received, and people don't forget them either.

How does a U.S. company based abroad use its public messaging to help neutralize whatever anti-Americanism there may be?

Sometimes it's most effective if a third party does it instead of you. What Prime Minister Tony Blair did in his speech in Parliament and what he has done since then has laid out the logic and thoughtfulness of the American response to this attack. That he spoke as a Brit did more to eradicate the idea that you could think badly of America than anything we could have done as Americans.

I'm also a firm believer in the intelligence of individuals. If you lay out the facts for people—perhaps dramatically or in an interesting fashion—reasonable people will make reasoned judgment. And they will almost always be right. But it has to be laid out with great respect for an individual's ability to understand, to follow your train of thought, and then act on something.

This is why I don't like the word *spin*. *Spin* is disrespectful. The underlying assumption of spin is that the individual to whom you're speaking is stupid. People are very smart. Your challenge is to lay things out in life so that smart people will understand and become advocates for whatever it is: for buying a product, for buying a share of stock, for working for a company, for supporting a nation.

It's been said that old rules and old assumptions are no longer valid. What assumptions are no longer true for you and your company, and what has taken their place?

I don't know that the old rules and old assumptions that relate to day-to-day operations of a company are no longer valid. We still have a responsibility as a company to do great work for clients. We have a responsibility as a company to produce a financial result that is expected and do it with pride. We have the responsibility of helping people grow inside organizations. I don't think the core values of company have necessarily changed.

It's the external decisions that surround those values.

People think twice about what they do and where they go. They think twice about how they're going to deal with someone, whether or not that someone has just been through a terrible situation. There's a very genuine effort from people to perhaps be more understanding, more tolerant of the fact that people have personal lives. And that those personal lives have an impact on them that goes beyond the company. There are certain sensitivities in the way we conduct ourselves and talk to each other that have definitely changed. But I think they've been changed for the better because they have urged people to be less caught up with themselves, more open to understanding of and interested in other people.

And I think that's good.

What does "investing in the future" mean now?

We have changed what to expect as assurance for the future. The recession plus the false gods of dot.com companies, coupled with the tragedy of September 11, have made people much less sure of what they thought was going to happen even from one day to the next. As a result we're much more humble. And that's exactly the way it should be. You can't predict the future, because you just don't know.

Isn't that contrary to the American hard-charging, make-it-happen way?

I don't think so. Just because we're not sure what the future is going to be is not a reason for not making decisions and doing things. You can be less sure of what the future's going to be, but how you implement what you decide to do should be done with all of the assurance and gusto that America is recognized and appreciated for—both domestically and globally. The way you implement your decisions shouldn't be cocky, it should be reasoned. But a decision that then gets implemented should be implemented with as much conviction as it was before. You have to get the thing done.

As far as the financial markets are concerned, that's a tough one. Their very existence tends to be focused on the short term. That tends to influence companies to make decisions designed to enhance quarterly results. That is not always the best thing to do.

Then again, there's also some humility in financial markets today. Many of these people who ran up the stock in these dot.com companies woke up without jobs.

What has enduring relevance in an environment of rapidly shifting externalities?

The values by which we make decisions. Values of doing your best to make the fair and right decisions in business. The values of being respectful of other people and appreciative of different points of view. Doing things with honesty and integrity. Again it comes back to what you do and how you do it. There's one element to all of this: trying to help people and encourage among people a sense of passion in what it is they do every day. Those are the best performing people inside a business.

Will there ever be such a thing as "business as usual" again?

Some people have used the term *new normal*. The concept behind that phrase implies that what was normal in the past is not normal today. In some point in time things will settle back down again. And one of the things about the human spirit is that a point will be reached in which things will get back to what in this new time will considered to be normal. Those things may not have been "normal" a year ago or two years ago. But there will be a "normal" sometime down the road. I'm not exactly sure what that will be or when people will begin to feel that it's there.

When people go against their judgment, they almost always make a mistake.

What are you certain of?

I have great confidence in people. People will do a great job if they're motivated. There is a great sense of confidence in the human spirit—the ability to be strong, to come out of a difficult situation in many cases better than they were than when they went into it. I'm confident that in the long run people will make the right decisions.

What are you uncertain of?

I'm very uncertain about the economic environment. It's going to be a tough time for quite a while, probably lasting through 2002. That makes things difficult. But these times create opportunities as well as hardships.

What is the essential ingredient for resilience?

Self-esteem. You have to have enough confidence in your own ability to make judgments and to accomplish things, and that when things are difficult you won't collapse. You have to have confidence in being able to make certain decisions, believing they're the *right* decisions.

Part of that comes from the ability to trust your gut. Having a strong enough sense of self will help you determine if something is right, doable, or wrong. Listen to what your gut is telling you about things and have enough confidence in yourself to believe it.

16

James Lawrence
Chief Financial Officer, General Mills

The finance function buys the insurance for General Mills. We used to be given elements of protection and coverage priced on the assumption that certain events would never happen. Now they are being priced on the assumption that they very well might happen.

If it's in the kitchen and you don't have to start from scratch, chances are excellent that it's a General Mills product. From breakfast (Kix, Total, Wheaties) to lunch (Colombo and Yoplait) to snacks (Fruit Roll-Ups) through dinner and dessert (Hamburger Helper, Pillsbury, and Betty Crocker), the $7 billion company probably had something to do with something you ate today.

General Mills' CFO Jim Lawrence has been tasked to making the company's finance function as world class as its reputation for its food products (including the packaging and marketing of them). The winner of CFO Magazine's "2001 CFO Excellence Award for Finance Leadership, Development and Training," Lawrence brings to his job his background as CFO of Northwest Airlines, as well as president of PepsiCola's Asia, Middle East, and Africa operations.

In this interview, Lawrence discusses the influence of U.S. enterprise in improving business standards and practices around the world:

- How U.S. corporate principles and standards promote capitalism worldwide
- The role of U.S. companies in influencing human rights progress globally
- Engaging team effort when effecting profound departmental changes

You were brought into General Mills to institute change in the finance department. How do you drive change instead of letting change happen to you?

In order to drive change, you have to envision what the change state should be. If you are at Point A, and want to move to Point B, you need to paint the picture of Point B, the "change state." Then you need to engage your colleagues and allow them decide *how* to get to Point B (and even *whether* to get there at all). Team members feel better if they can set the path of how to go from A to B. As the leader, you have to determine what degree of inclusiveness to allow, what degree of delegation to exercise, and how much time you are prepared to take for the sake of including all affected groups. This also includes determining how much dissonance you are willing to tolerate for the sake of engaging the hearts and minds of your colleagues. In turn, this depends both on your own temperament and how much room there is for delay and individual judgment.

Some environments simply are not appropriate for a lot of dissonance. My wife, for instance, is a surgeon. When someone works for her, she wants things done precisely. If a nurse or technician does not do it exactly how she wants it done, she is quite displeased. All of her personality, all of her approach to work is: "It will be done exactly the way I want it to be done, precisely 100 percent." Most people *want* a surgeon who demands that things be done to 100 percent specification. Not to 95 percent specification. But in contrast, in most organizations, leaders have to be willing to accept 90 percent specification or maybe 80 percent relative to what they want. You have to get a consensus as you work your way toward your goal.

It is nearly impossible to get proper depth of commitment and resonance if you say, "Here is B. Period. No discussion. Here is how we are going to get there. No debate. Get marching."

An exception, of course, is in crisis situations, where people recognize there is no time for discussion. As a group they know, "Anything is better than what we have now. I believe this leader knows where she is going. I could abandon ship, but if I stay and do what she tells me to do, it will most likely be the best outcome." Boom—they do it. Of course, it is best to have had the opportunity to build the relationships and have them in place *before* a crisis happens.

You have been credited with elevating the purpose of the finance department, transforming it into a valued and respected business partner, as opposed to an administrative cost center and staff function. What's the role of this kind of departmental leadership in driving a company toward a deliberate future?

It is not that there was a problem at General Mills—far from it. Finance was and still is made up of competent, solid, and great people. But it had been split up in an awkward way, with bits of the operation going in different directions, and people having bosses who were outside their function. In my own role, I was facing a larger question how to position the finance department to add more value to the company.

General Mills has long had a reputation of being a great company with great marketing talent. In recent years we had also begun to get a reputation for being extremely good on the supply chain, sales, and R&D end. Our CEO, Steve Sanger, said to me, "I would like General Mills to be at least as well thought of in finance as we are in those other areas."

Senior leaders really have two roles to play to drive their companies forward. They need to be responsible for their own specific function, and they also need to do what is best for the company as a whole. You do not want to have petty rivalries or tunnel vision among the different functions within an organization. As a leader, you need to drive your own function to do as well as it can, *and* you want to make sure all changes are for the overall benefit of your company.

In the finance function, we try to determine where to add value and what things we can do to help the financial well-being of our company. We then try to fit those ideas into the overall context of General Mills. We have had some success in doing that. But there is still plenty of room for improvement and growth.

And can you do that with a philosophy that it's not a question of limited resources, and that you don't have to take from one department to ensure the success of another?

The ultimate goal is the overall success of the company. The success of one function should not be at the expense of another function. It should be measured on how you make a contribution to the *success of the company as a whole.* Surely there are ways to measure individual performance, and you can do that separately from the success of the team. But we all want the team to win. We can all do well individually while we help the team collectively.

How can American companies demonstrate their corporate financial principles as proof that capitalism can be used as a tool for improving lives of people around the world?

The products that General Mills sells around the world are high quality. Most U.S. companies, with the ability to operate on an international level, do sell quality products. Secondly, the employment practices we have reflect the values and standards that exist within the United States. When they are applied abroad they may well be an improvement on those of the host countries.

Obviously, there are exceptions. Japan and developed Western European countries, for instance, have high standards and practices. But in certain ways our policies toward the inclusion of women in management may differ from those of many host countries, and we benefit from that. I remember in my management consulting days that we were able to hire truly outstanding Japanese women, for example, because they simply were not getting hired by traditional Japanese companies.

People in the host nations will often strive to match the business standards that we establish. For example, when I worked at Pepsi, the hygienic standards of our plants were much better than the norm in several developing countries. When people are trained in your plants, and then they go off to work for someone else, American standards begin to spread.

The American influence extends to foreign countries beyond things like food safety or fair employment practices. Take our adherence to the Foreign Corrupt Practices Act. American companies abroad are required to follow it. Those practices, while restraining us in some parts of the world, set a standard that companies of all nationalities can adopt. Local companies can also say, "We are going to do business the same way the American companies here do. We are not going to pay bribes. We are not going to give *baksheesh!*" Those are some of the ways American capitalism can show a good face around the world.

Those examples can also threaten carefully cultivated protections of entrenched power structures around the world, can't they?

Although I am an active Christian, my own hope for society is one of a secular democratic progress. In the post–September 11 world, I believe we should realize that we are facing a battle of antiprogressives against progressives. Of antidemocrats against a democratic political view. And of religious fanaticism against secularism. While America is a highly religious country, we are also highly secular in the sense that we believe that everyone should be allowed to have whatever religious views they want. In America, we do have fundamentalists who feel a positive duty to convert nonbelievers. Within those groups, however, the view is not universal, that in the absence of conversion, you are condemned. Even those who think nonbelievers are condemned, do not feel they should commit violence against others to make them see the light!

At the end of the day, no matter how deeply our *personal* religious convictions are held in the United States, as a *society*, we respect the fact that it is a matter of personal belief—not a matter of collective belief. The collective beliefs we share in this country, I believe, are essentially secular, even though many of them are value laden.

I personally believe that America projects this progressive democratic secularism through its capitalist system—and with our media and entertainment. And while it has been generally well received, there are parts of the world where this is seen as shallow materialism, lacking in morality, and driven by greed. That is particularly true in those societies where people are antiprogressive, fanatically religious in a collective sense, and do not share our democratic values. There, our way of life is seen as corrupting and provokes deep anger.

You don't feel that it's an imposition on other cultures for America and American business to manifest these principles abroad?

I think of our principles as "attracting" rather than imposing, and that is why I believe American principles will ultimately prevail. Our "Western civilization" is powerful because it is *inclusive*. It is based on people having the freedom and opportunity to pursue their individual interests. You do not even need to be *Western* to be part of it! We lead by example. To the extent our principles are attractive to people in other cultures, those cultures are changing.

Is it the role of American corporations to use their might to affect human rights progress around the world?

No. But I think it is a natural by-product of it. The role of American corporations is to make money for shareholders! But with each of us relentlessly pursuing the goal of increasing shareholder value within a political and social system that requires certain behavior, American corporations are going to spread our way of doing things around the world. Take the treatment of women. There are many societies in which women are treated terribly. American companies that operate within those societies are just not going to do that. And that has a positive influence in those societies. Just by enforcing our own standards and principles in our operations abroad, we are undermining the existing ways.

It's been said that old rules and old assumptions are no longer valid. What assumptions are no longer true for you and General Mills? And what has taken their place?

I am more concerned about the physical safety of the United States than I had been previously. It is clear the events of September 11 have raised the possibility of terrible outcomes that people did not expect. The finance function buys the insurance for General Mills. We used to be given elements of protection and coverage priced on the assumption that certain events would never happen. Now they are being priced on the assumption that they very well might happen.

What are you certain of?

I am certain of the progress of mankind. Things will be better in the future than they are today. And today's world is better than it used to be. I am confident the forces of progressive, democratic modernity will triumph.

What are you uncertain of?

I am uncertain of the exact speed of mankind's progress and what reversals we will take along the way. I am uncertain of the exact nature of scientific developments—or where they will take place. Technological advancement tends to spring up in one place or another, and you do not know where it will be, how big it will be, or when it will come. Nothing is smooth, nothing is without its dips and reverses. Nothing ever happens in a straight line. Progress is always curvilinear.

What is the essential ingredient for resilience?

You have to be able to take a hit. Take the defeat and move on. Like a goalie in hockey, you *are* going to get scored on. Once you have been scored on, let it go and focus 100 percent of your attention on not getting scored on next time! Pull yourself together and then take on the next challenge.

17

Howard Learner

Executive Director, Environmental Law and Policy Center

Good environmental performance is often the very best business practice as well. By being smart about how we do business and develop policy, we can achieve both *economic growth* and *environmental progress. That is a leading strategic opportunity for both public and business leaders in the twenty-first century.*

Traditionally, the environmental conversation has been divided into two camps: those who feel that pro-environmental initiatives must prevail, even if it meant the sacrifice of economic vitality, and those who feel that the environment question can be put off just a little while longer, boosting profits one more quarter. The Environmental Law and Policy Center (ELPC), a Midwest public-interest environmental advocacy organization, works on a different model. Its method is to discover and develop approaches that preserve and protect the environment, while offering compelling business opportunities to companies driven by the profit imperative. Its theory is that environmental progress and economic development can be achieved together.

With its staff made up of sixteen public interest attorneys, M.B.A.s, financial analysts, public policy advocates, and communications specialists, ELPC brings a strong and effective combination of skills to solve environmental problems. They are "public interest environmental entrepreneurs," identifying opportunities to improve environmental quality in the Midwest and then working actively to develop and achieve the potential benefits. ELPC also provides key legal and technical resources to local environmental groups through a combination of legal representation, economic analysis and public policy research.

As the executive director of the ELPC, Howard Learner is also an attorney specializing in complex civil litigation. He has previously served as the general counsel for Business and Professional People for the Public Interest, a public interest law center in Chicago. In this interview he discusses ways that local economic development and environmental concerns can serve each other in the traditional conversation:

- The enduring public passion for environmental issues
- The value of inter-city high-speed rail to promote regional economic vitality
- The increasing globalization of the environmental conversation as enterprise increases around the world

I've been interested in how environmental concerns have survived the current noise surrounding economic and key survival issues.

Fifteen years ago there was a perceived dichotomy between environmental issues and economic issues. When the economy was strong, environmental consciousness tended to advance. When the economy receded, public interest in environmental concerns tended to pull back. That's not the case now, however. Through 1999, we enjoyed the most robust economic growth in American history. Environmental values, both in terms of public opinion and economic data, grew significantly. However, even as the economy has receded, these strong environmental values have been retained.

There is also a generational shift. My parents' generation may have been generally concerned about our lakes, but they weren't what today we call environmentalists. Look at what has happened since we were kids: Earth Day was a pivot point for our generation, and these environmental values are reflected in our shopping decisions, business and civic actions, and recreational choices. If you look at the relevance and poignancy of environmental issues to people who are a generation younger, it's even higher on their list. There has been a seismic shift in the degree of importance of environmental values for people who are in their twenties and thirties. Today's teenagers feel even more strongly. This is going to play out in the values that people bring to the public arena and our political system. And it plays out in the values and the decisions that people make when they shop.

What accounts for the difference? It used to be that environmental concerns were considered a luxury to be thought about only after more conventional survival and business issues were addressed.

Environmental progress and economic development are not in conflict. Indeed they are complementary, and they can often be achieved together.

For example, there is tremendous interest right now in developing better inter-city rail service here in the Midwest. People are frustrated by air delays, and some people are worried about the safety of air travel. The development of the Midwest high-speed rail network is sustainable development in action. Trains pollute less than cars and airplanes. A downtown-to-downtown high-speed rail network spurs the regional economy. It will counteract sprawl by pulling jobs and business and people into our central cities. It's a good demonstration of how environmental progress and economic development can be achieved together in a way that benefits peoples' lives by providing a valuable additional option for business and leisure travel.

Interestingly, what we're seeing now, even in a time of economic downturn, is that environmental concerns are staying high on the public radar screen. Our environmental values are remaining high, and people increasingly understand that sustainable development works.

At a time in which the world's attention is focused on the heightened threat of terrorism and the financial meltdown of Enron, the largest energy company in the United States, you can still see ads on television from various businesses touting how green they are and proclaiming their environmental values. That's not an accident. It happens because the market research these days shows the strong degree to which more people are putting their environmental values into action, both in terms of their daily lives and their purchasing decisions.

The reason you see the growth of supermarkets like Whole Foods, and more traditional supermarkets stocking organic sections and healthy foods sections, is the realization that these environmental and health values are influencing people's purchasing decisions. Be it BP, Shell, and Archer Daniels Midland advertising a "green" corporate image, or Whole Foods providing a pro-environmental shopping experience, there's an increased recognition in the business community that the public's environmental values are being transformed into purchasing decisions that affect our economy. Better environmental performance is good business.

Do you see making pro-environmental decisions a patriotic thing? Is this part of the overall anthem of taking good care of our country?

It's more than patriotism. The rise of environmental values has been accompanied by a general rise in spiritual values in the United States. People see environmental protection as being both good public health—in terms of cleaner air, cleaner water, and fewer toxins—and good stewardship, in terms of preserving our natural resources and global environment for future generations. This is a deep environmental and spiritual value. We live in a society, not just an economy.

And you don't see that passion subsiding in the face of tightening wallets and paring down business operations?

That's not what we've seen so far. I don't have any doubt that if the economy were to completely tank, people would be forced to accept cutbacks in their quality of life. What has been remarkable over the last two years in a time of economic retrenchment has been the strong continuation of environmental values.

Virtually all the public opinion polling data shows increasingly strong values with each succeeding generation. As I mentioned before, the generation that came of age in the 1960s and 1970s was the generation that witnessed the first Earth Day. Environmental values were even stronger in the next generation. And, now, they're even stronger among teenagers.

Those values are being shaped at a time in which our environment and economy are increasingly global. Environmental issues are global issues. Excessive amounts of carbon dioxide emissions from India and China affect the atmosphere that hovers over the United States as well as over those countries. Climate change and clean water issues are global challenges. Americans cannot escape the global consequences.

The old paradigm says that environmental progress can only be achieved at an economic cost that would create a very unsettling effect on business in the United States and globally. But public and business leaders have come to realize the economic benefits of sustainable development.

Good environmental performance is often the very best business practice as well. By being smart about how we do business and develop policy we can achieve *both* economic growth and environmental progress. That is a leading strategic opportunity for both public and business leaders in the twenty-first century.

The long-standing parody is that environmentalists are tree-hugging Luddites who want to burn candles in the dark. But today's new environmentalists are leading technological advocates supporting, for example, new clean-energy efficiency, renewable energy technologies, and advanced car technologies. By contrast, some utilities and the coal industry want to keep running highly polluting power plants built forty or more years ago. Environmentalists are looking, instead, to the tremendous technological improvements in wind energy turbines and solar power, in fuel cells, and in modern energy-efficient high-tech lighting ballasts, which can both reduce pollution and reduce energy costs. This saves money for consumers and businesses. We should be using modern, new clean energy technologies to power the "new economy" of the twenty-first century.

The Environmental Law and Policy Center is working closely with a coalition of thirty Midwest businesses that manufacture and distribute clean energy efficiency and renewable energy products. Those companies include BP, Maytag, Andersen Windows, Honeywell, NEG Micon, Spire Solar, and a number of other leading businesses that are profiting by making clean energy products. They are part of the positive clean energy development solution to our global warming problem.

How do you expect high-speed rail to succeed when Amtrak has been suffering so mightily and is on the ropes?

Congress has demanded that Amtrak achieve two contradictory goals. On the one hand, Amtrak is asked to run profitable rail lines. On the other hand, we're asking Amtrak to continue providing service to small and medium-size towns when it cannot be profitable. As a nation we need to be clearer on Amtrak's mission: Is it to be a profit-making rail company? Or is it to be a public carrier that serves small markets even when revenues do not match expenses?

We already have one profitable high-speed rail line in the country, the Northeast Corridor linking Washington, New York City, and Boston. The modern, fast, convenient rail line is working. More people want to have that choice available to them.

Is it your vision to have this an Amtrak service or one that's provided by another company?

Amtrak should have an opportunity to bid to run it, and other private competitors should have the opportunity to show how they can do a better job. Don't make it Amtrak's automatic right or obligation. On the other hand, don't automatically exclude Amtrak.

There should be more public investment in our nation's rail infrastructure, just as there is public investment for roads, airports, and bridges. Studies have shown that high-speed rail in the best regional corridors can then operate on a break-even to profitable basis.

High-speed rail can be successful in the United States. It makes good environmental and economic development sense, and it shouldn't be limited to just the Northeast Corridor where, over the past decade, we've invested about $3 billion in developing modern rail service. In the Midwest and other regions, the logic of high-speed rail is becoming more compelling, and there is strong interest also in the Pacific Northwest, California, and Florida. There are plans to develop regional high-speed rail systems all over the country. Over the last forty years, our nation has disinvested in rail infrastructure. That's been a mistake. High-speed rail should be a fundamental third leg on our transportation stool. It's a good option for many people. There is no sound reason why the United States should be so far behind Europe and Japan when it comes to modern high-speed rail service.

Within a 400-mile radius of Chicago, there are ten major cities and a number of medium-size cities in-between. I work in downtown Chicago, and right now, to get to St. Louis, I have two choices: a 325-mile car drive—which is not a real choice—or air travel, which means roughly an hour, depending on traffic, to either O'Hare or Midway Field. Now with security issues at airports, you need to build in an extra hour, maybe two. Once I get on the plane, the trip itself is an hour. Then it's another half-hour or more on the other end. A business trip from downtown Chicago to St. Louis takes at least three-and-a-half hours, on a good day. It's a hassle, and it chisels away the savings in time that are supposed to be offered by air travel.

With high-speed rail, I could go to the train station, hop on a modern, fast, comfortable, and convenient train that would get me from downtown to downtown in the same amount of time as by plane. On the trip itself, I could use my cell phone, plug in my laptop, and even have a meeting.

Rail service can be time-competitive on a door-to-door basis up to a range of about 400 miles. Beyond that point air travel tends to be more time competitive.

Modern rail service located downtown attracts more commercial activity. There are two positive environmental impacts from this rail development: First, trains pollute less than cars and airplanes. Second, to the extent that downtown rail stations become active vibrant centers of transportation, they will serve to pull jobs, people, and businesses into our central cities. That will create a business vitality that's good in terms of our overall economy, and it will counteract sprawl. It's what is now called a "smart growth" development strategy.

Some businesses will make money on high-speed rail development. That's good. Companies should benefit from their participation in environmentally progressive products and services. BP, for instance, is one of the largest solar manufacturers in the world. It will clearly make more money if the solar energy development market grows. It's good for the environment, and it's good for economic growth. I would rather see BP and Shell making money developing solar energy for the twenty-first century than drilling for more oil in Alaska and the North Sea.

What are you certain of?

I'm certain that there is a transformation in the strength of environmental values in American society, and certainly in the developed nations, which is becoming even more compelling as we address global issues. Environmental progress and economic growth can and are happening at the same time. Businesses will make money, people will be employed, and we can live in a healthier environment with a better quality of life. Sustainable development is real, and win-win results are achievable.

What are you uncertain of?

I'm less certain whether politics and policy will keep pace with technological development when it comes to environmental technologies. Too often we find that politics and policy are debating yesterday's issues while technology is moving forward much more rapidly. For example, the debate in Congress about highly polluting old power plants is being outpaced by the advancements of wind and solar power, fuel cells, combined heat and power, and other new clean energy technologies. We need to begin to reshape policy to support the environmental technological development that is not only possible but that is already happening at a rapid pace.

What is the essential ingredient for resilience?

Intelligence, openness to new ideas, and integrity. All the computers in the world cannot truly replace smart, creative people exercising good judgment.

18

James C. Madden, V

Chairman, CEO, and President, Exult

Companies also act shocked when there is a downturn in the economy or things happen outside their control. But if you look over a long enough period of time, you'll see that these things always happened. And management almost always acts surprised. That's what surprises me.

Based in Irvine, California, but with offices throughout the United States and in Glasgow and Geneva, Exult is one of the few Internet-based B2B companies that have thrived despite the overall downturn in the dot.com economy. For its current success and future promise, Exult's management staff credits one major salient point: It was never a dot.com company. It clearly saw the distinction between using the Internet as a source of identity and using it strictly as a tool.

Today, this e-HR company counts among its clients Fortune 500 companies such as the Bank of America, International Paper, and BP. It assumes complete management, ownership, and accountability for all the people, processes, technologies, and third party vendors associated with the HR function in global corporations. By transferring much of the transactional, administrative, and operational responsibility for the HR function to Exult, global organizations achieve improvements in the level of HR services delivered throughout the company, reduce fixed HR costs, avoid significant capital investments, increase employee loyalty, and fortify competitive advantage.

One of Exult's founders, as well as its chairman, CEO, and president, James Madden began his career with Andersen Consulting, where he created and led Andersen's first outsourcing practice on the West Coast. After an additional stint with Booz Allen Hamilton, he joined MCI's $2 billion outsourcing unit in 1993 as vice president and managing director of the Los Angeles office, becoming general manager of the company's

Pacific Region in 1994. In 1995, he was named president of the U.S. and Latin American Divisions, and then corporate chief financial officer in 1997. During his tenure there, Madden was responsible for developing and managing more than $4 billion in long-term client outsourcing engagements. He also served as an active member of the executive steering committee for each major outsourcing client.

In this interview he discusses the prospect of high-tech based companies during an era of New Economy backlash:

- Surviving short-term economic impacts with long-term planning
- Introducing innovation to mature markets
- The new leadership skills necessary in times of global uncertainty and short reaction time
- Working with investors

Not too long ago, there was so much emphasis on attraction and retention, commonly called the War for Talent. Now, since September 11 and economic shifts, more than a million people have been laid off within only a few months. How has the War for Talent transformed itself, both in the immediate term and the long term?

I'm worried that many companies are reacting to external events by immediately and almost exclusively cutting costs, rather than also building a plan and taking action for future growth. It seems some mature companies may be recklessly laying off unnecessary numbers of people in a "knee jerk" reaction to September 11 or are simply using September 11 as an excuse to correct previous errors or cost issues and overruns that should have been addressed a long time ago in a systematic manner.

Using the airlines as an example, most of them reacted to the events of September 11 by focusing on cutting costs to cope with the fact there were fewer passengers. But you saw very little commentary from airline executives about what they were going to do to preserve the top line—meaning getting passengers back on the planes and making them feel safe and comfortable. A really astute management team would have given equal time to what they were going to do to make their customers feel more secure and keeping revenue up. So far I've seen very little evidence of that kind of conversation.

Let's not make decisions today that we're going to regret tomorrow. Mature companies are cutting huge numbers of employees, and I'm worried they may be losing valuable talent that could otherwise help them build their future. No one will convince me that those people being let go were all performers in the bottom 20 percent of their company. Some of the employees' companies are losing are the very ones they desperately need to keep.

A mature company must be distinguished from a small, rapidly growing company, and the mature company should strive to create a more stable, predictable operating environment based on a three-year view, not a ninety-day view.

It's understandable that many companies have temporarily put expansion and growth plans aside. But we're seeing very little dedication toward just to getting back to the status quo. What is the planning horizon now? Thirty days? Ninety days? Six months? I don't think there are many companies out there that are looking at a planning horizon of even two years. My view is that the CEO needs to be planning for at least three-years.

Yours is one of the few B2B businesses that has thrived through recent disappointing economic times. How do you explain your continued growth when so many of your peers are shutting down companies right and left?

We started Exult in late 1998, when this country was in the middle of all the dot.com hype. The prevailing message was that if you don't go on line, you're going to perish. And we had a lot of pressure from certain individuals to become a dot.com company. Instead we carefully thought through the question: Is our business about the Internet, or is the Internet simply going to be a tool in a service we're going to provide? We chose the latter, and we were very clear with the distinction from day one that the Internet was only a tool. And though the tool was powerful and unique, it also had severe limitations. It was not going to be able to do all the things we needed to do in terms of providing the services we wanted to offer in our marketplace. We knew from the very beginning that technology had its limitations, especially when you compared it to what you could do with bright and talented people coupled with robust business processes.

A second strategy has also made a big difference. We decided to go after customers that are very large, established organizations. It was risky enough to start a new company. We didn't want to have our customers be new companies as well. We saw a better market opportunity in the large, established Fortune 500 corporate world.

Finally, and perhaps most importantly, we had a clear economic-value proposition, not a "pie in the sky leap of faith."

One of the advantages of going after the small nimble start-ups as potential clients was that everyone was building a new way to work. So the marketplace would have been wide open for you. But instead you went after the mature organizations that had had generations of established practices and contacts. How were you able to introduce and insert this new way of doing things?

That has been the greatest challenge of our business. Large corporations do have entrenched, established cultures. We knew that for our business model to succeed with any individual client, we needed a senior executive champion within the organization who would sponsor and stay committed through the entire course of change. At an absolute minimum, it's the senior level executive in charge of human resources.

But equally frequent among our clients, it's the leadership of the CEO. A good example is John Brown, the CEO of British Petroleum. His view was that the company needed to change, and one of the ways to move it into what he calls the "world of digital business" was to make sure that all of the employees had the ability to understand and to work over the Internet. What better way to start than to provide a tool to the employees so that they could do all their human resource activities with the company over the Internet? That was a great step forward. BP has approximately 100,000 employees across a hundred countries. We work predominantly with employees in the U.K. and the United States—about 60,000 employees total. Of the 60,000, more than 55,000 employees regularly use the e-HR (Internet-based) services. Overall, the level of satisfaction with those services hovers between 85 percent and 95 percent, compared with satisfaction with pre-Web enabled HR services measured in the 60s.

One of the most enduring fears of employees in any kind of large organization is that their individualism gets lost, their talent gets underappreciated, and their own ambitions get ignored. This tool is a great way large companies can say, "You will not be overlooked. Here's a way you can grow your career and future with us."

Our clients are organizations that are committed to empowering employees. We could not have done it by ourselves. But it still takes strong leaders to say, "This is what we're going to do." And then go do it. In our case, the power of Web technology and e-HR truly empower employees.

People are saying now that old rules and assumptions are dead. What has taken their place in your business?

I don't completely agree with that assumption. We heard an awful lot two years ago from people riding the tidal wave of the Internet saying, "The Old Economy is dead, and the business cycle is dead." Both of those have been proven 100 percent false. The business cycle is alive, and, in my opinion, it will never go away. Companies are going to have to learn to live with that fact.

Companies also act shocked when there is a downturn in the economy or things happen outside their control. But if you look over a long enough period of time, you'll see that these things have always happened. And management almost always acts surprised. That's what surprises me. You shouldn't be surprised. You should expect it. If your vision of history goes back at least fifty years, you can say there is almost a basis for having already seen everything. And you should be ready for anything.

In another way, though, I do agree with that assumption of change. I do think some things are different. One is the force of globalization. If you're going to do business among the Fortune 2000, you cannot be successful in an isolated geographic marketplace. You can't just look at your competitor across the street. You can't just look at your competitor in the same country. You have to think about the market globally. You have to be prepared for competition to emerge from anywhere. And your competition could have all kinds of advantages over you that you need to be thinking about all day long.

And capital will be increasingly global. It will move in and out where it has to go to get the best returns. That means you have to be prepared for the negative. You never want to put yourself or your organization in the position of being capital starved. As we are now seeing that can happen very quickly. And it's happening to countries as well.

Finally, as a public company, you're going to get voted on every day by investors as to whether you're successful or not. That probably means we're doing business in a harsher, more fast-paced, information-based world. But it's a fact of business now. Your own performance record is going to be open for everyone to see. As it should be.

What are the new leadership skills necessary in this environment of global uncertainty and short reaction-time frames?

You have to be truly a leader, and not just someone who is "in charge." You need to be visible; you need to be there first before you can lead. You can't lead from a desk. You can't lead from an e-mail. You have to physically make yourself visible to those you're expecting to lead as well as to your partners, your investors, and your clients. It's amazing to me how many people in the months after September 11 ducked down under their desks and sent e-mail and voice mail communications only, rather than getting out and seeing their customers and employees.

And you need to talk straight. When it is bad news, tell it. When it's good news, tell it. When you don't know, say so and promise to find out. Hedging or speculating is one of the worst things you can do. People want to be told straight.

What about your own self-talk? One of the models of the hard-charging successful CEO throughout the years is the idea of the "can-do, I know my stuff, I know what's going on, I know where I'm headed" kind of leader. Today's business environment is shot through with ambiguity. On one level there's a huge opportunity for creative solutions. On another level, though, it's sifting sands. And I would think that would be very uncomfortable for the conventional leader.

A portion of the decisions we must make must be based on instinct, because we just don't have all the information. You have to make decisions based on a large amount of uncertainty because a decision has to be made. The implications are that you're going to be wrong every now and then. Hopefully, you'll be right more often than you'll be wrong. But you are going to be wrong. When that happens, admit it and then change course quickly. As has been said, "If you're going to fail, fail fast." Equally important, don't live in the past. Recognize the here and now and act accordingly. Almost every bad decision can yield a positive, new idea if you move on.

What have you learned from working with investors in these three years?

I have run a small, rapidly growing public company, and I have run divisions of large public companies prior to founding Exult. But before Exult went public, I also had the opportunity to run it as a private company. In this capacity, I have worked with some of the world's most sophisticated capital investors. And there are a lot of lessons to be learned there.

Money should not be viewed as a commodity. The $50 million dollars you may need to start the business isn't going to be worth the same number of dollars from one investor to the next. Depending on whom you're getting it from, that $50 million could be more or less expensive, and it could be more or less valuable. You need to understand as clearly as possible every single string attached to those funds. You need to do as much reference checking of your investors as you would if you were lending someone money for their mortgage.

So you need to ask potential investors detailed questions. What are their expectations in a board meeting? Do they want to act as they would in a traditional corporate governance board? Or are they going to help you manage the shop? Ask them how long they hold their investments. And don't rely exclusively what they tell you. Insist on talking to the CEOs or CFOs of their last ten investments.

And don't try to raise money without experienced help. It is really one of the single biggest mistakes entrepreneurs make. They go out and raise money maybe once or twice in their lives. But they're dealing across the table with private investors who do this full time. So right away entrepreneurs are immediately outnegotiated before they've even begun the conversation.

In our experience at Exult, we have been fortunate in having very positive experiences with our major private investors.

We follow this same principle in making sure our own clients are taken care of during the negotiation process. Our lead sales people and attorneys negotiate outsourcing contracts for a living. But they're going to sit across the table from a client who may have outsourced one project before. Maybe even none. So we advise them to get an attorney who negotiates outsourcing contracts for a living to represent them. It's not as altruistic as it sounds. It helps the client a lot but it also helps us. We'd rather deal across the table with someone who knows what they're doing. It just makes the process go quickly and efficiently.

Global political incidents are creating new alliances and re-energizing old animosities among nations. How can a U.S. company confidently establish itself globally when overnight an incident can throw its host country into turmoil?

By operating in a balanced way and not overreacting to political situations. We need to operate our businesses as if they are a representative of the United States in a global environment. U.S. corporations need to behave as ambassadors to investors, suppliers, employees, and customers so that they rise above the fray. I'd like to think most companies are positioned to do that.

This doesn't mean that U.S. companies—or even the United States—should behave as though we were the exclusive, moral shepherd of the globe. That's not our role. But I do think that it's our obligation to work with other countries and companies that share our views on human rights, for instance, to speak on behalf of those principles. But, as a nation, we don't speak out very consistently. We go after some countries where our personal interests are at stake. And we sometimes close our eyes to others. I think we need to be more even handed and act swiftly and decisively. Ironically, we tend to use political instability as a reason not to globalize.

Where does the corporation play a role in international affairs?

The corporation cannot act and behave like a government because it is not a government. Remember when our plane was shot down over China earlier in 2001? Tensions were quite high between the U.S. and China. But still there are many U.S. corporations that do business with China. Should they have behaved any differently in their day-to-day business dealings because of what was going on with our governments at the time? My belief is they absolutely should not have. They should have acted morally. They should have acted ethically. They should have acted in a businesslike manner. And my guess is that that's exactly what most of them did.

But at the end of the day, the U.S. corporation is still a U.S. corporation. And at some point you may have to change your operations in accordance with national interests. But don't get ahead of that. You shouldn't be setting policy. It is the government's role exclusively to set policy.

What are you certain of?

I'm certain of change. I am certain we will continue to adjust our business plans and make changes we can't yet think of today. What I spend half my day thinking about is, "What am I not thinking of? What could possibly catch us by surprise?"

What are you uncertain of?

I'm uncertain of the *rate* of change. While I'm completely convinced of the need for companies to reinvent themselves according to the rate of change, I don't really know how quickly that change will happen.

Today, Exult has six large clients for long-term human resource outsourcing contracts. These clients were early adopters. What I'm uncertain of now is the rate at which our concept will grow. Where is the tipping point? Does Exult need one or two more clients before a large number of companies will be willing to adopt our concept? I don't know whether that's going to happen in the next six months or the next two years. But I'm certain it's going to happen.

What is the essential ingredient for resilience?

To be resilient, you're going to have to accept the fact that there will always be change and uncertainty. You're going to have to accept the fact that there will always be things that are outside your control. And then you have to be willing to change your plans and expectations accordingly. Resilience for both individuals and corporations will depend on their ability to evolve and adapt, to anticipate what they can, and at least to respond to changes they might not have thought about week ago or even a day ago. If you're not adapting to changing markets and changing conditions, you're merely thinking of new ways to make your product obsolete.

19

Marilyn Carlson Nelson

Chairman and CEO, Carlson Companies, Inc.

Most companies are constantly looking outside their own walls for best practices in other organizations, so they can use them and operate their own businesses more effectively. As individuals, Americans can do the same by looking across borders for better, more effective ways of managing their lives and doing things.

Few economic sectors were hit as hard as the travel and hospitality sector by the aftermath of September 11. As the companies drastically cut their travel budgets out of perceived security risks, individuals also cut back their own discretionary spending on other travel-related services, such as hotels and restaurants. The resulting ripple effect has extended far beyond the airlines, and deep into other businesses and livelihoods, such as travel agents, hotel housekeeping, and waiters and waitresses.

The Carlson Companies have been feeling the impact in all these areas. From Carlson Wagonlit Travel to the Radisson Seven Seas Cruises to the Regent International Hotels (which includes a property on Wall Street) to TGI Fridays, all the Carlson Companies' brands and services have been affected by the economic uncertainty of today's worldwide marketplace. However, as the second-generation leader of this family-owned company, Marilyn Carlson Nelson takes the long view.

She also takes a global view, having earned a degree in International Economics from Smith College, with graduate studies at the Sorbonne in Paris and at the Institute des Hautes Etudes Economiques Politiques in Geneva. Since taking over Carlson, she has led a doubling of her private family company's capital base, and the expansion of its brands into more than 140 nations in the last seven years.

The growth has been fueled by unique transborder partnerships developed by Nelson. At the first international meeting with one such partnering company, the attendees were prepared to hear about the new "Carlson way of doing things." Instead, they found themselves discussing their life values and what was important to them as people. This value-centered approach has earned Carlson a place on this year's *Fortune* and *Working Mother* lists of "Top 100 Places to Work." Nelson, herself, appears in *Fortune's* list of "America's Fifty Most Powerful Women."

In this interview she discusses the challenges of leading a global business in one of the sectors most profoundly devastated by the economic aftermath of September 11:

- The effects of September 11 on global relationships
- The role of the U.S. corporation as a citizen of the world
- What investing in the future means today
- Business's role in long-term global economic development

How have the events of September 11 changed your business, and what is your outlook for the future?

The events of September 11 hit us dramatically, but hopefully short term. They impacted our travel agency business, our hotel business, our cruise business, and our restaurant business. Do we expect that the world is going to stop traveling? No. Do we believe that the drive to explore the world and meet people is irrepressible? Yes. Do we believe that thoughtful, rational people will find a way to take control of this situation? Yes. We're not atavistic in our thinking. We don't believe that we'll go back to some primitive time when we hid behind our walls. Free people are people of action, and we'll work together to create the world in which we want to live. It's not going to be easy, and I don't know how long it will take. But I do believe we will find a way to get enough control over our business environment so we can rebuild this industry.

Both our industry and the public are now discovering exactly what it means to have our transportation system directly traumatized. For the first time we're all understanding that the entire sky can actually be closed—that is beyond anything we could have ever imagined, and that has had a tremendous "ripple effect" through our economy, far beyond that of affecting just "travel." In fact, I think we need a new word to describe our industry. "Travel" connotes something totally discretionary, almost peripheral in nature to the economy. But transporting, hosting, and entertaining people—for either business or leisure—is absolutely vital to a service economy, such as we've become, and to the free flow of commerce. A better phrase might be *transport and hospitality*—it better describes the transport and hosting of the human resource, which is as important to a service economy like ours as the transport of capital goods is to an industrial society.

Have your relationships abroad been strengthened by the impacts the tourism industry suffered in the last quarter of 2001?

On the whole, what has happened has been extraordinary. For instance, the support the UK has given the United States and the support our UK employees have given us is unprecedented. The bonds between our countries and people are stronger than they've ever been. I was just presented by the British Foreign Secretary with the First Award for Responsible Capitalism, and one of the things we discussed was how circumstances have renewed our common interests in democracy and free enterprise.

Circumstances have also created new bonds where none existed before. Our industry has long been concerned that very few of the postindustrial countries have acknowledged that travel and hospitality are the heart of the service sector. The realization of this by government and industry just wasn't there—until now. Governments and other more "traditional" industries have now learned that their interests are bound with those of travel and tourism. Some estimates say that one in ten jobs around the world are travel- and hospitality related. In the United States, the ratio is one in seventeen. Because of the downturn in our industry, we could have three-quarters of a million people out of work from our sector in the United States alone. Those people won't be buying cars, or washing machines, or clothing.

Worldwide, the United Nations has acknowledged that nearly 9 million people are going to be out of jobs because of the impact of the recession in travel and tourism. Governments around the world are beginning to understand the impact of our industry and forming new and strong bonds with us.

Because of the very nature of your business, you bring your customer the chance to learn from other cultures. What can American companies and Americans themselves learn from other countries and the societal values that they represent?

As Americans move about the world, we learn by osmosis about true inclusiveness and diversity. There's not only social hope in this fact, but also an economic vitality in it. Inclusive cultures and corporations have the benefit of a wider range of thinking and points of view. Most companies are constantly looking outside their own walls for best practices in other organizations, so they can use them and operate their own businesses more effectively. As individuals, Americans can do the same by looking across borders for better, more effective ways of managing their lives and doing things.

As we operate in different environments and look for best practices wherever we go, we may find ways to get more productivity, less turnover, more innovation, and more creativity. And then we may adopt those ways throughout the organization, wherever we're located.

What cultural traits in other countries inspire you?

The French and Italian people are wonderful role models for us in the hospitality business. They appreciate fine food and wine, and the subtleties of flavor, and they take the time to enjoy them. I'm very inspired by our Asian and Latin American partners' commitment to families and family businesses. Many businesses have thrived for multiple generations in these cultures. I also appreciate the Asian long-term perspective. The people of Russia have a resilience that inspires me. I appreciate the Scandinavian people's early inclusiveness of women and their view of life: There's something metaphorical about deep winters and the blossoming springs that follow that helps them to understand that dark times are followed by light—that great sorrow and great joy are just shadow and light. That they are necessary parts of the human experience.

What is the role of the U.S. corporation as a citizen of the world?

Our view of corporate citizenship may be seen as lofty, but in fact, it's pragmatic. Its roots lie in the fact that we're a private company. You see, the role of the leadership of a private family business is as much stewardship as it is leadership. I manage this company as if it is in trust for subsequent generations.

Because I'm the second-generation leader of a family business, which will someday sustain my heirs and extended family, I see myself as a living link between the past and the future. The ultimate measure of my success, as well as that of my team and our culture, will be whether or not we can continue to add value to see the business prosper. This is an appropriate metaphor for what the citizenship role of a corporation should be: Can it ultimately say that it has been a link between the past and the future, added value, and helped generations prosper?

In the end, aren't all companies stewards of natural and human resources for subsequent generations around the world? A leader of a company who drives a magnificent but short-term result at the expense of the future ignores the fact that the scorekeeping is going to continue beyond the existing generation. The long-term sustainability of any business or society has to do with the ability of its leadership to think and act beyond the horizon of the current generation, rather than focus on one quarter of one year. America and its businesses are so young, compared with others in the world. We are only now learning to take the long view and act accordingly. It is a new role for us, but one we must play if we are to be truly understood and embraced in the long-term by other countries, companies, and cultures.

American business is very much an international player and finds itself on center stage, whether it likes it or not. Countries are looking toward American capitalism as either a promise for the future or—more ominously—a source of trouble.

So one of the roles of American business is to be a torchbearer for hope?

I'd like to see us be that. By definition, a viable business creates jobs. Having a job creates hope. Business's job is to (a) create value that people are willing to pay for, and (b) create a context in which people want to give of their time and their life's energy. What they get in return for working may be more than just financial. A job may be self-developmental, in that it provides skills, knowledge, or career-building opportunities. Or it may be environmental, in that it respects the importance of family and home life and shows it in the way it operates. These things aren't at the cost of the profitability of the company. Investing in these things is simply our view of what sustains long-term profitability—and hope.

How is investing in the future more than simply a financial transfer?

To me, the future has everything to do with human resources. Today, financial capital follows human capital and capabilities, the very thing that provides the energy, strikes the vision, and produces the innovation and results in the return. Leaders of today must be stewards of financial capital *and* stewards of human capital. It's a combination of the two that obviously provides the value-add in return.

 If you disenfranchise any group—the shareholders, the employees, the customers, or the communities in which you operate—if you don't keep everything in balance, the imbalance threatens the whole. Imbalance most often occurs when the market pressures are so great that employers start making compromises at the expense of their employees' satisfaction, often thinking that those changes are only temporary. It's a slippery slope, and the shareholders and customers ultimately become disadvantaged because the employees are dissatisfied.

 It's that employee profit chain: The satisfaction of the employee ultimately affects the satisfaction of the customer, which ultimately impacts the shareholder. We see it over and over again.

 I just mentioned that one of the key constituencies a business must invest in are the communities in which it operates. The strength of those communities and the strength of the system we operate in are part of our responsibility. Our company was one of the cofounders of the Keystone Program here in Minnesota. We wanted to create a quality of life in this state second to none. So in the 1960s, we and other Twin Cities companies created the Minnesota Keystone Program, in which local businesses gave 5 percent of their pretax income to the community. Later, a 2 percent level was established as well. At a time when the national average for corporate giving is less than 1 percent, it has become the correct thing to do in Minnesota for companies to give between 2 percent and 5 percent.

 At Carlson, we also encourage our employees to become more engaged and involved in the community. We have created a software program that allows employees to identify on line their volunteer interests, how much time they can spend, and exactly when. They can either go and look at the different volunteer opportunities, or opportunities come to them as weekly e-mails, based on their stated areas of interest. If suddenly this Saturday you wanted to work with the Hmong population and you were available between 10 and noon on Saturday, it would "push" an opportunity to your e-mailbox. The software then gives you an opportunity to register and tells you where to go. It even captures what size T-shirt you need for your volunteer "uniform."

Our interest in the communities in which we operate is not a marketing ploy. It's endemic to who we are.

The recent violent protests at the World Trade Organization's meetings and the fact that so many nations were represented in the World Trade Center tragedy brought home to a lot of people how thoroughly humanity is integrated through global business. How should we be thinking about business's role in long-term global economic development?

With regard to the World Trade Organization protests, I think that legitimate dissent and protest can be enormously important. But a violent, radical fringe threatens to shout down and drown out the voices of true debate and destroy the progress that legitimate dissenters have achieved.

Our long-term role in global development needs to be viewed as more than an opportunity transfer: It's also a skills transfer and a knowledge transfer—in both directions.

One thing we're very proud of in our industry is that in both developed or developing nations, we create a lot of jobs and stability. We offer to investors, here or abroad, franchised business models that are highly predictive of success. In developing nations, where the failure rate for entrepreneurs is more than 80 percent, the success rate for established franchise models, such as ours, is more than 90 percent. More success equals long-term internal stability and expansion. Almost without exception, a successful franchisee in a developing country goes on to franchise another one of our brands, or someone else's brands. Or that person or family goes on to develop their own business using some of the discipline, modeling, and approaches that they've learned through franchising.

Finally, we must come to a place where all parties acknowledge the interdependence of private enterprise and public interest. Certainly we must retain discrete roles, but we must collaborate more and create new solutions for global problems that no one sector can solve alone. There are limits to the capabilities of both corporations *and* nations. There is no such thing as a "corpor-nation" that can do it all unilaterally. At Carlson, we are always seeking improved methods of governing and operating globally and working across nations responsibly.

Would you say the world has gotten smaller since September 11, or bigger again?

September 11 made the world suddenly and violently shrink even more. But frankly, it is my opinion and hope that it continues to get smaller, in a less traumatic and horrific way, of course. The events of September 11 brought home all too painfully that what takes place in a single country half a world away can affect us to an extent no one imagined. So it's important that we become cognizant of the greater world issues and act accordingly. We must dedicate our energies both as individual citizens and as corporate citizens to making that happen.

What are you certain of?

I'm certain that the future holds exciting opportunities and that we can find solutions to the problems. The free enterprise system is the best way to drive innovation and create wealth for the greatest numbers of people. I'm certain that democracy is the hope for the world. And I'm certain that freedom is a universal objective.

What are you uncertain of?

I'm uncertain how the present global terrorism threat will impact or restrict freedom in the short term. Freedom depends on the free flow of people and ideas, and I'm uncertain of how much our progress toward those goals might be set back. I'm worried about the global spread of AIDS and other diseases and our ability to stop them soon enough. I'm uncertain about the science of global warming and where the long-term energy sources will come from.

What is the essential ingredient for resilience?

The first answer that comes to mind is faith. Faith gives one the perspective of a bigger, transcendent view.

I'm reminded of the parable of the talents in the Bible, where the master, who is going away, gives talents—coins—to his servants and charges them with stewardship of the money until he returns. One servant, who obviously has faith in his own ability and in God, risks it all but ends up multiplying his principle. He is the one the master praises, even though he could have lost everything. The master berates the other servant, who, you might say, was without faith, and who took the "safe" step of simply burying the talents for safekeeping. He made no good use of what the master gave him.

I've always understood the "investment/return" aspect of that parable. What I hadn't focused on until recently was the role of *time* in the story. There was no indication when the master was coming back. There was no date in the future the servants were planning and working toward, because they didn't know when the master would return. So the lesson: The only time we have is the time being. We don't know when we're going to be judged or when the summing up is going to take place. It may be this hour, or this day, or this week. As a result, there is an urgency for us to make the greatest possible contribution—the greatest possible difference—for the current moment, for the time being.

Interestingly, having that point of view focuses your attention, efforts, and energies. But it's also a relief. If you see yourself as a living link and not responsible for doing it all, you do the best you can with the time you have. And you can take comfort in knowing you're part of a continuum.

20

Marjorie Randolph

Senior Vice President, Human Resources, Walt Disney Studios

I'm sure that the Enron debacle will have an impact on how people are viewing their workplaces. But to me it all comes back to a deeper value. We work for many reasons, but I hope those reasons include more than just money.

It's not risking overstatement to say that for most U.S babies, it's very likely that their first friends (aside from Mommy and Daddy, of course) are Mickey and his pals: Minnie, Goofy, Donald, Cinderella, Jiminy Cricket, Sleeping Beauty, Snow White, Sleepy, and Dopey. They're in the songs of American childhood, dangling overhead a baby's crib in a mobile, on television, on DVD, stuffed and plush, and tucked into the corner of children's beds throughout the land. They're live and in person. And they're joined by others like Pocahontas, Ariel and Sebastian, and Simba.

As the children grow up, many pass through a phase when it's their cherished dream to run away and live in Disney World or Disneyland. And eventually they grow up some more and pass through a phase called "their life's work." Millions of grown children leave their Disney dreams behind. But thousands of them find a place for themselves in the world that Walt Disney created. Many of them, from artists to administrators, land in The Walt Disney Studios. This is the birthplace of many of the Disney characters that populate a land where everyone is happy to see you, and where mice wear four-fingered gloves, even in the height of summer.

While Marjorie Randolph was a law student and doing some work for an advocacy group, she discovered the magical power of a workplace where everyone treats each other with respect. And she knew that she wanted to invest her life's work in developing "respectful workplaces." After many years as a real estate attorney and then as general counsel for a major department store chain in California, she shifted her career to human resource management exclusively. She is now senior vice president of human resources for The Walt Disney Studios, the Disney business in which inspiration comes alive in the form of characters (both animation and live action) that audiences invite into their lives and hearts for generations.

In this interview Randolph talks about what it takes to lead a strong, highly creative, people organization into the future:

- Promoting creativity within a large corporate environment
- Branding the company as a desirable career opportunity over its competitors
- Keeping the internal branding message (to employees) consistent with the external branding message (to customers)
- Recreating the employer/employee relationship in a time of diminished loyalty

∽

Disney has historically been recognized as a company set apart from the pack of large corporations by the fact that it depends on positive world-changing creativity. But I think now most companies are coming to terms with the fact that we must all be able to revolutionize our little patch of ground with innovation. But the creative environment can be quite unnerving to the corporate frame of mind that likes things recognizable and easy to line up in tidy columns. What can corporate America learn from the way Disney employees are managed to boost their own innovative capacity?

We're in the entertainment industry, so obviously, creativity is the heart of what we do. Giving creative talent the leeway they need to generate products that are original and enchanting, all the while doing it inside a large corporate environment, has always been an interesting conundrum.

My first job at Disney was heading up human resources in Feature Animation, the group that originally did those wonderful movies that many of us remember from our childhood. Feature Animation is filled with some of the best artists in the world. And to me it was so entrancing to be surrounded by wonderful artists every day. It gave me the opportunity to understand how an artist—a creative person—might approach a problem differently than I might. The other thing it did for me was allow me to see inside the minds of highly creative people—how they view creativity, what it means to them, how creativity comes about, what the process is that allows them to have a creative thought and then express it, on paper or on a computer screen.

Learning more about that process helped me to get to the next step, which was to see in a whole new way how creativity plays a role in all our lives, no matter what we do. I had assumed that creativity of this magnitude was limited to the arts. But the fact of the matter is that creativity is necessary in the activities that I do everyday. Creativity encompasses the ability to open up our minds to new solutions—to not just do things the same way we've always done them. All of life is risk assessing and problem solving. We need to be able to think creatively to do that, especially in light of all the changes that are going on every day in both the workplace and the marketplace.

Every company must be innovative and creative. This isn't solely the domain of the artist. How do you institutionalize creativity when the function of the institution is to create a safehouse for productivity? That typically does not leave room for personal ritual or wacky behavior, even if it's that behavior that generates the next Big Idea that then brings in the money?

This is something that we struggle with every day. In a culture like Feature Animation it was just wonderful to spend time with the artists—and quite frankly they exhibit all kinds of behavior that you may think is wacky, but it works for them. It allows them to create. If you look at another environment inside our Studio, for instance, the creativity may happen in a very different manner. You need to be creative in your marketing but it's a different kind of creativity from that of the person sitting at an animation desk.

We're constantly searching for ways to ensure that the culture is an open one, which allows the employees enough freedom to create and try new things. Any large corporation may inherently have problems in allowing a lot of individual innovative behavior. There are always parameters, structures, and organizational issues within which you must operate. We are a large corporation, and we have all those boundaries, levels of comfort, and rules about what's okay. A large corporation has challenges in terms of allowing openness and creativity just because of its size.

But it's that innovative spark that could create the one valuable insight that would could drive a company's future success.

Absolutely. The leaders who can set up the kind of environment that encourages that spark are the ones who are going to be successful. We know we can provide three critical elements: to have heart and not be afraid to express that, to have fun, and to take pride in our product.

There are so many smaller, lively creative houses doing great work these days. And they may offer artists the chance to have greater creative control than they might working in a large production team at Disney. How do you competitively brand the opportunity of working at Disney? How do you keep Disney's brand as an employer fresh and irresistible?

We always say that we're the best. If you talk about animation we're absolutely at the forefront in both the beauty of traditional animation as well as the technological tools that give us enormous depth on the screen. The attraction for an artist coming to work at Disney is the body of work that's there from the past and understanding that the tradition of these masters of animation still holds. The Disney legacy is enormously important for people. People who work here at Walt Disney Studios believe in that legacy and care about carrying it forward.

When I first started with Disney in Feature Animation, we were recruiting at art schools around the country. That was the time many new animation houses were starting up. Some of them were sponsored by major studios, and some were smaller independent houses. Teachers would often ask us, "Why should we encourage our students to pay attention to Disney when there are all these new opportunities?" My answer was the same: "We were the first and we will be the last." We felt that many of these other organizations wouldn't make it. And indeed, many of them have folded since. The Disney brand itself is so imbedded in our culture, it's so long-standing, and it's known for a quality that anyone else rarely achieves. That's very appealing to potential employees.

The people I've interviewed for positions throughout all the different areas of the Studio are people who grew up going to Disney movies. They remember how watching these movies as children made them feel—excited, curious, happy. Now that they're adults, they want to be associated with the company that produces those experiences. That goes a long way for us. Those of us who work there take enormous pride in our product. We know that we have an impact on our audience.

Every child's dream has been to run away and go live in Disneyland— or Disney World. But we all know that if you spend enough time there you would begin to see the facades, the scaffolding, and the unpainted parts behind the scenery. Once you get to that point inside the company, how do you keep the brand refreshed—the magic alive—when employees can see the machinery behind the magic?

It's still a wonderful illusion, and I don't know that many of us ever really get over wanting to believe in that illusion, no matter what we know about the background. It makes you smile. It makes you scream if you're on the roller coaster. It makes you cry a little bit when you're watching *Lion King* on the stage and listening to *The Circle of Life*. Or even watching some of our wonderful live action movies. I saw *Remember the Titans* six times and cried every time I saw it. We can still believe in those things that make us feel better, no matter how much we know about the background and the work that went into producing it.

The messages that Disney delivers everywhere and in every way are, "When you wish upon a star, dreams will come true. You can be the best of who you are, achieve potential, bring magic into the world." As a company of employers and employees, do you sustain that message with your employees?

Yes, we try, but this is also a highly competitive business. We're a publicly held company, and we know that we must be successful financially. I think many people who work for Disney—and I happen to be one of them—tend to feel positive about life. And regardless of what kind of shape the economy is in right at this moment, it will change again. And we'll still be here, and we'll still be producing this incredible product.

We've heard a lot about the War for Talent not too long ago, and now a lot of people are getting laid off. What do you think will be the long-term story of the War for Talent? Do you expect the economy will cause the companies to cycle back into that?

In the technology arena, the War for Talent really hasn't changed. Finding great people with technological expertise is still more difficult than it is in other areas, even though dot-coms have gone belly up, and even though more technology talent is back in the marketplace.

In other parts of the business, it seems to me that there will be a moderating factor in the economy. There will continue to be growth, perhaps at a slower rate. People will find jobs, and the marketplace will control how quickly we get into this more positive viewpoint. But I don't think we'll ever return to a boom like that of the dot-com economy. My opinion is that we will see more moderate growth.

Do you think we're also going to have a sadder but wiser employee, and that HR is going to have to work harder to serve him or her?

That's a distinct possibility. Individual employees have come to the realization that the relationship between company and employee is not based on loyalty as much as it used to be. It's perhaps more like a business arrangement. Human resources plays the unique role of being a partner with the business, as well as a consultant to each individual within the business. There are some who say that HR's client is the business organization itself. But I disagree. A really good HR professional is able to maintain equal credibility with both sides of the employment equation—and in doing so makes the business stronger and more successful.

Loyalty has been replaced by the feeling of being a fellow entrepreneur sharing the risk. The relationship has evolved into one that says, "As long as this is good for me and I'm good for you, let's hitch our wagons to the same star." We may have thrown our employment contract out the window, but employment relationships still seem to

be built on the assumption that each given scenario is a good bet for both parties. Given what's happened with both dot-coms and Enron, the message seems to be that in addition to success not being a guaranteed thing—which it never was—you may not be able trust your partner anymore.

I'm sure that the Enron debacle will have an impact on how people are viewing their workplaces. But to me it all comes back to a deeper value. We work for many reasons, but I hope those reasons include more than just money. I think it has a lot to do with personal satisfaction. As an employee I don't know that I expect a tremendous amount of loyalty from my employer, but what I do expect (and therefore I assume other people feel the same) is to be treated with respect. Respect encompasses many things, but ultimately it's about overall treatment and taking pride in the product.

Employees should also be active participants in understanding the business side of their own lives and careers. This means they should understand how their company operates in its marketplace, how revenues and profits are generated, and what the overall financial trends are. Personally, they should review their retirement portfolios periodically to determine whether they still believe the investment mix is the best for them. And they should stay informed about the overall business environment and how their company is doing competitively. It's also important that each of us understands that we own our own careers and that we maintain our own personal marketplace competitiveness by continuing to expand our skill sets.

As an employer, how do you maintain that relationship of engagement?

By cultivating a listening culture. For people to take pride in what they're doing and feel that they are part of something wonderful, they need to know that someone is listening to them. It's a culture based on respect. To me respect encompasses listening, direct and honest communication, and organizational integrity. It is making sure people are treated fairly. It is deliberately creating an innovative and open culture so that people feel safe in sharing their ideas with others inside the company. If you have a respectful culture, it encompasses all of that.

The culture of any organization is set at the top. Most of us watch, learn, and take our cues from it.

What are you certain of?

The greatest certainty I have is the fact that business will continue to change. Technology is changing, people's attitudes are changing, and daily we are more aware of world changes, including new global markets and instant worldwide communications. My one certainty is that change will continue.

What are you uncertain of?

I'm uncertain of how the workplace will look in ten years. One of our challenges will continue to be the diversity of the workforce. The challenge always is to help people—of any color or race—to understand the value of someone who doesn't look or sound like them. We are all perhaps a little more comfortable with people who are just like us. As a result, the people who are in a hiring capacity may still tend to want to hire someone just like them because that feels comfortable. We have to continue sending the message to hiring managers that the value of a diverse workforce is so extraordinary that we have to overcome our discomfort. Our workforce and our customer base are the same group.

It's a wonderful thing from a business perspective. It's obviously also the right thing to do from a sociological and ethical perspective. And quite frankly it's so beneficial to all of us in terms of opening up our minds.

What is the essential ingredient for resilience?

We need to be comfortable with who we are. By understanding and accepting ourselves, we are able to understand and accept others better. We must be accountable, be *willing* to be accountable, and have a sense of self-respect.

21

Leonard D. Schaeffer

Chairman and CEO,
WellPoint Health Networks

Nobody can predict the future, but if you do a good job of planning, you'll be ready for whatever happens.

Safety and health were never more inextricably linked in the minds of the American public than they were in the months following September 11. One cataclysmic event on a single clear September morning seemed to be all it took to unleash another national nightmare: bioterrorism. And suddenly all those minds that are paid to dream up worst-case scenarios had a lot of work to do—but not just in imagining how a major urban emergency might play out or how a global war would be resolved. The scenarios now involved answering this question: How many different ways can a terrorist make an entire population sicken and die?

This question has an obvious sense of urgency for every individual living in a nation that is discovering just how vulnerable it really is. But for health-care companies, social health and safety are always at the core of their daily business plan. Named America's "Most Admired Health Care Company" by *Fortune* magazine three years in a row, WellPoint Health Networks is one of those companies. One of the nation's largest publicly traded health-care companies, WellPoint goes beyond the traditional health insurance companies and HMOs. Offering a wide range of network-based health plans, WellPoint serves 10 million medical members and more than 44 million specialty members in all fifty states.

Leonard Schaeffer came to WellPoint with a distinguished background in business management, both in and out of the health care arena, and both in and out of the public sector. His previous positions include vice president of Citibank, executive vice president and COO of the Student Loan Marketing Association, and administrator of the Health Care Financing Administration of the U.S. Department of Health, Education, and Welfare. More recently he was president of Group Health, Inc., one of the Midwest's largest HMOs, after which he managed the turnaround of Blue Cross of California, which had lost $152 million in 1987, and its ultimate transition to WellPoint, which has been profitable since 1993.

In this interview, Schaeffer discusses the impacts of terrorism and a changing nation on the planning for and delivery of best-quality health care:

- Anticipating future health-care demands in a time of rapidly changing economics and demographics
- Keeping a business model current with social policy
- Establishing healthy business relationships across diverse communities
- Standing ready to respond to potential terrorist threats

The entire environment surrounding health care continues to change. Every day there is a headline about new research or how a commonly accepted principle of what's right and what's wrong has been turned on its ear. How does a company like yours stay ahead of all these changes and anticipate what's coming so that you're ready to respond to it before it gets there?

Three threads run through the answer to your question. First you have the science base—it will continue to generate new technology, products, and procedures today and tomorrow. We have physicians, nurses, and other professionals focused on understanding the scientific advances and how they apply to practice patterns. They also participate in the industry's efforts to understand efficacy so that we're supporting the practice patterns, therapies, diagnoses, and efforts that are going to have the best outcome. In our business it's called *outcomes research*.

The second thread is the social values related to health-care delivery from one culture to the next. We serve so many different cultural communities, and it's important that the way we support health care delivery is culturally appropriate to our clients.

The third thread is economics. Our health-care system is extremely expensive. We spend more money than any given country on health care, and that's because our citizens believe that they are getting value. They believe that scientists can do things that are important to them.

So when trying to understand the future and trying to predict what's going to happen in the field of health-care delivery, you have to look at the scientific realities, the social values, and the overlay of what's economically possible.

Given the importance of social policy to both health care and the way priorities are set in this country, how do you fold social policy into your business model?

That social values thread comes to us first through legislation and regulations—health care is a highly regulated industry. It also comes to us through litigation. And it comes through a whole network of entities that have taken it upon themselves to try to understand a given disease state, like the American Cancer Society. There is also a social context for health care that we want to be sensitive to. We are the custodians of the money that our customers pay to us, and so we want to make sure that we finance the health care they need, when they need it, in the most effective manner, in the most cost effective venue. It's not just "You have a problem, we'll pay your bills." It's "We want to pay the bills for the therapy that's going to work in the least restrictive, most effective setting." A lot of time and energy are spent on outcomes research on how to find the best way, the most cost-effective way, to get high quality care.

What trends along those lines will be changing within the next five to ten years?

There will be huge changes. We're going from a medical science that has focused on the anatomy of the human being to a medical science that focuses on the atomic makeup—the *molecular* makeup—of human beings. We're particularly going to focus increasingly on genetics. We're going to move from a chemical environment to manipulating genes and molecules. A lot of drugs now work on a molecular level. It's becoming much more complex and much more arcane scientifically. Nobody knows how the genetic revolution is going to play out. But it will be possible that within a decade or two we'll be able to tell with precision which drugs will work with any given person and which drugs won't because of the genetic makeup. And we'll be able to predict with some precision what that person's health status will be over time if he or she is not treated.

That level of predictability is already being challenged by those who are interested in protecting individual rights to privacy—and all those things that go along with it—such as the ability to find and keep employment, for instance.

One of the values that's very highly developed in this country is that of personal privacy. There is already legislation on the books that prevents employers from discriminating against employees who show a high predictability for certain illnesses. As a country we view that as a violation of personal rights. Just because it can be done, that doesn't mean it will be done.

The other side of this argument is that the efficacy of particular drugs can be predicted based on genetic make up. Those findings are going to be used. People's genetic makeup will be analyzed by physicians, if it helps in their treatment. That will be allowed. We as an insurance company will not keep tabs on someone's genetic makeup, but it will be analyzed by doctors, and it will have a dramatic impact on how people are diagnosed and treated.

But again it's very hard to predict how these things will play out. All we know is that the world is going to change.

Globalism is also affecting health care and the acceptance of alternative treatments and approaches. How will it affect insurance companies' acceptance of *paying* for those treatments and approaches?

It's not just alternative therapies, it's also the globalized way individuals are learning about symptoms, conditions, and diseases. Because of the Internet, people, regardless of where they live or even what language they speak, are talking to other people who have similar problems. The science base is open to everyone. People are becoming much, much more sophisticated about their disease state and about the therapies that are available. It's the so-called Internet-positive patient who walks into the doctor's office with forty pages printed out and says, "I want the following drugs."

On one hand physicians want patients to know about their illness, take responsibility, and deal with it. On the other hand many times information that these people have gotten may not be accurate or their interpretation may not be appropriate. The question is whether people are able to use it appropriately if they're not trained clinicians. And that's a big issue around the world.

There is also a greater set of possibilities and a more expanded set of possible therapies that people tend to be interested in. There is a heightened interest in health-care practices and traditions cross culturally, and people are finding out about alternative therapies from all over the world.

And there's a historical component to how health care is defined and perceived. Health care gets redefined on a regular basis. Fifty years ago people with substance abuse problems were dealt with by the criminal justice system or not dealt with at all. Today they're dealt with by the health-care systems. Years ago when someone had what we call erectile dysfunction, we just didn't talk about it. Today they get Viagra, and Bob Dole talks about it on television. There's a constant redefinition of what health is and therefore what health care is. And it's always expanding.

Across cultures, of course, there are alternative therapies and practices brought in from other countries that aren't yet validated within the U.S. system. In our country the FDA regulates what can be considered an effective pharmaceutical. And our country has standards as to what is considered to be safe and efficacious. Many of these alternative therapies have not gone through that kind of review, and so they can't be reimbursed effectively through a health insurance plan.

We are on a regular basis redefining what health is and what therapies are effective in maintaining good health. The range of possibilities is greater than the range of accepted approaches. But that range is continually expanding. Here in California, for instance, we reimburse for chiropractors and acupuncture. Twenty-five years ago it wouldn't have been the case.

And how are these changes impacting your business?

It's a creative opportunity for customer service. By redefining health and health care, we are covering more therapies and treatments every year.

How else is diversity affecting your business both externally and internally?

We are headquartered and started out in California, which is an extremely diverse state. So for us, that's part of doing business. Our associates come from many different ethnic backgrounds and speak many, many different languages. Our services have to be delivered in culturally appropriate ways for many of our customers. For instance, we have a lot of people from Asian countries who would prefer to get care from individuals from the same nationality. Or it may be important culturally that women seek health care from other women. It's not our job to tell someone what's best. What we want to do is identify culturally appropriate sites so that people feel comfortable receiving the care that they and their families ought to get.

Our company is focused on the concept of choice. This differentiates us from the others. We don't think that we've figured out the single best way to get health-care financing. We never believed that the HMO was the answer. Or that traditional health-care financing is the answer. Americans want to exercise their prerogatives as consumers, and they have a higher level of satisfaction if they can choose the health-care plan that makes sense for them.

We believe that health care is locally delivered and locally consumed. While we are a very big company, we focus on local geographies and local offerings of choice. As such, cultural diversity is part of that kind of choice offering we provide our customers.

What is your philosophy toward establishing healthy business partnerships?

You have to be very focused on what you do well and then executing that so others can depend on you. The same is true in the partnership relations. We understand that we finance care and that our responsibility is for marketing, design, the timely repayment of claims, and all those sorts of things. We make promises to our constituents, and we try to keep those promises. And the constituents who do the same for us are the preferred partners.

But we do not practice vertical integration. We're doing more horizontal initiatives. I don't think a true vertical integration model has worked out. You have to do what you do well and be a dependable partner so that others who depend on you will feel comfortable. And, in turn, you have to find partners whom you can depend on. That's what our health-care networks are about. We identify physicians in the community who are high quality and affordable. We identify the hospitals similarly, and then we work together.

What does investing in the future mean now to you?

We're only as good as the last intervention a customer has had with one of our associates. So the first thing we invest in is our people—which includes their career development, training, and opportunities to have them grow and develop as individuals. We have created a meritocracy so that if you do your job you will do well here.

The second thing we have to do is invest in technology that helps us serve our customers. We're always looking for new ways to eliminate bureaucratic abrasion and make it easy for members, payers, physicians, hospitals, agents, and brokers to work with us. We've invested heavily in technology to do that.

Thirdly we have to invest in those activities that will allow us to reduce our costs, both our cost per unit of services and the number of services that we deliver. In our industry, because we do so much in the way of processing transactions, we want to lower the costs per transaction as well as the number of transactions that our customers must have with us.

How do you think we can use health care and its attendant economics as a model to neutralize anti-Americanism around the world?

The fact is that the United States pays for most of the research and development of health care in the world. Most of it is done here. Certainly most of the drug research is done here. And we export that by virtue of exporting drug therapies and diagnostic approaches. From a research and development perspective, we really do offer a tremendous amount to the world.

We spend a lot of money on health care, which is a key reason why our population is so productive and our quality of life is so high. Our message to the world is not that American affluence results in everyone having four cars. Our message is that more people are living longer and having better lives. We can be the beacon to the world by our example of using our affluence to create a better quality of life from a health perspective. Yes, as a nation, we have some issues with the uninsured. And we have some issues with people who don't take responsibility for their own health status. But we're achieving progress in both areas.

What assumptions are no longer true for you?

The biggest change is that the safety and security of our country can no longer be taken for granted. The dangers that are out there are now physical dangers, such as terrorism and bioterrorism. I think that we must think in much broader terms about what could happen. As a company we have to play a larger role in both the public health care and the public security infrastructures. I don't think we've conceptualized our company in that way before.

It is no coincidence that the consumption of drugs to help people with anxiety is going up. When someone comes in and says, "I'm worried because I think people are out to get me," guess what: They're not paranoid. It's true. People *are* out to get them. We're going to see mental health services increase, and we're going to see stress-related problems increase. We're going to see a whole bunch of things happen we never thought about happening.

I hope we never see a bioterrorist attack or another huge airplane slam into a huge building again. But it could happen, and we have to be ready for it. We have to redefine what is possible and what we have to insure our members for.

How can you even hope to create a model that will help you plan for, say, a mass release of smallpox?

We've got people working on it. We're working with the Centers for Disease Control and others to try to think through what we ought to do. Obviously, if someone were to release smallpox, there will be ways to deal with it. There will be smarter or dumber and faster or slower ways. We're in the process right now of reconceptualizing our future and being aware of a level of catastrophe that we never thought about.

We understand that if we had a tragedy in Los Angeles we'd fund every dollar that we could possibly fund. We wouldn't be sitting here thinking about our profit margins for that day. Clearly we have to have reserves. And one of the things we've focused on is being financially strong so we can deal with something like that. Up until now we never thought of—nor had anyone else thought of—the scale or severity of the tragedies of September 11 because it wasn't in our lexicon. It just wasn't in our minds.

To be successful in these uncertain times, businesses must be planning. But then we must be prepared to live with a reality that is almost guaranteed to be different from what we thought would happen. But by virtue of thinking it through we're better able to deal with reality. That's what planning is all about. Nobody can predict the future, but if you do a good job of planning, you'll be ready for whatever happens.

What are you certain of?

I'm certain of change. In our industry, the science base is always changing. This means the techniques to diagnose and treat health problems are always changing. And peoples' needs and expectations are always changing. Young people really are very minor consumers of health care. But as we age we use more health care. Also our family situations change. We go from being single to being parents. And we go from having parents who are young and vital to having parents who are much older. Our needs and expectations change.

On the business side, the competitive landscape is always changing. There are all sorts of challenges to the traditional health insurance company, which is what we were fifteen years ago, and so the company itself has to evolve. When I give a lecture here to our officers, it routinely starts with the message that all things are changing all the time. If the company doesn't change, we will lose out.

The once great companies are either gone or no longer significant players. And it's always because they failed to change. They found one thing, figured out how to do it well, and then did something called "institutionalizing it." Find a single way of doing things and then go out and find a lot of people who will prevent any change from that way of doing business.

That's the opposite of what you need to do. What you need to do is change constantly as the environment changes. We don't want to institutionalize a way of doing business; we want to institutionalize a way of changing.

What are you uncertain of?

The pace of change is very difficult to judge, particularly in the science base. We're always on the cusp of something huge and dramatic. The pace of change is rarely what you expect. In the business world the best example is e-commerce. That was going to change everything overnight. Of course it didn't, but the fact is that even though many of the dot.coms imploded, the use of the Internet is actually increasing and becoming much more effective. So, in addition to the pace of change, it's also the bets you make in terms of where to invest and what's the right thing to do now. Those questions are tough.

What is the essential ingredient for resilience?

It's a combination of not believing your own press clippings and never forgetting where you came from. When I joined this company in 1986, the company was insolvent. We only found that out over the next three months going through the financials. We had to go through an extremely difficult process of downsizing. We went from 6,000 employees to 3,500 employees. And we went from having 2 million customers to 1.8 million customers. We went through lots and lots of pain and agony. We are never going to go back there again. We are never going to make the kinds of mistakes that will lead us to having to lay off people who are innocent victims and who are trying their best. We don't want to repeat those mistakes.

It's easy to only look at your successes. When you overlook the mistakes you have had to overcome, you won't have the dedication and persistence that's necessary to overcome future struggles. You can't forget where you've come from. You can't believe that the momentum of the company is going to make the difference. You have to believe in hard work and working smart.

22

Theodore G. Shackley

Associate Deputy Director of Operations (retired), Central Intelligence Agency

I have heard former KGB officers say, "Given the current situation in Russia, why should we spend millions of dollars and years of research when we can obtain something that has value for a few thousand dollars via espionage?" And from their point of view, there's a certain amount of logic in that. From our point of view, understanding that, we need to do something to protect ourselves.

Over the last four decades, the Central Intelligence Agency has been plagued by scandals, and it has been the object of conspiracy theories, mistrust, distrust, suspicion, and derision. It has also been a high-performing organization of dedicated professionals, who have committed their lives to protecting the United States through the collection and analysis of intelligence all over the world. Performing the bulk of its high-value work in utter secret, the CIA is one of the largest, most influential organizations in the world that does not allow itself the benefits of a wide-open, full-fledged public relations campaign promoting its value to its customers—the American taxpayer. You will not see, for instance, its commercials on *Face the Nation*.

But since the absolutely unexpected and sudden attacks on September 11, Americans have had cause to think of the CIA twice in completely new ways. First in the ensuing hours, days and weeks after that attack we asked ourselves, "Why didn't the CIA pick up on this conspiracy before it was too late?" And then on November 29, 2001, the CIA announced that one of its officers, Johnny Michael Spann, was killed in a Taliban prison uprising. Spann would be the first American killed in combat in the conflict in Afghanistan. The CIA has gained new respect among Americans who freshly realize the role that the CIA plays in protecting U.S. interests abroad.

Ted Shackley's own story tracks the Cold War hot spots from establishing intelligence collection operations in Eastern Europe and the Soviet Union after World War II, to being station chief of Miami during the Cuban Missile Crisis. A career intelligence officer, Shackley served as base chief in Berlin from 1965 to 1966—when he was tasked to rebuilding clandestine assets after the erection of the Berlin Wall. He also served as station chief in Laos during the Vietnam war—during which he built a guerrilla army of 40,000 tribesmen. He went on to become station chief in Vietnam, chief of the Western Hemisphere division, and division chief of East Asia, before retiring in 1979 as associate deputy director of operations. But before leaving, he was to witness the politically driven move to gut the CIA of almost 1,000 seasoned, experienced intelligence officers—the infamous mass firing by then-CIA director, Stansfield Turner, that would be known as the Halloween Massacre—in favor of a more technologically driven organization. This would be a decision the nation would come to regret a quarter century later on September 11.

Shackley is currently president of Research Associates International, a risk analysis firm specializing in working for independent oil companies and manufacturers of products sold in worldwide markets and providing executive protection for senior corporate officials around the world.

In this interview, Shackley discusses the role of intelligence in both understanding threats and creating vital alliances:

- Unifying diverse groups with their own, disparate motivations to achieve a common mission

- The long-term price inherent in replacing human talent and experience with technological ability

- The relationship between American intelligence and American enterprise in their functions around the world

- How companies with international operations can manage and reduce their risk exposure both domestically and abroad

Is it better to be for a cause or against it?

It's more motivating to be for something. The historical examples that make that point are Fidel Castro's revolution in Cuba and Ho Chi Minh's reunification of Viet Nam by force of arms. In each war the positive message was simple and one that struck a responsive chord with its intended audience. Castro had great success in being *for* removing a corrupt regime, eradicating illiteracy, and treating all citizens as equals by phasing out the color line. Ho Chi Minh successfully sold nationalism and the reunification of the country to his people. He backed those fundamentals with the force of arms and won a protracted struggle against France and the United States. In so doing he gave up nothing fundamental to his wartime benefactors, Russia and China. As a matter of fact, in 1979 Vietnam went on to fight a short and successful war with China.

When it came to recruiting 40,000 tribesmen, what was your leverage? How did you capture and unify the energies of so large and disparate a group that had so much to lose and could have been completely demoralized?

This was a guerrilla force divided along ethnic lines that was influenced by geography. In the northern part of Laos, the predominant tribal element was the Hmong. In the south the participants were the Lao and Kha people. Each one of these groups had a slightly different motivator. In the north with the Hmong, this was a society that had been slash-and-burn farmers who were free to roam around the country. But their movements had been restricted by the war. And they had tribal leaders willing to resist the North Vietnamese in order to preserve the lifestyle that they had—or that they thought they could build in the future, which would be better than what they understood North Vietnam to represent.

In the South it was a matter of keeping the North Vietnamese from encroaching on traditional Lao lands. The motivation of the Lao and Kha was more materialistic. It focused on bringing people a better standard of living by setting up trading centers and water sanitation facilities, improving health care, and bringing the people into a money economy. That's how it was possible to unify these disparate groups under the overall banner of the Kingdom of Laos.

So we were actually able to unify and motivate these groups even though their separate motivators were so different. But they weren't mutually exclusive. Today in the United States, we have two kinds of motivators going on at an indigenous level: One is a unification of the population against terrorism, and the other is the preservation of the "American way."

What we're trying to motivate ourselves to do—as the nation focuses on the preservation of the American way—is to preserve democracy and the free enterprise system. This two-track motivator encompasses the right to be free from fear on a daily basis and the right not to have your property destroyed by an enemy force.

On the other hand, it seems that the big motivator for Al Qaeda is being *against* something.

They're against the cultural influences of Americans on their society. But they're also *for* a religion that they believe should be established and recognized around the world. The problem is that their religion is an interpretation of Islam that's not acceptable to most people. Most scholars of the Koran say Al Qaeda is not correctly reading or understanding the Koran.

You witnessed one of the most devastating transformations during Jimmy Carter's administration, when many of the most senior, most experienced intelligence professionals were summarily dismissed during what is now called the Halloween Massacre. Today, in the corporate arena, missions are regularly celebrated by one generation of leaders and then compromised by the next. Still, companies love to talk about vision, corporate culture, and mission. How can you sustain organizational focus when the company changes the rules, the priorities, even the leadership itself?

You have to depend on the dedication of your cadre. As I see corporate takeovers, when the mission changes, it's a different problem from what happened at the CIA. In the corporate sense, when the mission changes, the new team has to have a vision of where it's going with the corporation. In having that vision it has to take that message to the employees. Usually that means the CEO has to put on a dog-and-pony show, introduce himself or herself to employees, and articulate that mission. At the same time, that leader must appear to be flexible enough to receive and seriously consider employee input as to how that mission plays out in the marketplace.

In the CIA, when the shift took place during the Turner period, the world itself had not changed significantly. There was still an interest in Washington in working against the Soviet Union and China. The fundamental mission of the organization didn't change. What we had was a shift in the kind of approach we were going to take and how we would get intelligence. One of the specific items at issue was how to harness technical collection while reducing human source collection.

Which is a problem with private enterprise as well—creating the best formula for combining the two—human input and technology—in a way that's most appropriate.

You have to have balance in these activities. What came about in the Turner period was that we lost a certain semblance of balance. His view was that more had to be done in the technical collection arena. Everyone said, "That's fine, if you do that you're going to enhance your ability to get *capabilities* intelligence. But if you reprogram all these funds that you're going to save by cutting people out of the human source collection arena, you're going to degrade your ability to have intelligence on *intentions*. You're going to understand that the enemy has a lot of equipment that has certain capabilities. But what is he going to do with it? What are his intentions?" You won't know without the human sources to tell you.

That was not something the Carter-Turner team wanted to hear. And that's what caused the human collection effort to be gutted.

It also caused the brain trust of the clandestine collection organization to be gutted.

Once people in the CIA saw what was happening, it was time for some of them to bail out and go do other things. What Turner and others in his clique didn't understand was how long it takes to get human resources up to the level of proficiency that's required to get the spy job done. It takes years to develop language capabilities, area knowledge, and the experience of recruiting and managing spies. In today's world the new officers coming into CIA's clandestine service can't get the required expertise quickly.

The opportunities aren't there. And, up until recently, it was harder to recruit high-potential talent as spy masters because the opportunities for growth weren't as plentiful as they should have been. Without the experienced professionals that we lost in 1977, we didn't have the master/apprentice opportunities that we did in the 1960s and 1970s.

Hasn't this experience with Afghanistan demonstrated the argument against relying on technology and not so much on people? Wasn't it the judgment that goes along with knowledge collection that we needed to understand what was happening? What do you think of the comments made about the fact that our intelligence resources were so overwhelmed by the data they didn't have the human resources to sort it out and truly didn't understand the ramifications of what they were reading?

That is part of the problem. There is more information coming out of the technical sources than we can process. But secondly, the fact is that we simply did not have the human resources needed to put all this data in sharper perspective or those who could alert us to these developments on their own.

This problem isn't solely attributable to this emphasis on technical collection. There have also been executive orders issued restricting the kinds of individuals that American intelligence could recruit.

You can't hang out with the riffraff.

Right. You can't hang out with the bad guys. Yet you're trying to penetrate terrorist cells and drug syndicates.

Which strikes me as being supremely naive and so far above the fray that you really don't know what it takes to get the job done.

Right.

What's the role of American intelligence in supporting American business abroad?

It doesn't support American business. You can't go out and specifically collect intelligence if the beneficiary is going to be an American corporation. But there's a whole panoply of things that people can do that is designed to help American business. If American intelligence finds out that a foreign nation is attempting to penetrate an American company, it will go to that company, alert it to that fact, and work with it from a counterintelligence point of view to help it protect its information as well as neutralize the attempt by the hostile service to steal its material.

Do you find that American businesses are sophisticated enough to realize they may indeed be targets of this kind of activity?

There's an awareness generally in corporate America. But the awareness that there is such a threat doesn't necessarily translate into procedures within the corporate empire to define precisely what it is they want to protect and how they have to go about protecting it.

Each corporation obviously is different, and you have to define what it is that's most important to you to protect. Once you've identified that information, it's possible to protect it. You don't want to try to protect everything. What you do want to safeguard is the one or two critical items that make your product unique or cost-effective. How you developed the product or how it is produced can be sacrificed on the altar of cost-effectiveness. That in turn frees up resources to protect what is vital.

It seems the American social and cultural mandate has traditionally been to not be paranoid. Do you think that in our country, with our built-in open society philosophy, we're too naive and we should factor in more caution?

We should have more concerns, and they need to be focused on critical technologies. Those are the technologies that are key to our economic and military well-being. I have heard former KGB officers say, "Given the current situation in Russia, why should we spend millions of dollars and years of research when we can obtain something that has value for a few thousand dollars via espionage?" And from their point of view, there's a certain amount of logic in that. From our point of view, understanding that, we need to do something to protect ourselves. That was the trigger for the Economic Espionage Act of 1996. That legislation forms the basis for the crafting of enhanced industrial policies, new security procedures, and a proactive counterintelligence effort. Put into the jargon of American law enforcement, the totality of the effort that has flowed from this legislation sends a clear message to the industrial spy or thief. It is: "Be aware that there is a new effort to identify you, manipulate your efforts, and put you in jail for long periods of time." To put it simply, this means that the U.S. government has become more aggressive in finding corporate spies and throwing them into jail. It used to be that the FBI might not do anything, but now it has a separate operation dedicated solely to corporate espionage or theft.

As a society do we need to wise up even more?

Yes. Our long-term focus has been to assume Russia and China may still be bashing away at us. What we don't understand fully is that there are about twenty friendly, nonaligned nations that are also conducting economic espionage against us. Countries like Taiwan, Japan, South Korea, and India. Even our allies, Great Britain and France. France and Japan are probably the most active in trying to get economic intelligence out of the United States.

Does that mean employers should be prudent about hiring foreign nationals, especially from those countries?

They certainly should be screening them very carefully so they understand what they have. A lot depends on where within the corporate structure you're planning to use these people. If you're an American company with a subsidiary in France, you have no choice but to hire most of your employees in France. But then you have to understand what data is critical to your corporate survival and what risks you're incurring by exposing a lot of that information to foreign nationals. On the other hand, that's a risk that must be assessed according to the kind of industry one works in. There's a rule of thumb in the computer software industry that says that you really can't keep anything proprietary for more than twelve to eighteen months. By then it's either stolen from you or copied by someone else in another country.

When you're bringing out a new product, you need to have thought through what the time frame is in which your competitors are going to bring out a better product. Then you can start thinking about what you can do to protect your product during that time frame.

What leadership lessons can we learn from the Taliban and Al Qaeda?

The main lesson that has come out of our war with the Al Qaeda terrorists is a clearer awareness of how small forces have been able to match technology or enhance the role of certain kinds of technology to fundamental acts of terrorism.

You've been in so many different world political emergencies when it seemed as though if it were not handled just right, the world could come to an end. Here you are with Berlin behind you, Cuba behind you, Viet Nam behind you, and now we're looking at Afghanistan. Is there any sense of historic proportion we can draw from this?

The most important lesson is what I call not falling into a mindset trap. You have to be able to evaluate the constantly changing circumstances and come up with strategies of how you're going to deal with them.

So even though today's problem could end life as we know it today, that doesn't mean that it will be tomorrow's problem?

Right.

Which doesn't take away the importance of today's problem.

No. And it doesn't take away the need to be able to fully assess what may be our problems in the long term. And it doesn't take away from the importance of understanding that yesterday's solution may be completely useless to tomorrow's emergency. It's not good enough to say, "Okay, last time, I dealt with it this way, so that's what I'm going to do this time." You have to evaluate the new problems and decide how to proceed in the current context.

You have to deal with these items as they unfold. And even as you're dealing with them, expect that they will take strange twists and mutate in interesting ways.

What role can U.S. companies take in neutralizing anti-Americanism around the globe today?

I don't think they can. Corporations today should follow the guidelines of "walk softly and leave no footprints." When you're in a particular market, you ought to be very professional, low-key, emphasizing the quality of your product or whatever else is in your package that makes you competitive— whether it's financing or the ability to deliver spare parts quickly. You shouldn't be out there doing high-profile advertising or spectacular social events, parties, or corporate functions. You certainly don't want to get involved in political controversy in the country where you're located.

It would be hard to avoid all those activities if you're a Microsoft in Paris.

Being a Microsoft in Paris is one thing. Being a Microsoft in Bogota is quite another. When you advertise your presence and blow your horn in some countries, your expatriate manager is likely to get kidnapped or killed. Is your product so good or important that you really want to have a huge sign outside your building broadcasting who you are? Do you have to throw big cocktail parties, or can you figure out other ways to make your sales presentation, such as quietly going around and calling on clients?

Is it the American companies' role to actually promote Americanism abroad?

I don't think that promoting the American culture is part of the corporate role. If you're a good corporate citizen, then you're not flamboyant and you're not flaunting your alleged superiority in everyone's face. All you really have to do as an American company is to perform at a high level. You don't have to go out and trumpet the fact that you've just pushed out three local companies on a contract.

Do you necessarily have to include those local companies as partners?

In some countries you can't really bid on contracts unless you have a local partner. But it's not necessarily something we *should* do. That's something that should be decided on a case-by-case basis.

What are you certain of?

I'm certain that the United States is going to be the world's only superpower for the next decade. As a result, Americans have to expect to be in the forefront of world envy. So we should maintain a low-profile posture so we don't attract the wrong kind of attention to ourselves. Low-profile posture is not necessarily a submissive posture. You can be very competitive and aggressive in your business once you get into the transaction. But it's *how* you get into the transaction and *how* you conduct yourself that bring about the high profile that can lead to trouble.

What are you uncertain of?

I'm uncertain of China. I see that China is making a lot of economic reforms and progress. Yet its political system has not adjusted to the changes taking place within China or the world. China's military is engaged in a very ambitious modernization program, and some of those trends—such as the development of a blue water navy, the acquisition of submarines, and its desire to expand the reach of its strategic missiles—have nothing to do, in my view, with China being a regional economic power. Its military expansion, plus the kinds of things you see in Chinese military journals, where they spend a lot of time dealing with cyber-warfare, leads one to the conclusion that they see the United States as being the enemy of the future.

You have to keep asking yourself, "Is that inevitable?"

It's hard to say that in today's world they would attack us. But they're certainly developing that capability, and they're not bashful about saying in their publications that when there is a war, the real leverage they will have against the Americans is the cyber sector. They think they can disrupt it and paralyze us.

The response to this challenge is quite simple. First, we must bear in mind that intelligence is, and has to remain, the nation's first line of defense. Intelligence, particularly intentions data, is a critical force for maintaining peace. That is because it provides a restraint on war. And if war becomes unavoidable, it is an essential tool for achieving victory. Secondly, knowing the Chinese see our vulnerability as being in the cyber sector, we must make our information technology systems more secure and less prone to disruption by hackers, terrorists, or nation-states that seek to do us harm. Last, but not least, we must engage Beijing in a sustained dialogue on the broadest possible range of issues. This exchange should be designed to persuade the Chinese that we have interests in Asia but not hostile intentions.

What is the essential ingredient for resilience?

Staying educated and remaining receptive to outside ideas and information. Don't get locked into the thought that the way things are is the way things will continue to be. Recognize that there's no monopoly on original thinking and interpretation of events in your corporate structure. Listen to input from throughout all the ranks.

23

Ken Smith

CEO, President, and Founder, Jobs for America's Graduates

Given the nature and speed of change, nobody can plan much more than five years out. But what you can plan on is the demographics. And we know who the workforce is going to be for the next fifteen to eighteen years. They are here.

Jobs for America's Graduates, or JAG, is a school-to-career program implemented in 1,000 high schools, alternative schools, community colleges, and middle schools across the United States and the United Kingdom. JAG's mission is to keep young people in school through graduation and provide work-based learning experiences that will lead to career advancement opportunities or to enrollment in a postsecondary institution that leads to a rewarding career. With the help of state funding, and with the cooperation of more than 13,000 employers, JAG's mission is to establish state organizations committed to implementing the JAG Model for both in-school and out-of-school young people. This JAG Model Program delivers a unique set of services to targeted youth in high school, including twelve months of postgraduation follow-up services, that will result in the graduate pursuing a postsecondary education or entering the workforce in a quality job leading to a career.

For every generation, the one following is a mystery. Who are they? What do they dream about? What engages them and motivates them? But there's one thing we know for sure: For the next five to ten years we will not have enough qualified new entrants into the workforce. The actual projections expand and contract as economic optimism shifts in the light of various downsizings and layoff announcements. But it is generally agreed that the labor shortage will return as the current recession enters the recovery phase. And the shortage will last at least a decade. Therefore, it is also agreed that of the new grads leaving high school and beginning their college or working lives, there's not a soul to waste.

But some kids do fall through the cracks, through drugs, dropping out, or violent home lives. They need extra attention and assistance to keep them engaged in the process of building a future for themselves, their community, and the country. Jobs for America's Graduates is the nation's largest school-to-career system designed exclusively for serving at-risk and disadvantaged youth. Since its inception in 1980, more than 300,000 young people have participated in the JAG Model Program, which works together with public school systems and local employers to serve three distinct groups of young people: seniors in a specially designed school-to-work program; a multiyear drop-out prevention program for students in grades 9 through 12; and a drop-out recovery program serving drop-outs or young people in alternative school settings. Through adult mentoring, classroom instruction, job and postsecondary education placement services, and summer employment training programs, JAG's programs are currently serving almost 70,000 young people in twenty-seven states.

Ken Smith is the CEO, president, and founder of JAG. In this interview he discusses the future of America's entry-level job candidates and the need to make sure that everyone is given the opportunities necessary to be productive working citizens:

- The ongoing need to support disadvantaged youth initiatives even when the so-called War for Talent appears to be subsiding

- The core competencies necessary to successfully enter the job market

- The core competencies employers must have to successfully attract and retain entry-level employees

- The necessary partnership relationship that employers must have with local educational institutions to ensure that students are equipped with the skills, education, and positive expectation necessary to build a successful future

❧

Only a year and a half ago you were marketing Jobs for America's Graduates to very receptive companies here in the United States and

abroad, given the so-called War for Talent that we were experiencing. We're now cycling around economically where employers may not feel that same pressure to make sure the future pool is stocked with hirable talent. How do you keep your message consistently compelling regardless of what the employment market is?

The demographic facts don't change. And the demographics are negative for employers—even for those who don't expect to expand employment. We're going to need *all* these young people ultimately—if not tomorrow, then soon. And therefore we have to reach into this pool of young people who typically have not been as urgently needed, and who have not had the time and energy spent on them to make sure they're ready to be productive employees once they leave school. In the short term, given the current state of the economy, employers clearly won't have to rely on this population if they don't want to. But over the long term, the demographics will eventually demand the investment it takes to grow these young people.

Secondly our young people are primarily entering entry-level occupations. And the choices employers have for entry-level people who are willing to work, who show up for work on time, who arrive with enthusiasm, who want to learn, who want to grow in the company, and who will be truly thrilled to be there, are still in short supply.

What are the core competencies of individuals entering the job market in the next five years?

The needs for specific skills change very fast, but there are several core competencies that remain timeless: the basic skills such as math and writing; the confidence and the comfort necessary to be able to learn quickly through a variety of ways; and enthusiasm, energy, and commitment. If you have those, you will do well in the future under almost any circumstances. If you're missing one of those three elements, you're in trouble.

Einstein said that one of the fundamental questions that all individuals must answer for themselves is whether the universe is a hostile one or a friendly one. I would imagine a lot of these kids have the feeling that the universe is hostile. Can there be a program to help neutralize that feeling?

We'd like to believe that that's what we do. We use a highly motivational student organization for building self-esteem and a positive point of view of the future. More than 90 percent of these young people were never invited to join anything ever before. So the sheer act of inviting them to join the JAG Career Association and be an officer in their high school chapter is just an enormous confidence builder. We find that these young people aren't dealing so much with the assumption that the world is against them personally. It's more a matter of despair. They tend to feel that no matter what they do or how hard they work, they're not going to make it. So our primary mission is motivation. We have to recapture hope for the future within these young people for them to be successful. In the student organizations they get together weekly, they make decisions together, and they organize community assistance programs where they get to see how their efforts can directly make a positive difference—that they have value to someone else. They organize field trips to visit employers where they can see for themselves what good jobs and careers are really available. They start talking about going to college and how can we help them get there. And we outline the steps for them.

It's an expectation-setting process, which says, "you've got talent, you've got opportunities, here are some terrific jobs you may never have thought of. There is a vehicle for you to go on to higher education, and if you're willing to work hard, we can give you some great opportunities."

So it's more a matter of overcoming a sense of futility and a sense of despair, as opposed to the world being necessarily hostile. It's a larger issue in that some have just given up on their future before they come to JAG. And, frankly, in too many cases, the educational system has told them formally or informally, "You're not going to make it." The cards are stacked against them.

Do employers have to be more creative, more open minded, more aggressive in seeking out this particular population? Do they need to be more assertive with high school guidance counselors, for instance? Do their recruiters need to be more tolerant of certain backgrounds or behaviors? What should employers do to open up their receptivity to these groups of kids?

Employers need to understand that over time, if they're going to be competitive and beat their competitors, they're going to need to be looking ahead to the future of the workforce and where their future employees will come from: how do they reach them, how do they motivate them, and how do they get as much help from outside forces as they can?

Companies would do well to remember that the population is changing, which means that their customers *and* their employees are changing. Not everyone comes from the Cleaver family. So, internally, they need to be understanding and accommodating, within the confines of good business, of course. They need to be able to respond to challenges, such as the need for flexible schedules. And they need to be able to create a workplace where people can perform, learn, and be held accountable, for sure. There will need to be more training on the company time, preferably in a company facility. Employers will need to be tolerant—again, within reason, of course—of different hairstyles and dress. By that I don't mean that they need to tolerate things that are inappropriate.

Employers must also be able to listen well to their employees, always knowing what's on their mind, what motivates them, what issues they are facing.

Are we talking in terms of five-year increments into the future?

Yes, and that's really all. Given the nature and speed of change, nobody can plan much more than five years out. But what you *can* plan on is the demographics. And we know who the workforce is going to be for the next fifteen to eighteen years. They are here. So that is one of the few things employers can plan on. There are certainly going to be more disadvantaged, more minority, more female, and more young people with challenging backgrounds in the employee population who want to build a future for themselves.

Now, in order to accommodate these facts, employers must start by first accepting them as true. That's probably the most important thing. Then they must help their HR organizations understand this and make arrangements now to work with schools, guidance counselors, job training programs, and others to help find these young people, motivate, train, and then hire them for good jobs.

Should employers reasonably expect to have to include training programs on interpersonal skills, communication skills, even literacy?

Or would you like to see that America's graduates are graduating with the necessary core skills already in their pocket?

Employers have been—and must remain—demanding of the school systems to produce young people who are ready and able to go to work. And that means having those interpersonal, communication, and academic skills. When we spend $250 billion a year on education, like this country does, there is just no reason why we don't produce young people with those skills.

Having said that, it's clear that it's not happening in a lot of places. Any employer will tell you that. Therefore, employers have three choices. They can simply move the work offshore someplace where those skills are more readily available. Or they can say, "Let's work with external organizations who will do the final polishing." Or, third, they can say, "We have to do it ourselves." It's expensive, it's time consuming, and in some cases it will complicate the workplace. I'm not opposed to it at all. In fact, some companies do it very well. But, one way or the other, employers must find solutions for young people whom they really would like to hire but who are lacking critical skills. These skills have to be attained somewhere.

If you could name one barrier between these kids and employers, what would you call it?

Lack of knowledge about each other. Generally, employers don't fully understand the motivations, backgrounds, challenges, and barriers so many of these young people face. And these young people really don't understand the workplace, the requirements for success, the high level of performance requirements, the accountability, as well as the opportunities. They also don't have an understanding as to the wide variety of the jobs that are out there.

Do you see this as a matter of many local conversations being held across the country, or do you think corporations should look at this as a national conversation?

It has to be both. But in the end it will all get executed locally. Setting the expectations is the responsibility of the corporate leadership. And they must be public about it. This includes speaking at their Chambers of Commerce, Rotarian meetings, and HR leadership meetings on what they want the schools to do so they can hire young people with confidence that the skills needed to succeed on the job are there—day one.

How can this kind of story be used to promote American business abroad?

Reaching out to challenging populations pays even greater dividends internationally. Many countries aren't facing the labor shortage that is challenging the United States, but they do have groups in their communities that need extra support in building their lives. So when companies make this kind of effort to challenged populations abroad, it's a convincing demonstration of the company's real value to that particular community—beyond its own immediate self-interest.

One of the most effective strategies for counteracting anti-Americanism abroad, I believe, is reaching out to these populations in a visible, committed, aggressive, and sustained way. It goes a long way toward helping create value and an image that is important both for the United States and for that company. Clearly, the leaders of the business have to be very engaged and visible on those kinds of issues, being on the right boards, and reaching out in various ways to those populations and groups. Ultimately, their customers and the communities they operate in are going to appreciate that the company's heavy engagement in philanthropic activities may well benefit them in the long term.

This is one of the most effective ways companies can help deal with anti-Americanism. But if you're only going to serve the high end of the population, and if you're only going to hire the folks who are doing well in those countries, it may feed the sense of anger at the United States—unfounded as it may be.

What does investing in the future mean now?

It means investing time and energy to get community colleges, vocational and tech schools, and high schools oriented around your needs as an employer. It means clearly telling them how to prepare their students for the workplace. Invest the time now to understand your future needs and resources. What are the kind of employees you're going to need in the future, and where are they going to come from? How do we gain access to them now, and how do we make sure that we get what we want when we need them?

It also means investing in the community in ways that may seem merely tangential to your business interests. If you look carefully at the companies that have been consistently successful over a long period of time, you'll see that they're almost always visible, active, engaged members of the community. And they regularly target those issues that are the most concerning, disruptive, and potentially dangerous—both to their own business directly and to their customer base.

It's important to create the environment within your community that guarantees you the right kind of workers when you need them and good customers who will be buying your products and services. You need to be influencing the direction of that community and the use of the tax dollars and public activities that are the primary means of changing that community. A good, reasonably visionary company needs to be at the grass roots in the community it serves.

The economic clout of a company reflects a community's hope for the future. If that company leaves, how can it prevent hope from going away with it?

Good companies tend to plan for that eventuality, particularly in the last five years, when the speed of change and movement of work has been so rapid. If they're a dominant force in the community, they need to be thinking of their impact. If the day comes that they have to leave, they will have to invest time, energy, and money to mitigate the damage.

Is there a way a company can help develop and promote an independent mindset among its employees so that if that particular company does have to shut its doors, those employees will be able to say that they still have options and won't despair?

More companies are making it clear to employees, "We have a relationship for the moment, and we want you to stay with us—but, candidly, only for as long as we need you. In order to keep you interested in staying with us, we will invest in your training and development. This way you will have the skills and knowledge you would need to rapidly find other work should we choose to leave for whatever reason."

We help our JAG young people understand that nothing is forever, including a job. In fact, in some cases to get a better job they understand that they may have to move. We tell them, "When you have a job, take full advantage of it. Get all the training you can, learn all the skills you can. The economy and the world competition are such that your employer could go away."

We're trying hard to make sure our young people understand that they need to be a personal economic unit that is attractive to employers. That means constantly improving skills, aptitudes, attitudes, and abilities to make them so attractive that they could choose to leave for a better position—or if the employer chooses to leave they can quickly land on their feet.

What has enduring relevance in this environment of rapidly shifting priorities?

Offering hope is just crucial. It is important for employers and leaders at every level to make clear that there are terrific opportunities and genuine hope for the future. Yes, things are changing. And they're probably going to change again and again. But in that change process there's hope for you and hope for your family. The best way to boost your chances is to arrive with energy, enthusiasm, skills, and a belief in the future.

In many ways all of this change tends to create lots of new opportunities, although it may also create immediate short-term barriers for many people. But it has been the process of change that has already created so many good jobs and given us the economy that has gotten us this far. Change in general usually creates lots of opportunities.

What are you certain of?

I am certain that the skills we talked about are going to be essential in almost any economic and social environment. I have complete confidence that those prerequisites to success will continue. I am certain of the critical importance that this population presents to the American economy over time, even if there are bumps in the road. And our twenty-one years of experience demonstrate that young people will respond with great enthusiasm, energy, and success *if* given an opportunity and *if* given a helping hand to get there. People do want to succeed. Young people want to do well, they want to do the right thing, and they want to be a successful part of the American experience.

What are you uncertain of?

I'm uncertain of the future: How it's going to play out? What are the specific opportunities for us personally? What is the nature of the future jobs? Where is there going to be future demand? And where will the jobs disappear? It's tough to plan very far out.

I'm uncertain of what really does constitute the Old and New Economies, and whether there really is any long-term difference. And then there's great uncertainty about how our role in the world will ultimately play out and how it will affect individual opportunities for people in this country.

What is the essential ingredient for resilience?

Hope. You don't tend to come back if you don't have any hope. You have to have hope for the future. Hope gives you confidence in yourself, belief in your family, and the courage and patience to deal with your present circumstances.

William E. Strickland, Jr.

CEO and President, Manchester Bidwell Corporation

Hope, aesthetics, the area of the brain where the imagination lies, are essential to well-being, health, and business success.

As Bill Strickland tells his own story, he had been "a sixteen-year-old hostile kid in a predominantly black public school during the time of the riots" in Pittsburgh, Pennsylvania. Then he discovered a ceramics class offered by Frank Ross, who then went on to introduce him to other joys of being alive: great food, great music, great relationships. He wanted that for himself, but he wanted it in his own neighborhood.

Now, twenty-five years later, he has it, in the form of Manchester Bidwell Corporation, a training center located in what is still one of the roughest areas in Pittsburgh. But this is no ordinary training center: It houses a Grammy-winning jazz studio, a 350-seat concert hall that hosts an annual jazz series featuring the likes of Herbie Hancock, the Count Basie Orchestra, and Diana Krall. In the winter of 2000 he broke ground at an old industrial site for an orchid greenhouse, which already has eager potential customers in the major Pittsburgh supermarkets. He is now finalizing plans to repeat his vision of creating world-class technology and arts training centers in inner cities around the world.

His next destination: San Francisco to develop a similar center on a five-acre parcel on an abandoned Navy base, donated by the mayor of San Francisco. Among his supporters are e-Bay cofounder Jeffrey Skoll and, of course, Herbie Hancock.

In this interview, Strickland talks about creating a culture of hope and love of life as core elements in his business model:

- ◼ What it takes to be a renaissance executive
- ◼ Attracting and motivating employees who share the corporate vision

■ Using American leadership examples to promote a positive perception of American business throughout the world

~

You have said that it's important to be a "renaissance executive." Why is this an important concept for businesses at this time?

It's vital to the planet. We must create leadership both on the business and the social sides that really understands clearly that we're all on one planet and that we're all essentially built the same. The needs of people—whether they're in China or Afghanistan or the state of Kentucky—are essentially the same. The real issue to me is how we manage and distribute our resources in a way that can more effectively address the needs of all constituencies, not just a few. The leadership of the future will recognize the entire world as the market potential. Not just one country, one neighborhood, or one community. And successful companies are the ones that will really understand that and organize, identify, recruit, and encourage managers who think like that as well. Companies are talking about these issues, in the name of diversity. But most of them aren't really getting how deeply vertical and how broadly horizontal the sense of diversity must be.

So when we say diversity, we must include a sense of diversity in the way we find new solutions to old problems, as well as finding new product mixes?

Yes. Steelcase, for example, understands that its mission is not just to build good furniture but to provide creditable and good spaces for human beings to function in. One feature just happens to be good furniture. But it also involves architecture, aesthetics, and design, etc. Starbucks has also gone a long way down that street. It's beginning to understand that it's not just about fine coffee. It's about filling a variety of needs of that constituent group that happens to respond to that one product line. So now you find Starbucks selling jazz CDs, which is great, from my point of view.

So if I were to say, "For business in general, it's not just about profit, it's about all these other things," what would those other things be?

It's about values, it's about compatibility with humankind, it's about compatibility with the environment. Those are all elements that don't necessarily initially show up on a balance sheet. But over time they will.

Using this same idea but talking about personal success instead of company success, if I were to say, "It's not just about climbing the corporate ladder and personal financial success, it's about all these other things," what would those other things be?

Life. Let's start there. The successful career is one that's successful in life. Only one aspect is business. It's also the quality of how you raise your family. How you treat yourself as a human being. How you respond within the context of your community to the needs of your neighbors, your extended family, supporting the school and the church, and so forth.

How does hope play into this?

Hope is the fuel in my world. Without hope there's not really much point in getting out of bed in my view. Hope keeps the engine running. It's essential to how we're built as human beings. Instinctively parents teach their children how to rhyme, how to sing, how to color, dance, make music. Those are all inherently hopeful activities.

My argument is that hope, aesthetics, the area of the brain where the imagination lies, are essential to well-being, health, and business success.

Those are the areas that typically are not factored into a business plan.

I know. But they are in mine. If you accept the premise that hope is essential to life, you're obligated to organize your activities, professional life, and personal life in a way that supports that belief. You get people who feel that way on your company board. You hire people who feel that way in your operating staff. You devote a percentage of your resources to ensuring that that point of view is sustained, maintained, and nurtured within your organization. You play it out in terms of the environment where your work takes place.

We're under an obligation to reflect hope in all the things that we do, so that hope really becomes a lifestyle—a way of thinking, an attitude about how you live your life. Not just a set of statements framed on a wall. You have to be living this stuff.

You have said that it's time for the country to change the way it sees itself. What did you mean by that?

The country has got to see itself as the hope for the world, and not as a country that's beleaguered, inwardly focused, and depressed. We have the elements we need, the resources, the leadership, and the money to change the planet.

Your business story begins in 1968. But back then the entire social fabric among young people—especially among inner-city African-American young men—was built on anger, distrust of the establishment. How was it that you shook out of that group?

I never really was totally in it. I was raised to make my decisions based on what makes sense to me rather than what makes sense to the crowd. Secondly, I chose my heroes carefully. In the black neighborhood my heroes were people like Martin Luther King, Jr., who clearly was trying to think his way through problems instead of burn and kill through the problem. What he was creating in terms of his worldview suggested a vision that was more in line with the way I was raised by my parents, what made sense to me as a way of living on the earth. I adopted his values.

I also admired Sidney Poitier and was fascinated by the brilliance of his craftsmanship. I watched every one of his movies and wanted to be like that guy when I grew up. And I discovered Billy Taylor when Mr. Ross took me to a jazz concert one night. I was blown away by how articulate, brilliant, and smooth he was. There were 11,000 people in that room and he took command of it. And Quincy Jones, there was a man whose music I heard and loved. I picked people who made sense to me. I wanted to be like those folks.

In terms of putting together my values and my vision of myself and who I wanted to be, I was very careful on picking the right people to inspire me.

Were you tempted at all to bend your attention toward the anger, frustration, and annihilation that was being promoted among the young people in those days?

My thought was that the way to get out of this mess was not to add to it. I knew I had to go in a different direction. I knew I wanted to do something about this. So I thought, "Where could I most effectively do that?" My answer was the arts.

The arts isn't exactly the fast road to huge success.

That's true, but as the years have shown us, apparently I entered into a field that will ultimately bear more dividends for a lot more people than anything those other guys were talking about. Half the Black Panthers are dead and the organization is defunct.

But in 1968 the arts were also part of the anti-establishment scene.

There were parts of it that were and parts of it that weren't. The part that I wanted to be involved with came from Frank Ross, who was my art teacher in high school. He articulated a vision of living that I absolutely bought into: Frank Lloyd Wright, craftsmanship, ceramics, good food, having a cool house that celebrates all the craftsman-like qualities of the world, textiles, lighting, texture. Joy, pride, self-expression, those were all things I had learned from him.

When the school would close, I'd go over to his house and work in his studio. The pots were hip and he played great jazz: Wes Montgomery, Herbie Hancock, Antonio Carlos Jobim. And I said to myself, "This makes sense. This way of living makes sense."

But what I wanted to do is live this life in my neighborhood. That was the initial decision that launched this whole story. My bringing those two elements together.

When Herbie Hancock came to see us a couple of years ago, he walked into this world-class recording studio in the middle of Pittsburgh's roughest neighborhood and said, "What the hell is this?"

My answer: "This is my concept for a training center for poor people."

He asked: "Where did you get the idea for this?"

I said, "In part I got it from your music. In 10th grade, Mr. Ross would bring in these jazz albums. You were on piano, man. I fell in love with that music, and I'm going where that music's taking me. And if you think that's not true, how do you think you got here thirty years later?"

Herbie's now on the board of the center we're going to build in San Francisco.

How do you get beyond this immediate sense of fear and oh-my-god state that we sometimes fall into, especially when the economy and world affairs seem so uncertain?

You do it by having guys like me running around the country with a box of slides talking about hope and beauty. You talk about forming partnerships with other visionaries who get it. You do it by example. You do it in specifics. You build a center, then you build a second center, then you build a hundred centers. Once you got the hundred done, then you build five hundred.

In order to keep that energy going, do you also have to be able to peer over the wall that's in front of you and threatens to block your vision?

Sure. That's my thing. That's my game. That's what I do. That's why I'm doing what I'm doing. I've been able to put together a picture in my head that apparently makes some sense. And I live on the basis of that every day. Every day I listen to music. Now we have orchids in the deal, so I have orchids throughout the building. You have great food in the deal, you have wonderful music and jazz concerts going on, and all of a sudden you string together a way of living, and a way of operating your organization that propels that vision. That's why the thing works. It creates opportunity for change and hope and promise by virtue of the fact that it is what we do.

Even when I'm in a funk or down, the train is in motion, and it's pulling me along with everybody else. You eliminate the possibility of being depressed by creating structures that refuse to acknowledge depression and only will acknowledge hope.

The reality is that there's plenty to be depressed about right now.

There's also plenty to be excited about. Starting with sunup. Or taking one of these inner-city kids and putting him in a ceramics studio. All of a sudden the kid gets it, and ten years later he's working on his Ph.D., and he's got a family of his own. Or Nancy Wilson showing up and doing a drop-dead concert, and getting a standing ovation. Or it's producing her Christmas CD, and Oprah features it on her annual Christmas music show. Or it's taking an old industrial site in Pittsburgh and turning it into an orchid greenhouse. Or it's taking a decommissioned Navy base in San Francisco and turning it into a world-class arts and technology center.

Where's the hope? I just talked about it. And 100,000 things I haven't talked about.

How do you find people who get what you're doing?

They find me. I do a speech every other week someplace in the country, including the Harvard Business School. The kids all want to work for me at the end of the presentation. After a while you get pretty smart, and you get a sense of the people who really get it. Sometimes they don't, but no harm done. The gig is to keep looking.

I hired this guy Marty Ashby sixteen years ago. He walked in off the street after I built the center with this great music hall and I didn't have anyone to run it. He said, "Hey, man, I heard about you and I want to work for you."

I said, "What do you want to do?" "I want to build your jazz program."
"Do you have a reference or something?"

As it turns out he knew Billy Taylor. I happened to know Billy Taylor by then so I called him up. "There's this white kid named Marty Ashby who claims he's this jazz musician and wants to work for me."

He said, "Hire him before he changes his mind. He's brilliant."

That's where the jazz program came from. And sixteen years later, it wins Grammies. And we get on Oprah.

Does everyone who works for you have to get it beyond just being able to offer their skills like any other workplace?

No. I don't require the folks in the maintenance department to be visionary when they come to work. I expect them to unplug the toilets, keep the building spotless, and make sure the plants have water. But, as it turns out, they also have developed an internal sense of pride about the enterprise in such a way that they give out innovation. One of the maintenance guys loves plants. Now he's into laying out the courtyard with champion annuals. He wants to make the buildings showplaces for flowers. Inside and outside.

That tells you a lot, when the maintenance department internalizes the value system of the culture and begins to make contributions of its own. Any time day or night the building is spotless. Because they get it.

You are located in what you have called the roughest neighborhood in Pittsburgh. Why has your building had no vandalism?

We have built a sacred place. There are no cameras in the building. There is no anti-theft system in the building. In the seventeen years we've been open, we have never lost anything. There's been no graffiti. No police calls. No racial incidents. Not one drug or alcohol incident.

Can any building, any business, create a sacred place?

Yes. Sure. It starts with having a view of human beings that says they're sacred. And then you construct your enterprise based on that assumption, that value, so that the space you create, the way that you treat people, the environment you create that you work in, all of those things become a reinforcement of this point of view. And that's why it works.

When we built this fancy Frank Lloyd Wright–inspired building seventeen years ago, I put a $3,000 quilt up on the wall. It was the first thing I did when we moved in. The staff said, "What are you doing that for? They're going to mark it up or they're going to steal it." I said, "Leave it up there, because I want to know where the line is. If they steal it then we know we can't go that far. But I want to know. It's worth the quilt."

The quilt stayed up there three months, and then it stayed up there six months. I said, "Put another quilt up on the wall." It stayed up there six months. And I said, "Let's keep going." In the space of three years we put $150,000 worth of artwork on the wall.

Is there any excuse for business to say, "Well, good for you, but that's not for me?"

What's their excuse? I'm a black guy in a tough inner city neighborhood with poor people as my constituency. Hello? Everybody's up from where I'm sitting. And I am not a crazy-eyed liberal from the 1960s.

One of the principal values I'm talking about is that I live this stuff every day without being some guru. I want people to see what I do is normal, not abnormal. I want to put this in English and develop it in a way that says, "Hey man, this guy is talking about the way people live their lives every day." You don't have to go to church or become some kind of guru in order to do that.

You know, I'm also a director of the Mellon Financial Corporation. It's in the top ten among financial institutions in the country, with $1.3 trillion in assets, and $650 billion in active management. When I talk about my view in business I have a realistic perspective on this thing. I'm not just an artist sitting down in the neighborhood making pottery and looking out at the world.

Will there ever be such a thing as business as usual again?

I hope not. That's cynical. That says the world is a static and inorganic place. And that is not true. Life is not usual. We don't want it to be usual. We want it to be interesting, exciting, and multidimensional. We don't want to be gray, we want to be multicolored.

That means there is going to be some changing of the power chairs.

That's not going to hurt anybody. We have enough money to rebuild the world and still be cool. How many millions do you need? Don't get me wrong. I don't have anything against money. I'm a Republican. I love the stuff. I think it's great. But there's a point at which we don't need any more. At the end of the day you don't have anything. You're still going to die, and a $100 million isn't going to buy you ten more seconds. So why spend time chasing it? I think that on the day of your death, all you have are memories. You're taking nothing else with you. My strong advice is to have memories that are worth keeping.

The way you overcome death is to celebrate life. That's the only antidote.

How do we engage and motivate an empowered, impassioned, innovative workforce in these times of stress and strain?

By creating nurturing environments, that's how you motivate them. You give them a feeling that there's safety in what they do. Safety gives you the confidence that tomorrow will come.

How can we use American leadership to promote a positive perception of what America stands for around the world?

That question has its own answer. You use American leadership to promote the vision of this country. You get a guy like Strickland and some of his cohorts to build an arts center in São Paulo, Brazil, and then you let the whole world know you did it. Build one in Johannesburg, and then build one in Belfast, and then build one in Kingston, Jamaica—all, by the way, are countries and cities that have asked us to do these. So then the U.S. government says, "Hey, man, here's this black guy that has a very hip, world-class idea about how to transform economies. He's working with companies like Alcoa, PPG, Calgon Carbon, BASF, Fisher Scientific, Hewlett-Packard, and Cisco." And we're going to build these centers all over the planet. And we're going to have a big-time news conference to announce we're going to do it. Do you realize the impact that would have? And that's something we could do that wouldn't cost very much.

How do we continue to cherish the value of innovation and put our energies and hearts into creating the next Big Idea?

By creating places that preserve creativity and innovation. That's the best insurance policy. Out of that will come its own opportunities.

What are you certain of?

Good food is cool. Jazz is great stuff. Frank Lloyd Wright knew what he was doing as an architect. Spring's coming back in Pittsburgh. Life is worth getting up for.

What are you uncertain of?

I'd like to know how I am going to do this all over the planet in the next ten years.

What is the essential ingredient for resilience?

Hope. Hope is encouraged by the environment, design, music, culture, food. All those elements stimulate hope. And hope stimulates optimism, creativity, and promise. They're tied together.

Tai-chin Tung

Chief Financial Officer, Charles Schwab Investment Management

Change is a constant element of being alive. Throughout my career I don't think I've ever looked at things as "business as usual." Circumstances and conditions shift constantly.

Up until the mid-1990s it seemed as though playing the stock market—and being successful at it—was strictly the playground of those who were already rich. They were the ones on the inside track for getting in on IPOs, and they had money to lose on those off-days. When average Americans began wising up to the fact that they too could make money on Wall Street, the next step was to understand how it's done. This was also about the same time we increasingly saw advertisements for the financial services company, Charles Schwab Corp., often soundtracked to rip-roaring rock and roll.

Suddenly it was cool to be an investor. Suddenly, if you were born to be wild, it meant driving your desk like a Harley straight into the territories of previously unimagined wealth. It was just a matter of knowing how. And, through its offerings of free local workshops, on-line courses, advisers, and other financial services (some of which were tailored to specific demographic groups, such as women, the beginners, or people focused on retirement planning), Charles Schwab was everywhere. In the process, the company also earned a place on *Fortune* magazine's "100 Best Companies to Work For" list.

Today's CFO for the Charles Schwab Investment Management division, Tai-chin Tung, arrived in the United States from Taiwan almost twenty years ago as a young woman in her late twenties. With little money, very little English, and no firm, specific ambition, she took on almost all of life's profound changes all at once. New life. New country. New language. New culture. New ways of doing business. She is not a stranger to uncertainty.

In this conversation she talks about what it takes to develop employee commitment inside a large consumer products company:

- Creating a corporate culture in which all employees feel that their contributions are uniquely appreciated
- The evolving role of leadership
- Sustaining a mission- and values-focused environment as an integral part of achieving desired business outcomes
- How American companies should reassess their image both cross culturally and internationally

There is a lot of talk about passion and the drive for meaning inside corporate walls. Do you think companies are really geared up to handle that kind of exuberance from its employees? Or are we still in the lip-service stage?

I have worked for American companies for almost twenty years. But, until now, I never stayed with one company very long. Schwab is the only company where I've made a commitment to stay. And it's been six years now. A very major part of why I am staying here is that Schwab isn't giving you lip service when it comes to how it values the contributions of everyone who works here. The vision and values are being lived by all the employees day in and day out. It's so much a part of our culture that if a person is observed to be behaving outside our values, you'll hear someone say, "That's not very Schwab-like."

Our chairman, Charles Schwab, is very down to earth and very friendly. You'll see him walking down the corridors waving hello to people and calling them by name. In contrast, a few years back, I was at a major financial services firm in New York at a meeting in the boardroom. As I walked down the hall, I encountered a really distinguished-looking gentleman. He passed me without saying a word or even acknowledging that I was there. Later, the relationship manager with the company told me that this was their CEO. This man walked down the hall like he owned the world and had no time for anybody. But I was his customer! Wouldn't you think he could have thanked me for my business? One possibility, of course, is that his people didn't want to bother him and clue him in that a customer was on his floor. Doesn't that possibility tell you something about that firm's culture and values?

I am very unsure whether large corporations are ready to stand on their heads to reaffirm their values and vision. I've given speeches both in China and Europe about Schwab's culture. And people say, "This is unbelievable! Doesn't this cost a lot of money?" Their focus is still on the bottom line.

That kind of cultural reinforcement doesn't cost much at all. Corporate principles have to be lived minute-by-minute in everyday decisions.

Which comes back to the question about how people bifurcate their philosophy versus their behavior. Chuck's vision has always been that if you do things right for people, you would profit because people would grant you this trust that they would not grant anyone else. We have a very loyal customer base as a result. In everything we do we ask, "Is this good for our customers?"

To be able to reinforce such vision, it has to start from the recruiting stage. Schwab is excellent in categorizing the competencies it's looking for in its people. And during the recruiting process you're being told repeatedly what's important to the firm, and the stories are incredibly consistent. When I was interviewing with Schwab six years ago, I had thirteen interviews across the enterprises and up and down the ranks. In all the thirteen interviews, people were telling me that customers were number one. This is not all the same level of people, and yet you feel as though they're all quoting from a bible. That impressed me.

Senior people at the firm are expected to carry the vision and values. We just had a senior management off-site. The prevailing message was, "We are here to build a legacy and we are here to champion the vision and the values." It's less about the message, "You have to generate revenue, and you have to cut expenses." Yes, those things come with it, but what's more important is experiencing firsthand that the company spends a lot of time and energy making sure vision and values are always reinforced.

How can leaders create a results-oriented organization without sacrificing their own humanity, sensitivity, and creative urge?

I have always tried to remain true to how I feel, and that has served me well in developing sincere relationships with the people I work with. I may seem to have a very powerful job, and some people may look at me as a powerful woman—who might even be intimidating at times because of my position. But inside I am still a kid, and like a child, I'm interested in the other kids. I never want to lose that inquisitiveness and curiosity every child seems to have. I want to know who people are. I don't focus so much on their position or power in the company. I want to know and appreciate what they're like as individuals.

If you create that kind of caring environment that encourages everyone to be fair, empathetic, and responsive to each other's feelings, I think they'd be inspired to partner and excel. That's when you get the results you're working toward.

Has the role of leadership changed as the events of 2001 unfolded? How do we use leadership now to create a more deliberate future?

For business leaders, it's a matter of utilizing a different set of skills. When the economy is good and growing, and when people have a tremendous amount of resources, managing and leading is easy. In a time like this you not only have to have the skills to manage with limited resources, you also have to face a very big challenge in how you motivate and inspire people during uncertain times and a market downturn. This is the time for true leaders to emerge and reinforce their vision and values.

So is the threat to inspiration the lack of resources? Or is the threat to inspiration the fact that nothing is guaranteed—and disappointment could be over the horizon just as easily as reward could be?

Inspiration is something you can't touch and hold. How do I inspire people when I tell them to take that hill? Do I give them a big, false guarantee of what's beyond the hill? Or should I simply say, "Guys, I don't know what's beyond the hill. But we are bonded for the mission and if we fail we would still be the legacy"? That's the real leadership challenge for me. Sometimes even the story of failure in history can be inspiring. The intrinsic value in the mission's efforts survives whether the mission itself is successful or not.

What practices and disciplines should leadership assume to meet its changed role?

Leadership should regularly go back to the core values, reaffirm what they are, and rally people around them. Whether the market's up or down, your focus should always be on the people and customers. Make it your mission to meet the customers' needs no matter what the market is and you simplify everything.

When the time is good, if you focus only on your growth instead of reinforcing a vision and value to help the customers, when the time is bad, your people will be forced into deal with the ever-changing market without the certainty of working for the customers. You're going to face more instability and uncertainty.

How important is strong competition in the making of leadership? Are your competitors valuable to you?

You compete with yourself. You always want to outdo yourself for your customers. How do you excel? What are you bringing to the table? What kind of value do you add today versus yesterday? If you no longer bring additional value to the table, you shouldn't be here.

Of course, it's important for us to know what our competitors are doing. But I'm not too sure we should look at it as, "Oh, they've just come out with *this*; we should respond by bringing out *that* to our customers." We're much more about what our customers are telling us. How can we innovate to meet our customers' needs? Those are our priorities. What our competitors are doing is less important than what our customers are telling us.

Do you think that American companies can play a role in neutralizing whatever anti-Americanism there may be around the world?

To neutralize the anti-Americanism, it's very important for people in other parts of the world to sense that Americans have respect for them. Respect for their lifestyle, their values, and what they believe in. Whether we believe in those same things ourselves should be less important, but it's important to them that we respect them. What I find when I travel internationally, frequently, is that Americans abroad tend to behave as if we have no respect for other people's values. We judge and criticize. We don't mean to be arrogant, but that's how we come across. To balance our profit-making business and others' desire to be respected is a challenge for us.

America needs to be better at respecting the cultures of other parts of the world and better at sending its messages about what a great country we are as well. As someone who spent the first half of her life growing up in Taiwan, I could tell you that there is little unified idea of what true Americanism is. When I am abroad, other than ads for our consumer products, I never hear any commercial or campaign about all the reasons why America, as a nation, is wonderful. Or how America is a diverse group of people.

There's a wonderful pro-diversity and pro-tolerance commercial that has been on television since September 11, showing all these different ethnic groups and races saying, "I am an American." That's wonderful! But we need to show it to the world. We're too inward thinking; we really need to do it outward to others. In business, I believe we have the responsibility to show people who we are and what we represent as Americans.

What has enduring relevance in this environment of rapidly shifting priorities?

To me, our humanity and values have enduring relevance.

So the value of staying true to your set of absolutes and respecting the humanity of enterprise never shifts?

Right. Society continues to change over time. If it isn't what happened on September 11, something else catastrophic would happen in another part of the world. So how do you really go through life if you don't hold onto a set of values as your guiding principles? You must always remain true to yourself with a defined set of values to use as your guiding principles.

Values based on humanity, that's how I simplify life. It's not that complicated.

Will there ever be such a thing as business as usual again?

Change is a constant element of being alive. Throughout my career I don't think I've ever looked at things as *business as usual*. Circumstances and conditions shift constantly. A lot of people talk about innovation, changes, and "being a change agent." But how many people have you met who really embrace change? What you're assured of every day is that something will be different. Anything could happen tomorrow.

I want to live my life every day like there's no tomorrow. But that does not mean I want to live recklessly. You have to live with a passion, saying what you want to say and doing what's right. You are going to pass on your experience and knowledge, and even if you don't succeed, your hope is that you can inspire someone who can carry on after you.

What are you certain of?

I am certain that there are plenty of people in this particular society who have passion toward what they do. Their goal in life is beyond how money can reward them, beyond how position and power can reward them. I am also certain that ultimately humans are good.

Finally, I'm certain that processes, products, and futures will continue to challenge and innovate.

What are you uncertain of?

I'm uncertain of our commitment to extend our respect for humanity throughout all levels in our life. We forget how what we say and do has such a long-term impact on the next generation and the people who follow us. This applies not only in our family but also in our organization. Leaders like us need to remain conscious of how we can impact the future success of the generations to come.

What is the essential ingredient for resilience?

You first have to have a survivor's instinct. No matter what happens, you know that somehow you're going to make it. And the desire to excel beyond what others—or even you—expect. You don't just want to survive, to not quit, but you want to be better. When I came to this country I was in my late twenties, with very little language ability and no skills. I only had $200 in my pocket. Throughout the years it wasn't easy. I started out without any mentors or close friends. But what I found was a survivor's instinct and a desire to excel that I didn't know I had.

Resilience not only comes from one's inner strength, but also is replenished by human interactions. You must be able to continuously believe that people's kindness toward you is genuine and that your life goal is to bestow that kindness three or five times more on others.

William Bridges
Principal, William Bridges & Associates

It is a time when anything can happen. That has two sides to it: "Anything can happen. Oh hell. This is awful." Or: "Anything can happen—we can do anything we want to do."

No business book on change and its challenges would be complete without a discussion with William Bridges, the nation's leading consultant on managing the disruptive effects of change and capitalizing on the opportunities change provides. Bridges has been a leader in the field of transition management since the publication in 1980 of his best-selling book, *Transitions: Making Sense of Life's Changes.*

For twenty years he has worked with organizations to help them usher their employees through the changes they have to make with less distress and disruption. That work was the basis of his next best-selling book, *Managing Transitions: Making the Most of Change* (1991). His latest book, *The Way of Transition: Embracing Life's Most Difficult Moments*, traces his own personal transition as he coped with his late wife's struggle with cancer and the building of his life anew through what he calls the "neutral zone."

In this twenty-sixth and final interview, Bridges shares his thoughts on making the most from transitions in rapidly changing times and circumstances:

- Appreciating the roles of transitions and changes in creating progress
- Maintaining a reasonable measure of control over personal and organizational destiny through the transition process
- Understanding the uncomfortable—but necessary—neutral zone
- Using the cycle of change and transition as a time of opportunity

Transition and change are conventionally looked upon as bad-thing events, all very scary. How can we look at them in a different way— maybe even the source of good outcomes?

Everything we're trying to hold onto is itself a product of change. There's nothing in existence that didn't come into existence by replacing something else. The very things we call stability are products of change. Change is the natural state of things, and it's going to continue regardless of what we want.

The problem is our ability to process change at the rate it's coming at us. When change is slow, we get only a few doses of really profound change during a lifetime. When changes are more rapid, they begin to override our natural capacity to assimilate them. We don't so much assimilate change in some mechanical way that we can speed up to keep pace with the times. This assimilation process isn't a mechanical one, and it can't be turned on and off at will.

When change hits us, it sends us into transition. Transition, unlike change, has three natural phases to it. In the first phase we let go of the old situation. So it's an ending phase. In the second phase we're between the old reality and the new one. And the new one may not be at all clear yet. And the third phase is when we make a new beginning under new terms.

We can't just turn on a dime and become new people. That transition process is the only way we can get through change. We have to let go of who we were and go through this repatterning time and then come out new. The difficulty we're facing today is that this transition process is much slower than the rate of change that keeps coming at us. Changes have been occurring in days and hours. And the changes around September 11 were changes that happened in seconds. We're still reeling from the transitions we experienced after those changes.

Changes have been happening so quickly, and transitions happen much more slowly. And so the problem we run into in periods of high and frequent change like the present is that we fall farther and farther behind. We're still trying to get through one transition, when another change hits us. And we get started on that transition, then the third change hits us.

Most of us are running a severe transition deficit, and most organizations are, too.

How do we keep any control over our destiny if we're running a transition deficit?

Leaders need to play more of an active role in preparing the organization for the transition and leading it through the phases. This isn't a role that has been stressed much in leadership. It's all been about *change*. Leaders announce *change*, they envision *change*, they get the wherewithal to make *change* possible. But the transition process that will get people through the change is left out of the equation.

Leaders have to take a very strong role in bringing people through the transitions. Moses, for instance, is a transition leader. He takes his people through the same three phases. They leave Egypt, they are in the neutral zone a very long time, and then they arrive in the Promised Land and make a new beginning. So you have those three phases. In the neutral zone, the Moses organization is transformed. They go into the wilderness as slaves, and they come out of the wilderness as a strong independent group of people. So the neutral zone is the transformative part of transition. And it can't be rushed.

Of course, it says in Genesis that the generation that knew Egypt had to die off before they could enter the Promised Land. If you take that literally, that's bad news. That means everything is going to take astoundingly long. But if you take it symbolically, it's the attitudes and assumptions that fit the old model to have to die out. And, perhaps even more importantly, our attachments to the old ways have to die out before we can be a new people or organization. And that's the reality of transition, too.

When it comes to leading a group through transitions, the leader's role is three-fold:

First, articulate the ending. In the Moses story, this is told in literal narrative. By saying to the Pharaoh, "Let my people go," Moses is breaking the hold of the past.

Unfortunately, too many leaders simply try to bring about the future and they don't pay attention to letting go of the past. Leaders are great at proclaiming the future, but they don't necessarily like to say what's over. They associate that with bad news, and with disappointing or depressing people. Leaders may feel that they're risking alienating their people.

Second, manage this strange in-between state, which is a very creative state. This is potentially a creative, breakthrough place. But it's also very scary. A lot of people want to go back to Egypt or rush through to the

Promised Land immediately. According to the story, both of those approaches to the story are wrong.

Is there also a danger of identifying so much with the struggle that you don't move yourself along through the process?

That is true, especially today. We can get stuck in this in-between place. Especially if it seems a little bit interesting or it doesn't make many demands on us or we get so used to it. We risk getting bogged down in it.

Clearly, according to the story, and according to the transition theory, the task is to come out of it. *And make a new beginning, which is to get a new sense of identity, a new sense of purpose and clarity about the beginning.* And that is the *third* and, I emphasize, *last* role of the transition leader.

Most leaders try to start with that third role. They try to start with a new beginning. True, there are people who get a purpose very early and stick to it, come what may. They negate the in-between state. Others in the process of letting go of the old situation come up with a purpose to replace it. And then they enter the wilderness with that purpose clearly pictured in their minds. But most of us have to get used to the fact that that third phase will be a mystery until we move through and out of the neutral zone—when the time is right.

So would you typify what we're going through now as the neutral zone?

When you say "we," there are a lot of "we's" involved here. The whole society is very much in a neutral zone right now. We've been set up for a fall for a long time. The stock market rose higher and higher, and various kinds of activity got more and more unsustainable. Then the planes crashed into the towers. The ending that occurred then was like all the air coming out of a balloon. We really lost this inflated state that we had. We're very much in the neutral zone from that.

It's unfair to say that we're in the neutral zone only because of September 11. We're in the neutral zone after a period of enormous expansion, and something would have deflated us one way or the other.

How can we look upon this time as a time of opportunity?

The problem is that it's a confusing, frightening time. When it isn't clear what the rules are anymore, everything is up for grabs and the things that you counted on are gone. You're really thrown back to zero again. That's very scary for a lot of people, although it is also a situation that encourages creativity. It is a time when anything can happen. That has two sides to it: "Anything can happen. Oh hell. This is awful." Or, "Anything can happen, we can do anything we want to do."

In this case the task for us individually and collectively is to find the creative side of the neutral zone. We can use the chaos, confusion, and normlessness as an opportunity to try radically new things. And that is the opportunity we face now. There are things that could be done now that a year ago wouldn't have been done—internationally, nationally, organizationally, and personally.

The neutral zone changes the rules of the game radically. For instance, we find ourselves collaborating with potential allies who never would have been allies before.

You have similar kinds of opportunities for organizations. Most people see the negative side of it—the cascading effect of the layoffs, for instance.

But it's also true that at these times the possibility for true creativity is much greater. For example, every major step forward in the computer industry came during very hard times. These kinds of challenges automatically scramble the pieces on the board. They create a field in which innovation is more likely to take root than it is during stable times.

So how do you capitalize on the chaos?

Chaos isn't the kind of option most leaders would choose. That's too risky. They want to protect what's left and protect the growth they have. Leaders aren't very risk taking by nature; most of them are actually pretty conservative. But the breakthrough leaders are real risk takers. Most leaders who went beyond the competition did so by deciding to just go for it. Of course, there are lots of leaders who built their organizations one step at a time. And those are good leaders too, but those aren't the ones who thrive in a time like this.

In this time of transition, when everything feels very noisy emotionally, where can leaders find a peaceful place? What can they tap into to find some calm in the storm?

That calm can only come from inside. There are lots of leaders for whom that kind of introversion is almost an unfamiliar territory. They're very extroverted people. They get very nervous if they can't do something externally. But the renewal process involves going inward and really letting go of the old reality.

Now that feels like a risky thing, but it is the only way through. There's an interesting study by Arnold Toynbee, in which he writes about the pattern of withdrawal and return. This is a pattern that critical intellectual and political leaders have practiced through the millennia. He talks about how Jesus, Mohammed, and Buddha did it. Machiavelli and Dante did it—breaking away from a familiar reality and literally going into the wilderness or going into another country. This is the basic way that people get new insights, the new image they need for the next stage of the journey. That's a hard process under any circumstances, but in our extroverted society, turning inward doesn't appeal very much.

This kind of challenge and response pattern characterizes the behavior of really powerful leaders, and it provides them with a fresh source of leadership. This is how you find new alternatives and resources for renewal.

Maybe what we're in right now is not the New Economy but the Renewal Economy.

There were so many articles about the New Economy and the Old Economy, as though there was some kind of dividing line and we crossed it. Now it doesn't feel as though we've crossed anything. It feels as though maybe what we crossed was the Red Sea and all we've gotten ourselves into is the desert. And that desert is pretty wide and we're still slogging along.

And we have a lot to learn in the process. But I think we're really going to be transformed if we can hang in there.

What transformations would you like to see?

We can speculate, but in some ways life gets to decide that. I don't believe that we get to say what we'd like to see. It doesn't come from what we want. It comes from what life calls on us to do and be. I suspect that one of the things we really need is a way to recover a sense of the natural cycles of organic growth.

I think we're much more caught up in forces than we'd ever admit. They're economic and cultural forces that are cyclical. And so one of the things I hope for is that we come out of this with a great respect for these cycles. They are the things that will renew us—not just the willful decision that we have to do something new.

And we should just get used to the fact that we cannot engineer every little thing? That we will be acted upon and that itself is a transformation?

That's right. I think we're going to be dealing with a lot of stuff as it comes for a while. And like sailing through a very heavy storm, it isn't that you don't have a destination. You can set the compass and you can head for wherever you want to head for. If the storm is very heavy, the difficulty you have is not that you can't find the port, it's that you're in danger of sinking. There you are dealing with much more of an emergency situation, where you're just dealing with the storm as it comes.

How would you use the expression "exit strategy" in the context of your research on transition and your message for executives? What do you cash in, and how do you step out of it into your next iteration?

Leaving any place where you've been successful is a hard thing to do. Almost all people overstay their time. It's very hard to let go of a winning hand. If an exit strategy is a way to encourage an ending before the game does you in, I think that's a good thing.

Thinking preemptively in terms of an exit strategy is a smart thing to do, both personally and organizationally.

And we should be doing it consistently as individuals in our lives?

Absolutely. How in the world can we deal with the pace of change that we're facing without following an exit strategy? It isn't just weeding out things. It isn't like going through your life and destroying all your old relationships. It isn't like going down to the office and quitting your job right now. That's not what I'm saying.

We need to destroy the attitudes and ties we have to those things. And free ourselves up to develop better adaptive ways. Keep the job. But evolve within that job to new kinds of work within your role. And, yes, you may keep the relationship. But grow within the relationship and develop new dimensions to the relationship.

Do we also need to change the things we use to make us feel good about ourselves?

Again, life will tell you that. I certainly don't want to go through and start destroying everything in my life that makes me feel good about myself. But I'm getting pretty vigilant in my own life to identify what's working and what isn't. I realize how often in the past I stuck with things that had stopped working a long time ago. And by working I don't mean financially. I mean those things that are or aren't giving me the meaning, significance, beauty, whatever it is I need in my life.

What are you certain of?

I'm certain that the pace of change is going to stay at its present level for the foreseeable future. And any strategy that doesn't take that into account is going to fail.

What are you uncertain of?

I'm totally uncertain of what the content of the changes is going to be. There was no way to foresee September 11. What if next year there is a terrible climate shift, or a devastating political scandal, or what if we enter a period of profound deflation? I don't know what the changes are going to be, but they are going to be real and they are going to be big.

What is the essential ingredient for resilience?

Behind whatever doubts you have, you must have an underlying faith that you can start all over...that you can bring it all to a close and then begin again.

Index

AAAE, *see* American Association of
    Airport Executives
accounting standards, 8
acupuncture, 178
ADA (Americans with Disabilities Act), 60
Ad Council, 49–58
  and ad funding, 54–55
  and business as usual, 51–52
  changes in, 52–54
  responsiveness of, 50–52
  strategies of, 56
advertising industry, 49–58
  and economy, 56
  expansion of, 57
  unification of, 53
Afghanistan, 3
airports
  adaptation of, 24
  economic impact of, 21–22
  as economic indicators, 23
  security technology at, 24–25
  in smaller communities, 22–23
Aldonas, Grant, 1–11
  on Chinese economy, 4
  on demographic shifts, 10–11
  on human rights, 4–5
  on moral obligations, 6–8
  on reconstruction of Afghanistan, 3
  on resilience, 11
  on trade, 9–10
  on trust in government, 8–9
  on U.S.-China relationship, 5–6
Alexander, John, 12–18

  on inspiration from the ranks, 16
  on leadership, 13–18
  on mission and values, 17
  on resilience, 18
Al Qaeda, 187, 191–192
alternative therapies, 177–178
American Association of Airport Execu-
    tives (AAAE), 19–20
American Institute of Architects, 60
Americans with Disabilities Act (ADA), 60
"American Way," 187
Amtrak, 144–145
Andersen Consulting, 148
Andersen Windows, 144
anti-Americanism, 219–220
  and aviation industry, 26–27
  and community service, 88–89
  and cultural sensitivity, 47–48
  and solving problems, 33
  and third parties, 129
anticipation of market, 91
antiglobalization movement, 10, 17, 163
anxiety, 181
Appalachian Spring (Aaron Copland), 49
architecture
  and cultural sensitivity, 62–63
  and disabled employees, 60–61
  and future of skyscrapers, 61
  old rules in, 61–62
  power of, 66–67
"arc of crisis," 10
aviation, 19–27, 149–150
  adaptation, 24

and economy, 21–23
effect of threats on, 26
global aspects of, 26–27, 91
importance of, 21
role of, 20–21
and security, 24–25
Award for Responsible Capitalism, 159

Bain (consulting firm), 81
balance, maintaining, 80
Barclay, Charles, 19–27
  on airports and economy, 21–23
  on airport security, 24–25
  on global role of aviation, 26–27
  on love of change, 25
  on resilience and respect, 27
  on technology, 26, 27
Beamer, Lisa, 105
Belenko, Viktor, 42–43
Berlin Wall, fall of, 10
best practices, 41, 160
biotechnology, 31–32
bioterrorism, 31, 181
Black Panthers, 209
Blair, Tony, 129
Boston Marathon, 84
BP, *see* British Petroleum
branding message, 169–170
Bridges, William, 222–229
  on finding calm, 226–227
  on managing change, 224–225
  on "neutral zone," 225–226
  on positive aspects of change, 223
  on resilience, 229
British Petroleum (BP), 144, 146, 151
Brown, John, 151
Brzezinski, Zbigniew, on "arc of crisis," 10
buildings, high-rise, 60–61
Burson-Marsteller, 125
Bush, George W., 8
Bush, Laura, 51
business
  and education, 70
  effects of terrorism on, 111
  and global development, 163–164
"business as usual," 51–52, 131–132
business cycle, 152–153

business skills, 110–111

Cairo metro, 89
California, 112, 178
calm, inner, 226–227
capital, 152–153, 162
capitalism, 75
Carlson, Curtis R., 28–36
  on Exponential Economy, 35
  on knowledge economy, 30
  on motivation, 29–30
  on open environments, 32–33
  on responsibility, 31–32
  on technology, 33–34, 36
Carlson Companies, 157
Carns, Michael P. C., 37–48
  on competition, 39–40, 42–43
  on discipline, 41
  on greatness and circumstance, 44–45
  on leadership, 46
  on military adversaries, 38–39
  on patriotism, 43–44
  on readiness for challenge, 45
  on resilience, 48
  on respect for other cultures, 47–48
  on risk assessment, 41–42
  on voluntary partnerships, 46–47
Carter, Jimmy, 187
Castro, Fidel, 112–113, 186
Catholic Church, 65
celebrity CEOs, 16–17, 76–77
cellular technology, 72–73
Center for Creative Leadership, 12
Centers for Disease Control, 181
Central Intelligence Agency (CIA),
    184–185, 187–188
CEOs
  celebrity, 16–17, 76–77
  role of, 126–127
challenge, readiness for, 45
change
  acceptance of, 156
  adaptation to, 18
  certainty of, 182
  and competition, 40
  driving, 134–135
  managing, 224–225

change *(continued)*
  in media, 73–74
  as opportunity, 25
  positive aspects of, 223
  rapid rates of, 35
  rates of, 77, 156, 182–183
chaos, 226
Chicago, 145
China, 62, 63, 191, 194
  alliances with, to fight terrorism, 111
  American jobs competing with, 76
  benefits of trade with, 75
  business partnerships in, 71–72
  cellular technology in, 72–73
  competitive training in, 70
  emerging economy of, 4
  human rights issues in, 4–5
  market economy in, 6
  relations with, 5–6, 155–156
  transition in, 113–114
China Telephone Company, 71
Chinese (in California), 112
chiropractors, 178
Christianson, Clayton, 74
Churchill, Winston, 45
CIA, *see* Central Intelligence Agency
circumstance, leadership and, 44–45
Cisco, 121
clean energy technology, 144, 147
client(s)
  positioning of, 65
  value of, 36
coaching and enabling, 16
Cold War, 39
Colgate-Palmolive, 97
collaboration, 64–65, 110–111
  see also partnerships
college graduates, 94–96
colliding exponentials, 36
commitment
  of employees, 32
  engagement vs., 104
  and resilience, 48
Common Sense (Thomas Payne), 77
communication
  of leadership, 153
  and moral obligations, 7

as necessary skill, 110–111
  from senior management, 102–103
  with team, 46
communities/community service, 15, 98
  in foreign countries, 88–89
  investment in, 162
Compaq, 123
competition/competitors
  and innovation, 39–40
  and the Internet, 73–74
  joint ventures with, 103
  and leadership, 219
  and marketplace, 42–43
  partnerships with, 47
  and staying sharp, 66
computers
  Moore's Law for, 35
  personal, 34–35
Computer Shopper, 74
computer software industry, 191
Conlon, Peggy, 49–58
  on ad campaign strategies, 56
  on business as usual, 51–52
  on capitalizing on war effort, 56–57
  on changes in advertising industry,
    52–54
  on following instincts, 57
  on funding ad campaigns, 54–55
  on motivation, 53
  on responsiveness in advertising,
    50–52
consistency, 102–103
contextual leadership, 14
Copland, Aaron, 49
core competencies, 197
corporations
  creativity in, 166–169
  and global economy, 160–161
  and human rights issues, 138
  in international business, 155–156
  reactions of, to September 11, 149
  social responsibility of, 126–127
creativity, 166–169
Cuba, 21, 112–113, 186
culture(s)
  American influence on, 137
  and American partnerships, 122

architecture and sensitivity to, 62–64
and health care, 178–179
and leadership, 14
of leadership, 15
learning from other, 160
partnerships and foreign, 70–72
respect for other, 47–48
sensitivity training for, 63–64
similarities in, 87
customer service, 89–90, 104–105

Daly, Leo A., III, 59–68
on collaboration, 64–65
on competition, 66
on cultural sensitivity, 62–64
on mentoring, 64
on positioning of clients, 65
on power of architecture, 66–67
on replacement of World Trade Center, 67
on resilience, 68
on safety factor in architecture, 60–61
Daly, Ronald E., 69–78
on celebrity CEOs, 76–77
on change, 77
on changing media, 73–74
on fighting terrorism, 74–75
on foreign jobs, 76
on global trade, 75–76
on international partnerships, 70–72
on role of business in education, 70
on training workforce, 78
demographic shifts, 10–11
development, sustainable, 143
Dickerson, Ralph, 79–84
on benefits of philanthropy, 82
on resiliency, 84
on role of philanthropy, 80–82
difference, making a, 82–83
diplomatic skills, 111
directory printing business, 71–72
discipline, 40, 41, 100
diverse groups, unifying, 186–187
diversity, 110, 160, 173, 178–179
Doha (trade talks), 3, 10
Dole, Bob, 178
dot.com companies, 150

"double cube" rule (architecture), 62
drugs and drug research, 176–177, 180

Earth Day, 141, 143
e-Bay, 98
e-books, 73
economic impact statements, 22
economy
and advertising industry, 56
and demographic shifts, 10–11
impact of airports on, 21–22
knowledge, 30
and moral obligations, 6–8
recovery of, 123
and September 11, 149–150
and talent, 171
and transportation, 142, 144–146
education
and business, 70
fighting terrorism with, 74–75
and international partnerships, 71–72
investment in, 114
role of international, 109–110
e-HR services, 151
Einstein, Albert, on the universe, 197
Eisenhower, Dwight D., on capitalizing on war effort, 56
Ellis, Perry, 129
ELPC, see Environmental Law and Policy Center
e-mail, 54
employee profit chain, 162
employees
as active participants, 172
core competencies of, 197
and credibility of HR, 171
empowering, 152
evacuation of disabled, 60–61
investment in, 180
open environment for, 32–33
and personal meaning, 118–119
and philanthropy, 80–82
in post-layoff environment, 102–104
relationship with, 170–173
training of, 78
encyclopedias, 74
engagement, commitment vs., 104

Environmental Law and Policy Center
(ELPC), 140, 144
environment/environmentalism, 141–147
and corporate values, 142–143
and generational shift, 141–143
and global issues, 143
and politics, 146–147
and societal values, 143, 146
and technology, 144, 146–147
espionage, 189–191
E-Stamp, 115, 118, 122–123
ethical standards, 127
Evans, Don, 8
experience, 107
Exponential Economy, 35
Exult, 148, 150, 154, 156

faith, 68, 164–165
fast-tracking projects, 89–90
Feature Animation, 167–169
finance departments, role of, 135
financial capital, 162
financial information, 8
"first mover advantage," 98–99, 122
First National Bank of Omaha, 61
FitzGerald, Gerald, 85–92
on fast-tracking projects, 89–90
on growth from tragedy, 86–87
on heroism, 87–88
on human spirit, 91
on international partnerships, 88–89
on market positioning, 90
Flight 93, 105
Food and Drug Administration (FDA),
178
foods, 142
Ford Motor Company, 122
foreign assistance programs, 3
Foreign Corrupt Practices Act, 136
foreign nationals, 121–122
foreign risk, 191
France, 191
franchised business models, 163
freedom, 5, 9–11, 164
free enterprise system, 164
free trade, 9
Feng Shui, 63

Galli, Joe, 93–100
on corporate responsibilities, 96, 98
on developing future leadership, 95–96
on investors, 99–100
on leadership, 97–98
on resilience, 100
General Mills, 133, 135, 138
genetics, 176–177
Giuliani, Rudy, 45–46, 102
global aviation, 91
global economy, 9–10, 192–193
acting locally in, 88–89
benefits of, 75–76
capital in, 152–153
corporate role in, 160–161
and health care, 177–178
and human rights issues, 112
new relationships in, 159
role of U.S. business in, 155–156
and technology, 33–34
"golden mean" rule (architecture), 62
government(s)
moral obligations of, 7–8
trust in, 8–9
Great Britain, 191
GSD&M (ad agency), 51
Gutenberg, Johann, 77

Hancock, Herbie, 209–210
Harrison, Stephen G., 101–107
on leadership, 105–106
on post-layoff environment, 102–105
on resiliency, 106, 107
Haskell, Chester D., 108–114
on China, 113–114
on diversity, 110
on human rights issues, 112
on resilience, 114
on role of international education,
109–110
on terrorism, 111
health care
anticipating future of, 175–176
and diversity, 178–179
and globalism, 177–178
and social policy, 176
trends in, 176–177

heroism, 87–88
high-rise buildings, 60–61
hijackings, Cuban, 21
hindsight, 117–118
Ho Chi Minh, 186
Honeywell, 144
Hong Kong, 62, 63
hope, 106, 161–162, 206–207
hospitality industry, 158–159
HR (human resources), 171
hub-and-spoke air operations, 22
human capital, 77, 129, 162
human resources (HR), 171
human rights
    in China, 4–5, 113–114
    and global trade, 112
    and role of corporations, 138
human services, Internet-based, 151
human spirit, 91, 127, 132
humility, 105
Hussein, King (Jordan), 63

"I am an American" ad campaign, 51
illusion, 170
impedance matching, 118
inclusiveness, 160
India, 116, 191
information technology, 194
innovation, 97
    and driving business, 119–120
    introducing, 151
inspiration, 16, 46, 105, 127–129
instinct(s)
    following, 57
    for leadership, 153–154
insurance, 138
integrity, 32
intellectual capital, 81–82
inter-city rail service, 142, 144–146
international business/trade, 9
    American influence on, 136–138
    benefits of, 75–76
    combining cultures in, 122
    and human rights issues, 4–5
    partnerships in, 70–72
    promotion of, 2–3
    see also global economy

international education, 109–110
Internet, the
    as change factor, 182
    competition from, 73–74
    and health care, 177
    human services on, 151
    magazines about, 74
    as tool, 150–151
investment
    in education, 114
    in the future, 34–35, 201–202
    in human capital, 77
investors
    caring about, 99–100
    interference from, 123
    working with, 154–155
Irish Republican Army (IRA), 111
Iron Curtain, 34
Islam, 187
"I will fight terrorism" ad campaign, 52

JAG, see Jobs for America's Graduates
Japan, 76, 136, 191
Japanese (in California), 112
JFK International Airport (New York),
    87
Jobs for America's Graduates (JAG),
    195–196, 198, 202–203
John Paul II, Pope, 65
joint ventures, 103
Jones, Quincy, 208
Jordan, 63
Joy, Bill, on smart people, 34

Kapoor, Sunir, 115–124
    on economy, 123
    on hindsight, 117–118
    on innovation, 119–120
    on international business, 122
    on investors, 123
    on land of opportunity, 121–122
    on luck, 120
    on New Economy, 120–121
    on optimism, 116–117
    on personal meaning, 118–119
Keystone Program, 162
King, Martin Luther, Jr., 208

knowledge
    to fight terrorism, 74–75
    selling, 71–72
knowledge base, transfer of, 89
knowledge economy, 30
Komisarjevsky, Christopher, 125–132
    on leadership, 127–128
    on public relations, 129–130
    on resilience, 132
    on role of CEO, 126–127
    on social responsibility, 126–127
    on values, 130–132
Kuwait power company, 89

language, use of, 111
Laos, 186
Lawrence, James, 133–139
    on driving change, 134–135
    on international trade, 136–138
    on progress of mankind, 138–139
    on resilience, 139
leadership, 13–18
    changing role of, 17–18, 127–128
    and circumstance, 44–45
    and competition, 219
    and culture, 14
    culture of, 15
    developing future, 95–96
    and driving change, 134–135
    future of, 206
    heroic acts as signs of, 87–88
    inspiration for, 16, 46, 105, 127–129
    instinct for, 153–154
    models of, 97
    and risk assessment, 41–42
    shared, 18
    training for, 105–106
    and trust, 46
    visibility and communication in, 153
Learner, Howard, 140–147
    on environment and economy, 141–147
    on global economy, 143
    on rail service, 142, 144–146
    on values, 142, 146
Lee Hecht Harrison, 101
Leo A Daly (firm), 59, 63
Levin, Gerald, on inner human being, 29

Lincoln, Pat, on colliding exponentials, 36
listening, 172
Live Brave Coalition, 52
long-term planning, 149–150
"Loose Lips Sink Ships" ad campaign, 52
loyalty, 171, 172
luck, 120

Madden, James C., V, 148–156
    on global economy, 155–156
    on Internet as tool, 150–151
    on introducing innovation, 151
    on investor relations, 154–155
    on leadership, 153–154
    on long-term planning, 149–150
    on resilience, 156
Madrid, 111
magazines, Internet-focused, 74
making a difference, 82–83
market, anticipation of, 91
market economy
    in China, 6
    and moral obligations, 7–8
marketing agreements, 90
marketplace, competition and the, 42–43
Maytag, 144
McGruff "Take a Bite Out of Crime" ad
    campaign, 56
MCI, 148–149
McKinsey (consulting firm), 81
meaning, personal, 118–119
media
    changes in, 73–74
    fragmentation of, 53–54
mental discipline, 100
mentoring, 64
meritocracy, 180
Microsoft, 122, 123
Midwest, 142, 145–146
military adversaries, 38–39
mindset trap, 192
Minnesota, 162
mission, 17
money, as motivator, 30
Monterey Institute of International Studies,
    108–109, 110
Moore's Law, 35

moral obligations, 6–8
Moses, 224
motivation
    making a contribution as, 29–30
    and nurturing environment, 213
    voicing opinions as, 128
    war as, 53
Motorola, 72–73

naiveté, 31
National Crime Prevention Council, 56
Native Americans, 112
NEG Micron, 144
Nelson, Marilyn Carlson, 157–165
    on change, 173
    on effects of September 11, 158–159,
        164
    on global economy, 163–164
    on global relationships, 159
    on hope, 161–162
    on inspiration from other cultures, 160
    on investment in human resources,
        162–163
    on listening, 172
    on resilience, 164–165
neutral zone, 225–226
New Economy, 120–121
Newell Rubbermaid, 93–96
New York City, 67
Northeast Corridor, 144–145

"old rules," 61–62, 90, 130
Omaha, 64
open environments, 32–33
opinions, voicing, 128
optimism, 116–117
Oracle, 122
outcomes research, 175, 176
Owen, Wilfred, on war, 44

parable of the talents, 165
paranoia, 181
parking lot revenues, 23
partnerships
    international, 70–72, 88–89
    voluntary, 46–47
passion, 78

patriotism, 43–44
Patton, George, on war, 44
Payne, Thomas, 77
PB Aviation, 85, 87, 88
PC Weekly, 74
Pentagon, 15, 19
Pepsi, 136
persistence, 27
personal computers, 34–35
personal meaning, 118–119
philanthropy, 80
    benefits of, to corporations, 82
    benefits of, to employees, 80–82
    and intellectual capital, 81–82
    and self-esteem, 81
planning
    long-term, 149–150
    value of, 181–182
Poitier, Sidney, 208
politics, environmental issues and,
    146–147
Pope John Paul II Cultural Center, 65
Port Authority of New York and New Jer-
    sey, 85, 87
positioning (in marketplace), 90
positive attitudes, 170–171
post-layoff workplace environment,
    102–104
privacy rights, 21, 177
profiling people, 24–25
progressive democratic secularism, 137
public relations, 129
purpose, 77

rail service, 142, 144–146
Randolph, Marjorie, 166–173
    on branding message, 169–170
    on creativity in corporate environment,
        166–169
    on employer/employee relationship,
        170–173
readiness for challenge, 45
recruitment, 104
Red Cross, 51
Red Herring, 74
"renaissance executives," 206
Repsol, 62–63

research, outcomes, 175, 176
Research Associates International, 185
resilience, 147, 194, 204, 229
  and acceptance of change, 156
  and adaptation, 18
  and clarity of principles, 114
  and commitment, 48
  and experience, 107
  and faith, 68, 164–165
  and honesty, 183
  and human freedom, 11
  and market sense, 92
  and mental discipline, 100
  and optimism, 116
  and passion, 78
  and persistence, 27
  and self-acceptance, 173
  and self-esteem, 132
respect, 27, 172
  for current employees, 32
  for former employees, 103
  for other cultures, 47–48
responsibility, technology and, 31–32
revenues, parking lot, 23
reward system, 33
rights, *see* human rights; privacy rights
risk(s)
  of company failure, 8
  leadership and assessment of, 41–42
  and standards, 40–41
Roosevelt, Franklin D., 50
"Rosie the Riveter" ad campaign, 52
R.R. Donnelley Print Solutions, 69
Russia, 43, 190, 191

"sacred places," 212
safety issues, 138
  and architecture, 60–61
  and health care, 180–181
Sanger, Steve, 135
Saudi Arabia, 64
Schaeffer, Leonard D., 174–183
  on change, 182–183
  on changing health care, 177–178
  on health-care, 175–176
  on investing in people, 180
  on personal privacy, 177

on planning, 181–182
  on resiliency, 183
  on social policy, 176
Schwab, Charles, 216
Seattle (trade) riots, 10
secularism, 137
security, airport, 24–25
security laws, 7
self-acceptance, 173
self-awareness, 83
self-esteem, 81, 132
senior management, communication from,
    102–103
September 11 terrorist attacks
  aviation affected by, 20–21
  corporate reactions to, 149
  effects of, on business, 158–159, 164
  world trade affected by, 2–3
Shackley, Theodore G., 184–194
  on business and espionage, 189–191
  on foreign risks, 191
  on keeping a low profile, 192–193
  on mindset trap, 192
  on resilience, 194
  on unifying diverse groups, 186–187
Shanghai, 71, 72
Silicon Curtain, 34
skills, business and diplomatic, 110–111
skyscrapers, 60–61
Smith, Ken, 195–204
  on core competencies, 197
  on creating a positive attitude, 198
  on economic clout, 202
  on future workforce, 198–199
  on promotion of U.S. businesses, 201
  on training needs, 200
social policy, 176
social responsibility, 126–127
South Korea, 191
Soviet Union (USSR), 34, 39
Spain, 62
Spann, Johnny Michael, 184
speed (transportation), 21–22, 23
spin, 130
Spire Solar, 144
SRI International, 28, 29, 32, 33
St. Louis, 145

standards, 136
  accounting, 8
  ethical, 127
  and risk, 40–41
Starbucks, 206
Steelcase, 306
stewardship, 161, 162, 165
straight talk, 153
Strickland, William E., Jr., 205–214
  on the arts, 208–209
  on creating "sacred places," 212
  on hope, 207–208
  on leadership, 206
  on motivation, 213
  on personal success, 207
  on resilience, 214
success
  of company as a whole, 135–136
  of corporation, 98
Sunbeam, 123
supermarkets, 142
sustainable development, 143

Taiwan, 191
talent, 171
tariffs, 7
Taylor, Billy, 208, 211
teamwork, 127–128
technology
  and airport security, 24–25
  cellular, 72–73
  "clean," 144, 147
  effects of, 36
  and environment, 144, 146–147
  and global economy, 33–34
  investment in, 180
  opportunities created by, 26, 27
  and partnerships, 46–47
  and responsibility, 31–32
  use of, by Ad Council, 54
telecommunications market, 117
terrorism/terrrorists
  ad campaigns against, 52
  and business changes, 111
  and health care, 181
  impact of, 164
  knowledge to fight, 74–75

lessons learned from, 191–192
and profiling people, 24–25
and sense of urgency, 39
and technology, 31–32
unification against, 187
see also September 11 terrorist attacks
"the wall," 84
third parties, 129
time factors, 165
trade, international, *see* international business/trade
training
  basic skills, 199–200
  of employees, 78
  for leadership, 105–106
  of local partners, 89
"transport and hospitality industry," 159
transportation
  air, *see* aviation
  environmental issues related to, 142, 144–146
  speed of, 21–23
travel industry, 158–159
trust
  in government, 8–9
  and leadership, 46
Tsola, 115, 117–118
Tung, Tai-chin, 215–221
  on anti-Americanism, 219–220
  on competition, 219
  on creating a results-oriented organization, 217–218
  on leadership, 216–217
  on resilience, 221
  on vision and values, 217
Turner, Stansfield, 185, 186, 188

United Kingdom, 111, 116, 159
United States, as land of opportunity, 121–122
United Way, 51, 79
urgency, sense of, 39
U.S. Air Force, 37–38, 40
U.S. Congress, 147

value(s), 17, 129, 130–132
  of clients, 36

value(s) *(continued)*
  environmental, 142–143, 146
  systems of, 96
Verizon, 15
Viagra, 178
Vietnam, 186
voluntary partnerships, 46–47
volunteers/volunteerism, 15, 83, 162–163

Walt Disney Studios, 166–173
war, 44
  capitalizing on, 56–57
  as motivator, 53
War Ad Council, 50
War for Talent, 171
Warsaw Pact, 39
Washington, D.C., 64, 65

Wellpoint Health Networks, 174
Whole Foods, 142
Wired magazine, 74
wireless data services, 117–118
women
  in management, 136
  treatment of, 138
World Bank, 3
World Trade Center, 60, 61, 67
    see also September 11 terrorist attacks
World Trade Organization (WTO), 3, 6, 10, 163
World War II, 50, 52
Wright, Frank Lloyd, 209, 212
WTO, *see* World Trade Organization

Yahoo!, 74, 123